Telling Stories, Writing Songs

AN ALBUM OF

Foreword by Sam Phillips

Introduction by B. B. King

TEXAS SONGWRITERS

Telling Stories
Writing Songs

by Kathleen Hudson

 University of Texas Press, Austin

Requests for permission to reproduce material from this work
should be sent to Permissions, University of Texas Press, P.O.
Box 7819, Austin, TX 78713-7819.

(∞) The paper used in this book meets the minimum requirements of ANSI/NISO Z39.48-1992 (R1997) (Permanence of Paper).

Library of Congress Cataloging-in-Publication Data

Hudson, Kathleen, 1945–
   Telling stories, writing songs : an album of Texas songwriters / Kathleen Hudson ; foreword by Sam Phillips ; introduction by B. B. King—1st ed.
       p.   cm.
   Includes discographies and songwriters' biographies.
   ISBN 0-292-73135-3 (cl.) alk. paper—ISBN 0-292-73136-1 (pbk.)
alk. paper
   1. Composers—Texas—Interviews. 2. Singers—Texas—
Interviews.

ML390.H878 2001
782.42164'092'2764—dc21
   [B]   00-023682

Dedication

To my family for their unwavering belief and endless love:
Annabel and David, Lisa, Jessica, Anthony, Clayton,
David Jr., Charlie, Carolyn, and John.

For *all* those who have loved me and believed in me.
I did not do this alone.

Contents

Telling Stories, Writing Songs

Foreword

Texas has the greatest amalgamation of human cultures, yet great individuality, in our Grand Old USA. On a personal level, Texas means an awful lot to me. Reason number one, but many more: after Memphis, that's where I started Elvis Presley's career.

When I first began promoting Elvis's recordings, I was extremely discouraged with the response I got from towns and cities in other states. For example, I remember coming through Louisiana, where my dear friend T. Tommy Cutrer, one of the great radio personalities ever, ran a great country program at KCIJ in Shreveport. He told me, "Sam, you and I have been friends a long time, but I just don't know whether I can play Elvis or not."

I also remember the reaction of another good friend, Fats Washington, who was then working at KENT Radio in the same town. I said, "Fats, I've got 'That's Alright Mama' on one side and 'Blue Moon of Kentucky' on the other." He said, "You are crazy, Mr. Phillips. I've always played your rhythm and blues records, Junior Parker and B. B. King, but this man Presley just sounds so country that he shouldn't be played after the sun comes up in the morning!"

So I headed for Dallas, and I remember running into one of the few dust storms they have in Central Texas. When I got to the Big State Distributing Company, the company that distributed Sun Records in the Dallas area, the lady behind the counter, Alta Hayes (who later became the record purchasing and sales general manager for Big State) said, "Sam, you look like hell."

It was Monday morning, and I was trying to catch all of the jukebox operators and the regular store record buyers so I could talk to them. I believed in Elvis and this record so much I had literally exhausted myself physically and mentally. Alta said, "Sam, based on the early reaction to the sample record you sent me, you have got a hit." Though the record broke first in Memphis, it took off in Dallas and then spread back to Shreveport, and the rest, as they say, is history.

Texans, then as now, have a lot to say to me. If you give them what they want in Texas, they will flat let you know in appreciation. If not, guess what?

One of the reasons for the widespread acceptance of country (hillbilly) music was Bob Wills and his Texas Playboys' innovative western swing. His influence had a lot to do with what I felt about music. Western swing was, and is, music with a "feel good" sound that continues to be a fundamental major influence in country music today—but not nearly enough!

Blind Leon Payne, out of Houston, was a major songwriter the minute he wrote "I Love You Because," one of my all-time favorite songs for both lyrics and melody. Leon's songs stand the test of time for people, and that's the best of all rewards for a songwriter.

Another reason I love Texas is its vast variety of songwriters and musicians and the real diversity of its people and their tastes—what they honestly feel and respond to. Because of this, I know that Texas will always be a *great* place for music. Music succeeds because of the emotional contact it makes with the individual personality. That's the beauty of it. No matter the type, category, tempo of the music, it is your own personal experience as you listen that makes you respond. Usually, for the musicians who are performing (be it record or stage), it is the thing they love doing most in life. Without the genius of the songwriters, none of this would be possible.

I'm very protective about the individual spirit and what the individual can do if the opportunity is present. I don't think you'll ever have to worry about that spirit in Texas. A lot of people really don't think about where in the hell we would be without music. I don't care if it's from Arturo Toscanini or Bob Wills, John Lee Hooker or Elvis Presley. Music is a profound part of our lives, and Texas has contributed immensely to this, one of the emotional staples of living.

That brings me to the final idea I want to express. Kathleen Hudson, by nature a seeker, has the background and education necessary to do a book of this kind, as well as an understanding of human emotions and a beautiful appreciation of music. She's got that rare gift that allows a musician and songwriter to feel free and open up. I'm fascinated by her, and I believe this project has the potential to be the Bible of Texas music.

Thanks, Kathleen, and say hello to people I love—Texans.

Sam Phillips

Preface

Roadhouse, coffeehouse, concert hall, or honky-tonk, I go to a Texas music show with three distinct perspectives. First and foremost, I'm the biggest fan of every singer-songwriter in this book. You might even call me a fool for people who are out in the world making a difference in the quality of our lives by telling their stories and singing their songs. And every artist in this book has indeed changed my own personal life in some measure great or small. What they have shown me about the art of living has made this oral history adventure I started in 1986 worth every minute of my investigation.

That brings me to my second perspective. I've been a Professor of English at Schreiner College in Kerrville over the past fifteen years. I'm not just interested in what this generation of culture makers has to say about what it means to be Texan; I'm also on a search for what word-smiths and songsmiths say about the art and craft of actually creating music. And because my classroom is a sea of world cultures with readings and assignments and performances from everywhere, I'm always looking for the common interests through which we can join hands and partici-pate in a deeper humanity.

Finally, I'm the founder and president of the Texas Heritage Music Foundation. I was so overwhelmed by the impact the people in this book have had on my college students that I simply began to write a newspaper column to keep all the alumni informed on what was happening where. And through hard work and community support, I soon found myself showcasing the talents of these Texas songwriters wherever and whenever possible. And that has led to some very interesting things. Call it coinci-dence or kismet, but at the same time Bob Dylan was producing an album to commemorate the centennial of the birth of the legendary Jimmie Rodgers, I was putting a tribute concert together. When Willie Nelson, who sings on the Dylan record, found out, he agreed to come down to the Hill Country and close the show for us. He stayed two hours after the concert just to sign autographs and shake hands.

Cooperation has been the spirit of this project from day one. B. B. King was the first to set me straight and give me "permission to speak." After the Memphis Blues Awards in 1986, I requested an interview. He didn't get back to me right away, and I was wondering what I was doing standing around the stage door with all these wild ideas in my head. Later, at the all-night party at the New Daisy, he sent his manager to find that "tall woman from Texas." He remembered his promise and kept it. His remarks, along with an exciting conversation with Sam Phillips, set this book off on a long and wonderful ride.

And every interview in this collection was conducted in the field. In Texas, I've covered the waterfront—from Crider's in Hunt to the Broken Spoke in Austin, from the annual Fourth of July Willie Nelson Picnic in Luckenbach to the Cactus Cafe on the University of Texas campus in Austin, from John T. Floore Country Store in Helotes to a small empty room in Lubbock. In spite of the size of the take, these songwriters played and I followed with my dancing shoes, camera, and tape recorder.

What do these men and women have in common? Being accessible. Although Rod Kennedy's Kerrville Folk Festival brought many songwriters to town, just as many really went above and beyond the call of duty to help me. Sonny Throckmorton accepted an invitation to speak to a group of creative-writing teachers in Hunt. Kinky Friedman showed up at the Hill Country Cafe for breakfast with me after he took in the camp laundry. Ray Wylie Hubbard played a wedding for Greg and Rene McGlaughlin in Kerrville. Tanya Tucker, in spite of playing the biggest party in Texas, the YO Social Club in Mountain Home, still had time to sit and talk.

I interviewed James McMurtry, for example, over good food at the Liberty Bar and Grill in San Antonio. He had written only five songs at the time. He later visited my classes and played a small local coffeehouse. Three Columbia albums later we met again and talked. Townes Van Zandt took me for a canoe ride at his home in Nashville one hot afternoon and played baseball with my children in the "Meadow" at Quiet Valley Ranch on another. Johnny Rodriguez offered me great support even as we shared the passionate music of Johnny Gonzalez at Flores Mexican Food in Austin. During one chorus, Johnny dropped to the floor clutching his heart. We were all overcome—*muy apasionado.*

I met Guy Clark at a music conference at Midem in 1996, and when I needed more information, he agreed to yet another talk, this time on the French Riviera. And listening to and interviewing Texas songwriters on a different continent also opened my eyes to another Lone Star quality: the stamp of authenticity. Texas music has that rough edge that some true aficionados in the world want. Europeans know the distinction; they understand heritage and roots. That's why Aschi Maurer showcased Texas songwriters at the Frutigen Songwriters Festival in Switzerland and why Katy Moffatt consistently blows European audiences away. Texas music always carries Claude Nobs, who founded the Montreux Jazz Festival. He was listening to Stevie Ray Vaughan on his sound system when I attended a press dinner at his chalet. It was great background music for an international gathering. That evening Flaco Jimenez sat in with Dylan, and Lou Ann Barton brought Texas blues to the stage.

A third characteristic that came through these conversations is the underlying passion in these songwriters. Look to Johnny Copeland for a performer dedicated to spreading the news. With a machine in his chest to regulate his heart, he eagerly shared his story over the phone. He died shortly after our third time to talk and I think his last words will remind us of how undying is the sound he left behind. Reading every interview will, I think, reveal that what distinguishes Texans is an awareness of space out here, a willingness to step out into new areas and approach new horizons.

Many people deserve a mention. I thank the performers and their management, the club owners who understood the project (Steve, Griff, David, Joe, Jud), the many friends who listened to me talk about this for years, and KFAN radio in the Hill Country—they play all the artists in this book. I also want to thank my own family for giving me a foundation from which to launch this project, especially to David and Annabel Pillow, my parents, who encouraged me to live the life I love. A writer who does not show up in this book, but one who has influenced the many literate Texas songwriters, has helped the project more than he knows. Leonard Cohen always agrees to an interview with me when he plays Austin. In our conversation, I get in touch with the commitment and integrity of a creative life that I value so much. Our talks have kept me on track. The many students in my English classes at Schreiner College have inspired me. Shannon Smart started off taking a class and ended up transcribing many interviews. Her love and support made a difference.

Finally, Kirpal Gordon, a great New York writer and adopted son of the Texas Hill Country, helped me prepare all of my materials and discover nuances that have made this a better book. I also had a timely phone call from a woman named Joanie Whitebird who has been involved with Wings Press and Texas literature and arts for thirty years. She went over the manuscript, shaping the form. C. J. Berkman and Larry Gunn both read the entire manuscript as friendly editors.

I'm forever altered by the conversations I've had. I want to share them with a larger audience because telling our stories and singing our songs make a difference in the world. I acknowledge the University of Texas Press for sharing that commitment by publishing this collection. Theresa May, the editor at the press, is another woman committed to the arts and one who moved me into another realm with the work.

And now the work moves on as you bring your own story to the reading.

Acknowledgments

Thanks: The Pillow family, my children, Kirpal Gordon, Larry Gunn, Shannon Smart, Blake Holloway, C. J. Berkman, Schreiner College, Ma Parker, Ray Tena, Shirley Gerlich, Lori Hughes, Glen Alyn, Rod Kennedy, Joanie Whitebird, all my students, Ziggy Scharton, Dan and Sandy and Michael at AC Print, *Kerrville Daily Times*, volunteers of the Texas Heritage Music Foundation, Larry McMurtry, Leonard Cohen, Sam Phillips, B. B. King, Theresa May, University of Texas Press, Landmark Education Corporation, Jeanne and Robert Slobod, Past is Prologue Program, Janice Kennemer, Roxy and Judy Gordon, Jack Happ, all my friends who listened and listened to me, Casey Monahan, all the artists who gave of their time, and all those still unnamed and still thanked!

Apology: This is not a definitive treatment; it is a collection. Many worthy and significant songwriters need to be represented. Perhaps another book; perhaps a series. Red Steagall conveys the life of the cowboy. Buck Ramsey, before he died an early death, brought the cowboy life to a new level of understanding. Andy Wilkinson writes in the cowboy genre and brings new ideas to light. Freddy Fender has given us many Latino classics. Country stars Clint Black and Clay Walker have stories to tell. This collection represents various voices and diverse experiences. What they may have in common is a clear perspective on the edge. This group of songwriters have all entered the woods where there was not a trail.

Introduction

A great deal of Texas music has been inspirational to me as a blues musician, particularly three immortals from the Lone Star state. My all-time musical idol was a Texan named Blind Lemon Jefferson, the best ever in folk blues. I keep his records with me even today. Another Texan who greatly influenced me—and all blues style—was T-Bone Walker. Nobody has ever been able to capture the sound of T-Bone—they still haven't done it. Lightnin' Hopkins, another Texan, is someone whose music I have tried to emulate all my life.

Trace the music back. It was called "country and blues" before I left Mississippi. "Country music," like Willie Nelson said when we co-hosted the Blues Foundation Awards in Memphis in 1986, "is nothin' but the white man's blues." In fact, Willie has that nasal sound that most of us blues singers wish we could get—as well as that certain something in his voice, that tone that makes the bluesy songs he sings bluesiest of all. I know that sounds funny coming from a blues guy, but I was always crazy about Bob Wills and Willie Nelson.

I met Willie in 1969 in Nashville. I was playing a tune called "Nightlife," and just as I got started, one of the guys in the band touched me and said, "Look over to your left—there's Willie Nelson!" I almost fell off the stage. After the show he came back and spoke to me. Of course I didn't find out until later that "Nightlife" was a tune he had written. We hit it off that first night.

From then on, whenever we played the same town, he'd come to my show the nights he had free and listen. That's how we got to become the best of friends. I played some dates with him in 1984–1985, traveling through his state on what they called the Texas Bash. He told me if ever he could help in any way that he would. So I said the same thing to him. And then he called to ask me to do Farm Aid, which was a great honor. Then when the Blues Foundation was formed in Memphis, Willie gave us a big boost.

When I left my job as a disc jockey in Memphis, my next stop was Houston. I worked out of an agency that was run by a lady called Evelyn Johnson, Buffalo Booking, from about 1952 to 1960. That town has been very good to me.

I like to think the blues as we do it is like a mother tree with many branches of music that's sprouted from it. I think Texas has always been a home for good music and will continue to be a leader as far as musicians are concerned.

Music is akin to the air—everybody breathes it—and the air in Texas is rich. It doesn't necessarily have to be popular as far as the rest of the world is concerned, but we'll hear something that nobody else is doing, and we'll latch on to it.

That's how it grows. That's the story.

I like to think that there's much more to learn and I feel that I'm learning all the time.

B. B. King

Telling Stories, Writing Songs

Talking Texas

Larry McMurtry

When I said Willie Nelson didn't have an effect on me, I don't mean to put him down. I think that what he achieved after a long struggle is invaluable. I always admire artists who endure and prevail. I think success in the middle years is more impressive. Early brilliance is early brilliance. It can be smiled upon or frowned upon. But I really admire people who succeed and keep it going in the middle years.

The final interview for this project was with Larry McMurtry, the only Texas writer to win the Pulitzer prize for fiction. We met at 10:00 A.M. at his bookstore, Booked Up No. 1, in Archer City, Texas, on Monday, June 1, 1998. The temperature by noon read 111 degrees at the bank. It was a hot and dry Texas day. As I stood in the place that shaped both McMurtrys, father and son, I was reminded that both place and story are significant in the Texas writing scene. I looked across the square at the burned-out shell of the Royal Theater, the original last picture show in Archer City.

After Larry walked around the square, opening all four buildings of Booked Up, we sat down to talk. His genuine interest in the project took me back to another time I spent with Larry. We both attended the New Folk concert at Rod Kennedy's Folk Festival one rainy Sunday. We were both there to hear a new songwriter, James McMurtry. Larry had not received a Pulitzer prize for *Lonesome Dove* at that time, but he was still the voice of Texas literature. I didn't know then that a final conversation with him would bring this phase of the project to a close. But I've always liked a circular walk, agreeing with T. S. Eliot when he said, "At the end of all our exploration we shall arrive at where we started and know the place for the first time."

Hudson: Larry, you just heard James play here in Archer City at a benefit for the Royal Theater. Ray Wylie Hubbard and Steve Fromholz were also on the bill. The first interview I did with James was at your suggestion. He had written about five songs. Now he's working on his fifth album. Let's talk about last night's show.

McMurtry: I only got to hear three songs. Curtis, his son, had spent the week with me, and he was tired. I took him home to bed. I have rarely heard James since the very first record and the very first tour. I was on the road a lot at that time, and I intersected with him in Wisconsin, North Carolina, and a couple of other places. This show was not a typical show for James because he did not have his band with him. The other two are more folkie than he is, and the show pulled him back to a folk approach.

Hudson: I know he likes the idea of getting people to dance.

McMurtry: He likes that very much. The show was entertaining, but it was not an opportunity for me to listen to a typical "James" performance, now with all that he's experienced.

Hudson: What was your perception of him as a kid with music?

McMurtry: We moved to Virginia when James was seven. We switched cultures. He'd grown up in Houston, and we moved to a small, rural community. There were bluegrass shows on Saturday nights. I'm sure that had an effect on James. We moved into Washington several times. That didn't work. When he began his musical life, it was with bluegrass festivals, which he went off to by himself. I know that in Tucson he was still folk oriented. He went to old fiddlers' conventions.

Hudson: At that time did you think he was going to make music his life?

McMurtry: I thought so, but you never really know. There are so many ways you can get sidetracked. For a long time, I knew he was going to be a really good guitar player, but I didn't know if that was going to be his private kind of solace, or whether it was going to develop professionally. I don't think anyone knows that. I didn't know I was going to be a writer until I'd written three books. I could easily have been something else. It doesn't have to be something you continue with your whole life until you've done it so long you don't have any other good alternatives. But I knew in the first few times I heard him perform that there was a lot going on in his songs, both musically and dramatically. The point I would make is what I notice with James is the complexity of his music; it's not real simple. It's complicated. The emotions that he deals with are complicated. A lot of his songs are about distance; they're about distance down the road; they're about distance between people. You don't find very many people who deal with that over and over as well as James does.

Hudson: When I entered the graduate program at Texas Christian University, my major professor, Jim Corder, said in my first rhetoric class, "I want to quote Kenneth Burke and say that we have nothing in common but our separateness." I knew, then, that distance and connecting were primary concerns of mine, as well. I resonated with that statement.

McMurtry: I know when I've listened to his songs with friends my age, they say, "My lord, what has happened to our children? How did they get that dark?" That's a valid response, I think.

Hudson: My first response to his song "Crazy Winds and Flashing Yellow Lights" was to wonder how he captured a woman's perspective so well.

McMurtry: People ask me that as well. It's one of the easiest things to do. That transference is easy if you have any imagination at all. It's much easier to write about women than about men your own age. In any given book of mine, the women characters are much better realized than the men characters the same age. We're really interested in women, and we're not really interested in men. If you want to write about emotion, if you want to learn about emotion, you go to women, you don't go to men. They don't reveal emotions. The father of the English novel, Samuel Richardson, made his pocket money writing love letters for illiterate village girls. That's where the novel began with *Pamela*, and it was always keyed to women's ability to express emotions.

Hudson: All the years I've had of watching James and knowing him keep reminding me how much I love the writing.

McMurtry: He's a wonderful songwriter. There's no doubt, he's a wonderful songwriter. He was a ragged and raw performer when he started, and now he's a sophisticated performer. I noticed that this weekend (May 30, 1998). The thing that you notice, always, is the writing of the songs. They are very complex songs and are beautifully written. He doesn't write real fast. This new album, except for the first one, is the quickest.

When he met Mellencamp, he had an opportunity, and he wrote several more songs for the first album, quickly. He wrote some in the studio. He sort of resists writing. It's kind of hard for him, but it's gotten easier these last couple of albums.

Hudson: What do you imagine about his response to the McMurtry name? He's writing close to a giant in literature.

McMurtry: One of the things I'm proudest of is that he could find a way to do what he wanted his own way. He didn't relate much to what I was doing. And he started at a time I was at a peak in my fame. I cast a long shadow at the time he began working. And now he's forged a career that is very independent. People know James. He has a really good following.

Hudson: He seems to have his own space.

McMurtry: I'm very proud of that. But he does have a form of narrative, too. A gift, in some respects, to tell stories.

Hudson: As I drove into Archer City, I saw the American Legion Hall he told me about. I had heard stories of this place, of a mailbox with bullet holes.

McMurtry: The ranch house is just a mile off the road. You can see the bullet holes. That's the family ranch which James now owns. His great-grandparents' ranch house. That house was built in '28. A larger house burnt down in '27. He has a deep attachment to that house, that place. So do I. We reacquired it at the time James graduated from high school. I bought it from my mother and brother. It's a Montgomery Ward house. James needs it now as a psychological resource, a place to go write from time to time.

Hudson: Now, on to the music. As you were growing up and turning on the radio, did you discover any favorite types of music?

McMurtry: I have a few attachments. Country music was the only music at that time. It was the background music to my life and almost anybody's life in this country. We grew up with Roy Acuff, Hank Williams, people who were popular in the late '40s and early '50s. We didn't get radio until '42 or '43. I remember Jimmie Davis and one or two programs out of Fort Worth. The Light Crust Doughboys at noon. I don't know that they made that much of an impression on me. When I went to college at Rice, I had a roommate who was classically trained. We subscribed to the Houston symphony tickets. Most of my modern attachments pertain to a couple of years when I went to the symphony. I don't listen to music very much. It's a strange thing. Some writers listen to music when they write. I don't because I can't hear my sentences correctly. I spend a lot of time, just on sentences. Those are, after all, the building blocks of anything you write.

I need to hear my sentences in my head so I write in silence. I can actually write in a hubbub of people. I can write in the kitchen, and life can be going on around me. But music can't be going on around me because that's direct competition for the sentence I'm trying to form. I've found three or four twentieth-century musicians I really like, Stravinsky, Bartok, and Mahler. I listen to them over and over again. I don't listen to much else. I don't have a radio on.

Hudson: Did Willie Nelson's voice ever penetrate your world?

McMurtry: Never meant a thing to me. I knew Willie Nelson before I ever heard him sing. Not as a friend, but I saw him on the street in Austin before I ever heard him sing. I am very unusual in the degree in which I don't listen to the radio. I never listen, and I go away from it if someone else turns it on. It is mental competition, in a way. I write quickly, and I don't spend very many hours a day at the typewriter. But I have something of what I'm doing in my head most of the time, and I can't keep it if I'm listening to something. For the most part, I don't listen. This has always been a problem with almost everyone I've been related to. Of course, kids like to have music going all the time.

I don't have a television set on the first floor of my house. I have one in a guest room so people can watch television. As I get older, this is getting worse and not better. I realize that I'm sixty-two and only have so much time. The better I can concentrate on reading, the better, the more satisfied I feel. I listen to the few people I really like. The kids who work here have radios scattered around, and that doesn't bother me.

Hudson: Does this bookstore pull you away?

McMurtry: That's my relaxation. I've already written fifteen pages today. I'm through. I'm rewriting now, but I've done my literary work for the day. That's always been the way I've done it. I write early in the morning and do the bookshops the rest of the day. I will occasionally need music. When I was finishing the *Terms of Endearment* books, a tetralogy, I wanted to listen to requiems, so I listened to five or six of the great requiems for about a month, to find out which one seemed to apply to what I was thinking about and trying to do.

Hudson: And there's a country music background just living here.

McMurtry: You can't totally avoid it. When I was a cowboy working on the ranch, the radio was always on in the pickups, so I heard the country music of my day. But I've probably heard less contemporary country music than anyone of my day because I just don't turn it on.

Hudson: Have you and James ever talked about writing?

McMurtry: I don't think so. Once in a great while we'll have a general conversation about art or something that's popped up. I've wanted a time or two to get James involved in the music of some of the movies I've done. He's not wanted to, probably correctly. That possibility is always there. When he's fifty years old, he may want to do some of this kind of music.

Hudson: I introduced the interview with James by saying that you had told me to talk to him.

McMurtry: That's because he thinks about what he does. He's useful to talk to because he's more polished in a lot of ways than he likes to appear. He has a sophisticated intelligence. You can hear it in his songs, immediately.

Hudson: He said you commented one time on the fact that songwriters get immediate feedback.

McMurtry: That's right. Writers don't, and when we do get it, we don't want it. I finish my books and I forget them. I don't want to talk about them. It's usually a year after I finish that the book comes out. I don't think about those books, I don't remember them very well, and I certainly don't have anything to say about them. But a musician isn't like that. His repertoire is both recent and old. I'm never going to read the book that I wrote forty years ago. It's not even in my head.

Hudson: When I read *Moving On*, I had an immediate reaction to Patsy. Her story was my story in places. I had an overwhelming sense of identification. James expresses things over and over that I feel but have never found the words to express.

McMurtry: That's what it's supposed to do.

Hudson: What about Kinky Friedman in this world of music and literature. Do you ever run into him?

McMurtry: I run into him almost every day, it seems like. From the East Coast to the West. And I like Kinky. I liked his group when it was Kinky Friedman and the Texas Jewboys. I had a friend who wrote a rock music column for *Newsweek*, and he took me down to see Kinky over twenty years ago. I heard "They Ain't Makin' Jews Like Jesus Anymore" right off the bat. He's a lot of fun.

Hudson: A thread that runs through these interviews is reference to Bob Dylan, Leonard Cohen, and sometimes Kerouac. What do you suppose that is?

McMurtry: Did you read the wonderful piece in the *New York Review* a couple of weeks ago called "Creating Country Music"? It's about the famous Folkways collection of American music done in the '70s, and it's about music that would have influenced Dylan and Cohen. It was put together by Harry Smith, a strange guy who lived his life in the Chelsea Hotel in New York. Very eccentrically learned. He collected all sorts of music recorded from 1923 to 1930. Very primal and unsophisticated. The point he makes is that the earlier you get it, the rawer and more extraordinary it can be. There's this person, Fiddlin' Dave Carter, and his daughter Moonshine Kate, who he captured. He got black stuff, stomps and hollers and fiddlin'. The Dylan generation was very influenced by that collection. It's available now on CD from the Smithsonian. It's as good an article as I've read on American music. You should go read it.

Hudson: You spoke once at a museum in Fort Worth on the state of Texas literature and created quite a furor. Do any of those comments work with music?

McMurtry: I remember my complaint at that time. Literature needs its history. Writers need to know the history of the forms they write in. And I think it must be true for musicians. Or maybe they only need to know four or five deep influences and do not need to know the history of the form. I can see a musical generation coming out of three or four influences, three or four people. I see these influences in this collection. When I said Willie Nelson didn't have an effect on me, I don't mean to put him down. I think that what he achieved after a long struggle is invaluable. I always admire artists who endure and prevail. I think success in the middle years is more impressive. Early brilliance is early brilliance. It can be smiled upon or frowned upon. But I really admire people who succeed and keep it going in the middle years.

The Art of Listening

Darrell Royal

Why are you asking me about Texas music?

We met to talk at the Pedernales Golf Course in 1985. Darrell's relationship with Willie Nelson is legendary, and the location was fitting. My conversation with Darrell helped launch this series of interviews. I last saw him in 1996 at the Saxon Pub. He was listening intently to a songwriters' showcase featuring Sonny Throckmorton and Freddy Powers. He would not talk to anyone during the show. I loved watching the look on his face as these men sang hit after hit. The owner, Joe Ables, sat close by, also listening. Several weeks later Darrell was honored in Austin by having the stadium named after him. Willie played a private tribute to him. Darrell Royal is a man who knows a good song when he hears it. Once at a Speaker's Day Party with Gib Lewis, Darrell took me to his RV parked out back. "Just listen," he said. We heard Willie Nelson sing Alex Harvey's song "No Place but Texas." "I was with them when they recorded that just last night," Darrell added. He loves to share the music.

Royal: Kathy, I want to ask you a question first. Why are you asking me about Texas music?

Hudson: Darrell, your friendships with Texas performers are well known, and you are known as a man who cares about music. Maybe it's those listening parties you throw.

Royal: I had a brother, Ray, who had a crystal radio set out in the garage. My first memory is in grade school. I'd go out and put on that headset and listen to a station in Del Rio, Texas, across the river. Rajah Rayboy would tell you anything you needed to know about your future. I think it was fifty cents or so, and he'd look into his crystal ball. I had to listen to Rajah Rayboy's spiel for thirty minutes to hear two country songs. The first songs I remember were the old Jimmie Rodgers songs, somewhere around the '30s. "T for Texas," and "Waitin' for a Train."

Hudson: Many people stand out in the history of Texas music. Who comes to mind for you?

Royal: I'm not qualified to say who influenced what because I'm not a musician. I just know what I like to hear. I'm an avid listener. I did pay attention. Floyd Tillman was important. I was in junior high or high school. The La Vista Theatre had a drugstore next door, and I'd go there to listen to the jukebox. I listened to Floyd Tillman. I'd put my nickel in there to hear him. I never dreamed that one day I would meet Floyd and become a close friend of his. He lives close by—in Marble Falls. We see each other a lot, and I go hear him play music a lot. I've heard his influence passed on to others. Willie will be the first to tell you that he was a big fan of Floyd's back in the beginning. He influenced Willie and his songwriting. With the kind of chords and the different types of music. Floyd Tillman, they tell me, was almost pop.

Hudson: Do you have any favorite songs?

Royal: You bet I do. One that's been playing a lot now is Willie's Christmas song, "Pretty Paper." I asked Willie where he got that song. He said he was in Fort Worth every year, and before the old Leonard's Department Store there was a platform. On that platform was a man who had no legs. He'd move along the sidewalk pulling himself with his leather gloves. Every Christmas Willie would see him pulling himself along, selling papers and pencils. He wrote the song that played each Christmas. I also like a song he wrote called "Healing Hands of Time." It could be applicable to a love affair or a loss in the family.

Hudson: Do you think that "simplicity" is an attraction?

Royal: I think most music that people understand and hum along to and enjoy is a simple approach. I used to listen to the Lucky Strike Hit Parade and try to guess which songs were coming along. My love for music is not restricted to country music.

Hudson: Was there a point in your life when you noticed that you really paid attention to lyrics?

Royal: You know that Jimmie Rodgers song about the water tank? It never really occurred to me what it meant. When I got older, it struck me that this old guy was walking and waiting on a train. If you really put yourself in the position to understand the lyrics, you get more enjoyment.

Hudson: New songwriters?

Royal: Sonny Throckmorton from Brownwood compared to a Harlan Howard is a "new songwriter," but he's written fourteen number one songs. He's one of my favorites. I like Whitey Shaffer from Whitney, Texas. He's written a bunch of George Strait's songs. He's written a bunch that got Mo Bandy kicked off. He's one of my favorite songwriters. He used to hang out with Lefty Frizzell. He was with him darn near every day of his life the last ten or twelve years Lefty lived.

Hudson: What songs do you remember best?

Royal: I can't think of the George Jones song . . . about the guy who died, stopped loving her today. I heard this song played for six or seven years. Glen Martin, a songwriter who wrote "Is Anybody Going to San Antone?" likes to sing and get in guitar pullings. He played that song over and over. We must have heard it for six or seven years before George came along and decided to cut it. Then it became a big monster. Glen quit singing it at picking parties after George cut it.

I heard "Cold Fort Worth Beer" at picking parties by Whitey Shaffer for many years before George Strait cut it. Now we all know it.

Hudson: I know you have these picking parties and insist that people listen. Tell me about them.

Royal: I used to do that more than I do now. We didn't organize it. One would wander into town, others would join. We'd get together and play golf and all be at the house. Someone would ask for a guitar, and it started. Musicians are artists. You can't organize them. They like to pick when they want to pick, not because they feel obligated. It doesn't have the same energy, the same feeling. The best picking parties might have thirty or forty people there, or there might not be but four or five. The group can get too big. It becomes a performance instead of sharing.

Hudson: I know you've had a lot of special moments with musicians when everything became magic. Let's talk about one of those.

Royal: I had one not too long ago. I was in the recording studio—Willie's nice enough to invite me when he's recording at the Pedernales here. One night he was recording "Kathleen," a Bing Crosby song from way back. Everyone in the studio had a real warm feeling about it. He put his guitar up after playing it one time. After listening to it, he said, "Let's go to something else." He knew he'd nailed it. Everybody in there knew he nailed it the first time he sang it. Willie just had so much feel on the thing, and he had musicians he liked and was comfortable with. Freddy Powers was on it. Deanybird Reynolds and Johnny Gimble. It was just magic.

Hudson: Do you go to many of the public performances?

Royal: I do, though I don't enjoy public performances as much as I used to. It's hard to capture that magical feeling in a large concert. People are wandering around and talking. People come up and talk to me all the time. It's very distracting.

Hudson: It is exciting when the song works, though. I've been there when the crowd suddenly got quiet and entered the song with the performer. The hush sets in.

Royal: Pretty hard for a hush to set in. I'm talking about a show with three thousand people or something.

Hudson: What about female performers?

Royal: I like Juice Newton and Anne Murray. I like Janie Frickie. She does a great job; the backup singing she does adds a tremendous amount. I like the raspy voice of Sammi Smith. I don't understand why she's not still out there.

Hudson: What is it about the Texas character, the state and environment, which relates to the music?

Royal: First of all, we're rather large; we're almost four states in this area. We've got a pretty good possibility of something happening. I can't think of anybody who's had more lasting influence than Bob Wills, the western swing he brought to country music. The first one to have drums, the first one to have horns. It kinda had a big band sound, and it remained country. I have a hard time just identifying "Texas" music. I don't really have that distinction. Country music is enjoyable; I like the instruments. I like the excellent guitar pickers. I also like Sinatra and Ella Fitzgerald. Ella, by the way, recorded some of Floyd Tillman's songs. Bing Crosby recorded Floyd Tillman. He's a country music writer, but he's been recorded by Perry Como and a bunch of others.

Hudson: Do you hear much about the contrast between a Nashville sound and the Texas sound?

Royal: You hear them talking about it all the time, but I don't know what it means. You really lose me with that. I just know whether I like it or I don't. I don't try to classify it; I just enjoy it.

Paving the Way

Willie Nelson

I didn't really change anything. I came back to Texas when the music scene was already going on. Everybody says I started something, but I didn't start anything so much as join an already growing movement, a legion of people who like good music, no matter what kind, who like to listen to and play whatever they want to.

I heard Willie first in Fort Worth. I was attending Texas Christian University, working part-time for the Ranch Training Department. I sat at a big table in Panther Hall with these "cowboys" and watched a short-haired Willie sing "Mr. Record Man." I bought that first purple album on Liberty Records and played those songs over and over, discovering that I, too, was some sort of "outsider," who also felt a longing for something else "out there."

His generous spirit has always been present. I watched him stand onstage at John T. Floore Country Store in Helotes in the spring of 1995 and sign autographs on shirts, hats, tickets, guitars, and one bare chest as he talked with every fan after the show.

Willie carries a faraway look in his eyes even as they penetrate the object of his vision. His spirituality is ever present, and I've often sensed light surrounding him as we spoke. This man knows who he is in a way that defies articulation. He just knows. Listen to his music, watch his career. Willie has a story to tell and a way to tell it.

Hudson: Who influenced you?

Willie: A lot of different people. Floyd Tillman has been one of my heroes. I learned a lot about writing from him. Also from Leon Payne, a San Antonio boy who wrote "I Love You Because" and many, many more great songs. And there's, of course, Hank Williams and Lefty Frizzell and Cindy Walker. As a picker, I learned Bob Wills and Django Reinhardt, among a lot of other good people.

Hudson: I had a long talk with Floyd, and he calls your name.

Willie: And I'm calling his. That's the way it is.

Hudson: Talk about Farm Aid.

Nelson: The reason we're doing it is because the problem still exists—the farmers still not making enough money and they're going out of business at an alarming rate. We think the farmers shouldn't have to use poisonous pesticides all the time on the foods, and there's laws that require them to do that, and it's not the farmer's fault. If the farmer doesn't do it, he can't get the loans from the government. All these things are the issues we want to talk about—healthy food and the environment, showing how it's all related. Music has the ability to bring a lot of people together, and while they are together, they know they're there to help a good cause, and I think that's why Farm Aid concerts have been so successful.

Hudson: You've been performing so well for so long. How do you keep it alive?

Willie: We do tunes that we love to do, and we do songs that we think the audience would love to hear. If we can get that energy exchange going from the beginning to the end, then we've accomplished what we wanted to do. But it requires the audience and us together to get off at the same time—to "take it to the limits," to steal a phrase. I think we do what we really know how to do best with the songs we pick and the way we play 'em.

We're like electricity—we follow the line of least resistance and it works. We do lots of things off the top of our heads, and the band is good enough to follow me. That happens all the time.

Hudson: In spite of such legendary status, you've seen plenty of criticism.

Willie: We're dealing with it a lot better now than we did at the beginning. But it doesn't matter if it was then or now. We still have the same battles to fight. We still have people who would like to see things done their way, especially nonartists who don't hear the music but know the bottom line.

This is the hardest thing to deal with in the record business, but we still sing the songs we want to play and play 'em the way we want to play 'em. It's still and will always be a daily battle—there's not anyone that doesn't have to go through it every day.

Hudson: You're an extremely prolific songwriter. When do you know it's time for you to write a song?

Willie: It's like labor pains. Whenever you get an idea, you've got to write it; whether it's good or not, it just comes out. Usually, if I get somewhere by myself, it's a lot easier. If I don't get somewhere by myself, these ideas will come, and I'll get too busy to write 'em down, so I'll miss a good idea or miss a good song.

So every now and then I like to just take off down the highway with just me in the car by myself or get off somewhere. I like to spend the day on horseback sometimes. The world looks different on horseback. Or on a bicycle. Just out moving around by myself. Once I get by myself I can think more clearly. No one can write with a lot of noise and things going on around you.

It seems like the more you get in this business, the more noise and confusion you can run into, and it's harder to really concentrate on writing a song. But I know the secret is to get away by yourself.

Hudson: How do you choose songs that other people have written?

Willie: A lot of times folks like Fred Foster and Chips Moman, people who do the producing in Nashville, a place where a lot of the good material winds up, show me things. They have access to a lot of songs that I don't. They don't travel as much as I do. They sit in one place, and writers and publishing houses bring them the material. Songs. So they collect it all, pick the ones that they like, and they bring them to me. I listen to 'em, and if I like them then we record them.

Hudson: What about all those Texans who have moved to Nashville?

Willie: That's where the store is. To sell a song you have to go to the store.

Hudson: Just about every Texas singer-songwriter I've interviewed—well over two hundred performers—cites you as a major inspiration. Not just your music but the way you've "de-colonized" country music, brought it back to its roots.

Willie: I didn't really change anything. I came back to Texas when the music scene was already going on. Everybody says I started something, but I didn't start anything so much as join an already growing movement, a legion of people who like good music, no matter what kind, who like to listen to and play whatever they want to.

I'm probably one of the most bragging Texans you'll ever run across, and I also realize that there's other music in other states. But Texans go everywhere.

The Writer

Floyd Tillman

Foremost, I'm a writer. I think I have made my living as a writer, and I think I'll be remembered longer as a writer than I will be as a singer.

During the years preceding World War II, Floyd Tillman pioneered in the employment of lead single-string guitar playing and was one of the first country musicians to play an electric guitar. Before 1941, he began his reputation as one of country music's greatest songwriters, having written "I'll Keep on Loving You" and "It Makes No Difference Now." He became known as a singer of distinction with such songs as "I Love You So Much It Hurts" and "Slipping Around." According to Bill Malone in *Stars of Country Music,* "With his lazy, drawling style performed with a baritone voice that somehow suggested a rural Bing Crosby, Tillman built a new career as a country stylist."

    I drove into Hunt, my barrel horse in tow. We had two missions that night—one to run around those three cans in the fastest possible time; the other to talk to Floyd Tillman, country music legend. We were meeting at a legendary outdoor dance hall, Crider's, named after a Hill Country family. The huge spreading oak (since burned down) reminded us that Texas music is an integral part of the environment—trees, rivers, and lakes are also part of the scene. Floyd has many friends in the Hill Country. We sat down on a bench behind the cafe; my barrel horse was tied nearby. Floyd didn't blink an eye at the unusual "approach" to an interview. Instead, he smiled warmly, blue eyes lit up with curiosity, and welcomed me. Floyd, with his many years of experience, brings an authentic voice to the series. The man who wrote the first cheating song to be played on the radio, "Slipping Around," is still an active force in the Texas music scene.

Hudson: Crider's is an institution in this part of the country. You and your music are certainly an integral part of the entire country music scene. The first thing I'd like to talk about are some of the very early influences on you.

Tillman: The first time I got interested in country music, I was about ten years old. Nineteen twenty-four was the year, and my neighbor had a phonograph, and the boy I was running around with said, "Let's go over and listen to our record player." It was the type you wind up, and he put this record on: "The Prisoner Song" by Vernon Dalhart. I thought that was the prettiest thing I'd ever heard. I didn't care much about music until I heard that. The music didn't have a name then; it wasn't hillbilly, it wasn't western, it wasn't cowboy; it was just music. I heard that side of it and we turned it over. The other side was "The Wreck of Old 97." I thought "Well, that's kinda' nice." It was different from what I'd been hearing on phonographs before because most of it was a bunch of horns, and I couldn't understand it at that age. So I picked up a harmonica and started learning, and I played "The Prisoner Song," but I didn't care anything about singing. I did have two brothers who were interested in music, and the oldest one started taking a course, and he taught my other older brother how to play. I was pretty young, but they taught me a few things. I wasn't that interested in learning to play music. I was more interested in radios and electronics, things like that.

Hudson: Let's talk a little bit about some of the labels that have been applied to country music as well as to your own music. How would you describe your music?

Tillman: I think they first called it cowboy music because there were a lot of songs like "He Was Just a Lonely Cowboy." But that wasn't a good name, and some people picked up the word "hillbilly," and I don't know where that came from. It was "hillbilly" officially for a long time, and they had what they called a "hillbilly hit parade," and that lasted clear on through World War II. I'm getting ahead of my story now, but during that war, I made records while I was in the army. Axis Sally got a hold of some, and Tokyo Rose, and they played the songs we made on Decca, played them overseas, and the boys heard them. They used them for propaganda purposes.

Hudson: Worldwide exposure. So how did Jimmie Rodgers fit into the category "hillbilly," and what was your impression of him?

Tillman: I heard him a lot. I was in Post, Texas, that's West Texas, near

Lubbock and Sweetwater. I was a messenger boy for the Western Union and railroad, and I would ride down the street and hear Jimmie Rodgers. It was almost like having a radio on your bicycle. You could just ride down the street, and when we had a new record—everybody had the record—and you could hear "He's in the Jailhouse Now." You'd ride from one door and then hear it at the next door. It was really amazing how many people bought Jimmie Rodgers records. Naturally, he influenced me a little bit, as he did many other people.

Hudson: He had a short but powerful career.

Tillman: Like Hank Williams. When he was starting out, I had a band in Houston, and Hank was our guest. We paid him twenty-five dollars, and he had one song that he was singing, "Move Over Little Dog, the Big Dog's Movin' In." He said if he ever got a band he was going to get one like mine. But then he told me, "I ain't got nothing to do for the next three days, and if it's all right, can I just come along and sing with you? I won't charge you anything." So he sang with us for three nights free.

Hudson: You have watched a lot of different trends come and go in music. How do you account for having maintained your place throughout?

Tillman: I haven't exactly *maintained* my place. I got out of it for two years and played in what they call a pop band. It was in the Big Band days because I could make more money with them playing guitar and lead. This was a band in 1936, and the leader heard me play with this hillbilly band and asked me if I could read music. I said, "No, I can read the chords but I can't read music." He said, "That's all right; you've got a good enough ear to pick it up anyway." So I went to work for them for fifteen dollars a week, which was pretty good money then. I worked for them for two years. They had two girl singers, and these girls couldn't sing certain songs because there were supposed to be men singing love songs about a girl. A girl can't sing about a girl too much, so they asked me if I would sing. They'd heard me sing for a hillbilly band, so I did it. Songs like "Lilly Marlane," "In the Mood." I got to writing songs because I had written some in my hometown in Post before I left home, but I didn't know how to get them recorded because songwriters were very scarce. I bet there weren't three or four of us in the whole state of Texas that wrote songs, especially for a living. Commercial songwriters were mostly in New York in Tin Pan Alley or just a handful of people all over the country. Some were on the West Coast, but songwriters were very scarce. Not like now.

Hudson: Texas is rich with songwriters now.

Tillman: I turned out one called "It Makes No Difference Now," and because it wasn't a good song for this pop band to play, we didn't ever play it. After two years I decided to go back to hillbilly and see if I could get a hillbilly band to get it recorded. I started singing it; we got so many requests for it, we almost used it for a theme song. Jimmie Davis heard the song. He came by and wanted to buy it. He offered me two hundred dollars for it. I held out for three hundred. I sold it to him. But I found out later you sell a song for twenty-eight years. I got it back twenty-eight years later, and my first royalty check was ten times bigger than what I sold it for originally.

Hudson: Do you have some specific songs that came from the years you spent doing pop music?

Tillman: I wrote "The World Keeps You" and "I'll Keep on Lovin' You." I wrote about my car, by the way. I took three hundred dollars I'd saved up and put half on a new car, a 1936 Chevrolet, and I had it half paid for. A new car just cost six hundred dollars then. I loved that car so much I said, "If the world keeps on turnin' as I'm sure it's bound to do, I'll keep on lovin' you."

Hudson: When you got back into what you were calling hillbilly music, western swing, what do you see happening to your music as you moved along in the country field?

Tillman: I think as a writer, I had made more money from the pop singers than I had from the country singers. Perry Como sang my records and Bing Crosby, Ella Fitzgerald, the Mills Brothers. They were probably selling more records than the country music, hillbilly as it was called back then, and I did pretty good—more so as a writer than I did playing with a band. I'm getting ahead of my story, but I did form a band after I got out of the army. I kept this band together for about six or seven years. And I was writing a lot. During that time I wrote "Slipping Around." We were coming back from San Antonio that night, and we stopped at Charlie's Barn about two or three o'clock in the morning for a cup of coffee. I heard a woman talking on the phone. She said, "Honey, you call me tomorrow and if a man answers, hang up." I thought, "That's a funny conversation, maybe she's slippin' around." That gave me the idea for the lyrics, which I wrote on a napkin. We finished it the next day, and I never thought it would be played on the radio because some of those disc jockeys wouldn't play lyrics where someone was tied up with someone else. In fact, when it got on the Hit Parade later on, they sent me a wire saying, "We have to censor this line for the networks and add another line." I guess I had it coming.

Hudson: A lot of musicians and songwriters today feel your name and influence have been most important to them, including Willie Nelson. You've seen that wonderful review he wrote on you, put out by the Country Music Hall of Fame. That was such a compliment. If you were to look at artists now, who's going to make a difference?

Tillman: It would be sheer guessing, and I'm not a very good guesser as to what's going to happen. But I do know things go in cycles. Country music gets up real big, then it goes down, and it gets big, and it goes down. Rock 'n' roll will eventually slow down. Big bands will come back again, and I think jazz will come back.

Hudson: But that blues stuff is always there, right?

Tillman: Blues will never die.

Hudson: You hear some blues in your music, right?

Tillman: Yes, when I was writing for the guitar, I got a hold of a record by Lightnin' Hopkins playing the blues.

He was playing real blues licks on the guitar, and during my air appearance I didn't sing unless I had to. I just wanted to play lead guitar. That was all I wanted to do because it was unusual for anyone to play lead guitar when I started. But the only bad thing, they had no amplifiers when I started playing, and it wasn't loud enough. One of my brothers had a metal guitar, so I'd borrow his metal guitar and play so that they could hear me. But it still wasn't as loud as an electrical instrument. Then in 1935 Ted Daffen, who later on wrote "Born To Lose," used a steel guitar. He was a Hawaiian guitar player, and he wanted to learn how to play country music, so we hired him in the band we had. He also had a car and a sound system. He was good at electronics. He had what they call a Volutone. It was an amplifier with a little thing you put under the strings to make the guitar louder. I loved that thing so much I offered to trade him my $150 Model A Ford for it. I had paid $150 for it; it was a 1929 model Ford. He took me up on my offer. I think it was the best deal I ever made, because people would just stand around and watch me play electric guitar. That's how I came to get the job with that pop band—not because I was a singer or songwriter, but a guitar picker. Later on I had to sing to get my songs started.

Hudson: How do you see yourself first and foremost?

Tillman: Foremost, I'm a writer. I have made my living as a writer, and I think I'll be remembered longer as a writer than I will be as a singer.

Hudson: How do you know when it's time for you to write a song?

Tillman: You don't know. A song just comes through you, just like babies come through a woman. The good songs do. Of course you can write a commercial song, and sometimes you have to squeeze it out. But the idea in songs just happens. You're riding along, and you have something in your mind, and you write it down. Sometimes you get an idea from what somebody said, like "Makes no difference now anyway." That wouldn't be a bad name for a song. But you don't write it until you feel like it.

Hudson: Marcia Ball was in a bar real late one night. Everybody was fooling around the bar and the waitress said, "That's enough of that stuff." And Marcia said, "That's a song." She put it on her *Hot Tamale Baby* album.

Tillman: That's the way they come.

Hudson: How do you account for the fact that some people are in tune to or receptive to these songs? I mean there are a lot of songs that have passed through you.

Tillman: I think a lot of it's luck, and maybe the timing's just right. I do know that I've seen great songs written, and maybe ten or twenty years later they would come out and make a hit, but it wasn't the first time they came out. It must be something to do with the timing or the mood everybody's in when a certain type of song comes out.

Hudson: But I was thinking about the songs that come through you if you are a transmitter. Someone else may see some of those same things, but they don't come up with the songs that you do. So where do those powers of observation and feeling come from?

Tillman: I think it's just intuitive. Maybe it's the difference between a good artist and a bad artist. A good artist can pick up good songs where an artist that doesn't make it cannot recognize it.

Hudson: I feel real lucky to have gotten a hold of you before tonight's sesquicentennial celebration and dance.

Tillman: I'm looking forward to this night. I've got Scott Randolph and his band, and they sound real good.

Hudson: Is this a special part of the country for you?

Tillman: Yes, I love the Hill Country.

Living to Write

Sonny Throckmorton

Writing is like living. They're one and the same. I live, and I report on what I do. It's a continuation of what I have done.

I first heard Sonny at a songwriters' gathering for an Austin television show produced by Bill McDavid and Freddy Powers. We were at Bill's house waiting for the crew to set up for filming. Sonny was soft-spoken, unassuming and humble. I knew he had a long list of awards and years of experience. His willingness to talk and share his story was part of his charm. His sincere way of wrestling with each question to give a complete, honest answer was also part of his charm.

Several years later I invited him to speak and perform at the Texas Association of Creative Writing Teachers (TACWT) Conference at Heart of the Hills Camp in Hunt. We talked again before he told this group his own perspective on the writing process.

Sonny is first and foremost a writer, but when I heard him perform his own songs at the Saxon Pub in Austin, I heard "This Is When the Cowboy Rides Away" for the first time. I heard Sonny's story in his performance, and I even heard my own story. Sonny Throckmorton is a performer; he delivers a song straight from the heart.

Sonny is living in Brownwood, raising a family and working on an album of gospel music. The Internet is creating possibilities for marketing his music that were previously impossible. And he's excited about the possibility and change. The following conversation took place September 6, 1996, at the home base for Hammerhead Publishing Company with Bill McDavid and Freddy Powers.

Hudson: I'd like to begin with a saying by Chogyam Trungpa that Allen Ginsberg often quoted, "First thought, best thought." Let's talk about exciting moments for you.

Throckmorton: One of the highlights for me was being inducted into the Songwriters Hall of Fame. That was very exciting for me. Also, there were several years that I was honored as Songwriter of the Year. Just writing a song and getting done with it and knowing you've done a good piece of work, that day is exciting to me. And, I like entertaining. It's a love-hate relationship, but I like to get on stage and try to warble through my stuff. Music is exciting. And the day I found out I could make a living with a guitar was very exciting to me. 'Cause, lazy as I was, it was a hell of an option for an old boy who was going to have to dig ditches.

Hudson: What were you doing with your life when you discovered that?

Throckmorton: Well, when I discovered I could entertain, I was about six years old. My dad was a preacher, and I had two older sisters. They sang, and I became part of the trio. They had me doing harmonies by the time I was seven. The people in church were an appreciative audience.

Hudson: Where were you at this time?

Throckmorton: My dad was a Pentecostal preacher, and we traveled all over America. I was born in Carlsbad, New Mexico, and raised in California and Texas. More in Texas than anywhere, all over Texas. Dallas, Borger, Aransas Pass, Spur, Wichita Falls. I would say whenever I was a kid that if I ever left Texas, I wanted to come back. I didn't spend much time where I was born. All my family was born in Texas. I lived in Nashville about twenty years, and I'm in Brownwood, Texas, now. My dad and sisters lived there.

Hudson: Some songwriters I've talked to have been interested in books; others tell their life stories in their songs. What are your influences?

Throckmorton: The greatest influence I had to be a songwriter was my dad. He was a preacher. You put sermons together much the same way you put songs together. He preached a sermon one time about when Peter and Paul were thrown in prison, and he tied in the fact that the earth was the Lord's footstool. They started singing and getting happy, and he said God was sitting on his footstool and started patting his foot, and the prison fell down. Writers who influenced me are Fred Rose, Roger Miller, Curly Putnam, and, of course, Willie. I haven't emulated any of them, but

I soared with them. When they soared, I soared doing my own deal. I don't reckon I really copied anybody.

Hudson: What's difficult for you?

Throckmorton: I've always been in tune with melody. With lyrics, you put up your antenna, and you look for great ideas. You're working all the time. The people you meet and the life situations will give you ideas for songs. If you've got your antenna up. That's a given. It's the simplest, yet the hardest thing to do, just to be in tune. I lose track all the time.

Hudson: Writing is like that?

Throckmorton: Writing is like living. They're one and the same. I live, and I report on what I do. It's a continuation of what I have done.

Hudson: What accounts for this urge to "report"? Is it ever urgent?

Throckmorton: Yes, the good ones are. For example, "The Way I Am," a song I wrote for Merle Haggard, came to me after I had been through a lot. Writing can be some of the best therapy one can do.

Hudson: Do you have a daily practice?

Throckmorton: Yeah, I drink coffee in the morning.

Hudson: Do you keep a daily journal?

Throckmorton: No. I only write when I feel like it. I would think it would be better for me if I did, but I don't. There was a time I would go in and sit and write and think. I get into a place of deep thought at times and come out with a song.

Hudson: Is there a particular place where you like to write?

Throckmorton: I prefer being in a car. On a long trip, by myself. No radio. But, I'm also very lazy, and that forces a discipline on me.

Hudson: You say you're lazy. I don't see that.

Throckmorton: Oh yes, I'm very lazy. If I weren't, by now, instead of two or three thousand songs, I would have written forty or fifty thousand. I can write three or four songs a day. I've written as many as two hits in one day.

Hudson: You have a gift.

Throckmorton: I think I do. The first song I wrote I was in church, and my father was preaching this long-winded sermon that I'd heard before. I wrote a gospel song while he was preaching. I didn't know what it was. I thought I was some kind of weirdo, and I was afraid to tell my male friends I'd written this song. But, I would sit down and say it to this woman, and she started crying. I knew right then it was a gift to be able to reach out and touch someone. I also think it's a craft. It's both things. When you develop the craft, there's really no stopping you. When I was young, people would tell me that I didn't really want to do this. I should be a lawyer or an engineer. The odds of writing a hit song are about one million to one. I'd agree, then say the odds were twenty to one. I went right ahead and did what I wanted.

Hudson: I know lots of men who wake up about forty and hate what they're doing.

Throckmorton: I was about forty when I wrote "The Way I Am." I went through a phase where I hated music and songs. I moved to Brownwood and said "To hell with it," for a while. I've been in a burnt-out stage. I'm just now coming out of that.

Hudson: What hobbies do you have?

Throckmorton: I love to garden. I love to walk places I haven't been before. I love to hear music.

Hudson: Were you influenced by politics?

Throckmorton: I've written songs that poked fun at certain aspects of political life. But I'm not into politics; I'm into songwriting.

Hudson: Pick a song you like and tell me the story behind it.

Throckmorton: Probably one of the funniest songs was called "Trying To Love Two Women." The Oak Ridge Boys had a number one record with that. I lived on a farm, and I'd driven up my driveway to get my paper. I had to drive out and turn back in. I pulled up in my neighbor's yard, and he said to me, "Are we too loud down here?" Then he added, "If you hear shooting down here, would you call the cops?" I asked him what was wrong, and he said, "Well, I'm trying to love two women." So I backed out of the driveway and had the song written by the time I got back to the house. I made a demo of the song and thought it was a really weak song. I couldn't believe the song made the album for the Oak Ridge Boys. I said it would probably be the last song released on the album. It ended up being the first hit single. It's still a big hit in Europe. I guess it fit a lot of people. Sometimes it takes life to show you what a song really means.

Hudson: What is a characteristic of Texas songwriters?

Throckmorton: Free. I think that Texas has always been the breeding ground for a new species of music. What a wonderful mix we have here. Everything from German to Mexican to hillbilly. It all comes together in Texas. The people here don't seem to care. We have a freedom here. If you go to Kentucky, you're nailed down to bluegrass. Why, in Texas, they're into all of it, and they like it all. If it's good. That's the only thing they require. There's definitely a freedom of expression, a freedom of flow that doesn't exist anywhere else I know of in the world.

Hudson: Do you have a favorite song?

Throckmorton: No.

Hudson: A favorite style of music?

Throckmorton: No. I'm a Texan. I love it all.

Our next conversation took place in February 1999 at the TACWT Conference in Hunt. We sat on a stone wall near the Guadalupe River and talked.

Hudson: Describe your experience with the music business.

Throckmorton: I'm just as excited by being in the music business, and I've had hits in the '60s, '70s, '80s, and '90s. I've had a pretty long productive run, and that is kind of exciting.

Hudson: When you started in the business, did you have a vision of what could be out ahead of you?

Throckmorton: I always had the vision that I would always do good in the music business. I never doubted it. More talented people were out there, but they dropped by the way. My attitude is like I do life now. I let it flow, and it goes, and I figure it is going in the right direction if I don't get in its way.

Hudson: When I spent time around Townes Van Zandt, I really became aware of some of the struggle surrounding the creative process. What is your experience with struggle?

Throckmorton: Well, I pretty much struggled. I reached my thirty-fifth birthday, a deadline I'd set for myself to be successful. I had to feed a family, and when I was thirty-five, I had been fired from three big publishing companies. I always got the deals, but they would last a year, and then they would get somebody else. The last guy I had signed with was Roger Miller. He's a sweetheart. I signed with him, then moved to Texas. Before I left Nashville, a friend of mine told me to go by and see Don Gant, who had just come to work in the trade. I called Don, and I said, "I'm going to Texas, and I sure would appreciate it if you could get some of my songs cut. I could sure use the money until I can get on my feet."

He asked me if I had any hits. I said I did. In fact, they had already been at Tree Publishing (where Gant worked now), and I had been fired. I took him twenty songs. He listened to fifteen and wrote down thirteen. He went to a staff meeting the next morning and said, "If you don't know what a hit is, here's thirteen of them! Go pitch these songs." I started getting cuts right and left. Some of the same guys who fired me had to call me back and rehire me. I kind of enjoyed that.

I'm fifty-seven now, and that happened when I was thirty-five. After that I was probably the hottest songwriter for five years. All because I went back and let someone else listen to the songs. I had a run from '77 to '80. I'll tell anybody who does anything: you know you have to love it, first of all, and don't even do it if you don't love it.

Hudson: Let's talk about writing.

Throckmorton: I write from my heart, and I don't actually write anything; God writes it all. That's to start off with, and I don't mean that as a religious fanatical statement. I'm one who believes I can't outwrite God. The things that happen in my life, the big and courageous stories I see around me are real. I can get most of my story there, and I'm real smart if I stick with that text. If I ever try to create it in my head, it's never been worth a crap. I've experienced the stories in my songs.

Hudson: One of my favorite Sonny songs is "This Is Where the Cowboy Rides Away." The night I heard you sing it at the Saxon Pub was magic; the sky just opened up and the song struck like lightning.

Throckmorton: Well, bless your heart. That was a hard song. Casey Kelly and I wrote this. He had been with this lady who had been jerking him around for a long, long time. He finally escaped from her, and it broke his heart. I had one that pretty much did the same thing to me. We sat down until the spirit really moved on that one. It was truly one of those songs that you just don't sit down and grab something. We waited until it came. I'm proud of those kind of songs.

Hudson: Do most come to you that way?

Throckmorton: I've labored real hard on some, but I must say some of the bigger ones came real quick.

Hudson: What are you imagining ahead of you now?

Throckmorton: I want to do a gospel album, because I have never done one. I've got ten or twelve gospel songs that have been burning a hole in me. I want to get in the studio, and I own my own studio, so that is not a problem. I got a call right before I came here from some people in Nashville. They sell products over the Internet and are very efficient at it. They are going to do a Texas writers series, and they have a system where they can put 160 songs on a CD. I wouldn't mind somebody cutting some more of my songs. It's nice to have a hit now and then.

Hudson: You're speaking to a group of writers and teachers tonight. Dr. David Breeden, my colleague at Schreiner College, writes poetry, novels, and screenplays. He has translated Beowulf into modern verse and that is on the Internet. You just met Clay Reynolds, and he's written six or seven novels. This group is really going to be interested in what you have to say.

Throckmorton: I wish I had a chance to hear what they have to say!

Young and Restless

James McMurtry

I just get a little more irascible all the time. At performances, I get louder and more obnoxious as I go. The sound that I really prefer to play is in rock clubs for rock crowds because they just have a better time. A lot of times I have to bludgeon promoters into believing that.

I interviewed Larry McMurtry for my dissertation at Texas Christian University in 1981. He spoke at a Texas Images conference in Denton several years later. He told me he had a son in San Antonio who was writing songs. Another year passed, and I was at a book signing for *Texasville*. Larry reminded me again that his son was writing songs. I called him that day, and we set up a meeting at James's favorite hangout in San Antonio, the Liberty Bar and Grill.

By 1996 James had three albums out on Columbia, and he was searching for a new label. He had received huge critical acclaim, but the masses had not discovered him. Not enough record sales to keep him on the label. His performance had grown from a solo gig in a folk club to a trio that rocked the crowd and inspired folks to dance. James liked people dancing.

Our series of conversations reveal an artist at work, an artist growing, an artist facing both success and failure.

Hudson: Let's trace your travels. You've spent time in Archer City, and before that in Arizona.

McMurtry: I also spent a summer in Alaska. That was kind of interesting.

I was playing music in a little roadhouse. Instrumental background music, three hours a night, six nights a week. I never went anywhere. It was at a time in my life that if I didn't go certain places, it didn't matter because I would be back. Like, I never went to McKinley Park because I figured I'd be back next year.

Hudson: Alaska's a long way away to think that you would be back.

McMurtry: But every place was like that. My ideas about traveling were that I'd like to go places and live there for a couple of months and see how the locals acted, rather than touring around with the regular tourist crowd. When I started up there, everybody kept telling me to read John McPhee. I didn't want to read. I don't like to read anyway. I like to discover things.

Back to Tucson. It was okay. I had gone to prep school in the East, and Arizona seemed like the next step. I went to Woodbury Forest School in Virginia. The kind of school where they would toss you out if you had fun.

Hudson: What made you decide to go out to Arizona?

McMurtry: I was curious . . . about who went there and why. I was accepted by UCLA and Rice. If I had been serious about education, I probably would have gone to one of those schools. But who goes to Tucson? Somebody must go to Tucson. Mostly midwestern kids who didn't want to study. Or Eastern kids who didn't want to study . . . like me.

Hudson: Has your family been together all the time you were growing up?

McMurtry: I'm an only child, and my folks split up when I was about three, maybe earlier than that. I always saw a lot of both of them, but they never were together. My mother teaches English at the University of Richmond. She's a really academic type. She keeps trying to get me to go back to school. It may happen someday, after she quits bugging me to do it.

Hudson: So you went to a prep school, spent time with both parents, then tried college. Those influences must be important.

McMurtry: Yeah, but I sort of goofed off. I tried to cram two years of schooling into four years.

Hudson: In your travels and various jobs and school what were some high points for you? What are you, twenty-five now?

McMurtry: I just turned twenty-five about a month ago. It's really weird, like waking up from the dead or something. Now I'm getting interested in things. I'm not sure why. But I did write. I was talking to you on the phone about how I wrote fragments for years and years. I stuck them into a box, never made anything out of them. In the last year, I've been building some of that into songs. When I don't have any new ideas, I go through the box of possibles. Take a couple of lines and try to build a song. Like laying bricks, or something.

I'm curious to see what other people do with my songs. I have a friend in New Mexico, Tish Hinojosa, who plays some of my songs. I usually send her my songs just to see what she will do with them. There's one I've got that I'd like to hear Nanci Griffith do, if I can get it to her. In fact my father just called this morning, she's a big fan of his, and mentioned her. I'd like to send her something saying, "Here, I know you like my dad's stuff; here's some of mine."

Hudson: Are you involved with the new work of songwriters and musicians here in San Antonio?

McMurtry: Not really, I'm kind of a recluse here. I've got a couple of musical friends, including Steve Chicetti. He's been a solo artist for a couple of years.

Hudson: Have you approached the Leon Springs Cafe?

McMurtry: Several times. For some reason, I don't seem to hit it off with those people. I did an audition there once. Tish was playing, and she let me play on one of her breaks. I was real nervous. I don't know if I really screwed up the audition or if they just don't want solos or what. [James has since played several very successful gigs there, including one just prior to his record release of *Too Long in the Wasteland* on Columbia.]

Sid Fly played out there regularly for a while. I showed up about a year and a half ago. I had this song I had been playing around. I think it was the first one I ever copyrighted. It was about small-town life. Sort of *The Last Picture Show* goes to song. Sid had heard it. He asked me to get up and play my song during his break. I said sure. By the time the break rolled around, Steve Chicetti [now calling himself Steve James] and Rex Foster had appeared. So there were more important musicians there, so he got them up on his break. I was hanging around till the end. Finally, I got up and left. I always felt uncomfortable when I went out there.

Hudson: How do you deal with the "Larry's boy" aspect? I'm sure you're aware that it can be helpful.

McMurtry: I plan on capitalizing on that the best I can. It's not a hindrance right now, at all. It was for a while. I sort of got tired of it. I think it's a real good time to be "Larry's boy." Opportunity knocks.

Hudson: He just won a Pulitzer Prize for writing about this area in *Lonesome Dove*. There is an interest in regional material. In the record business, CBS just signed Rattlesnake Annie, a traditional folksinger, and the O'Kanes, who include lots of bluegrass licks in their songs. There seems to be more interest in regional material, even at a national level. Asleep at the Wheel is now on CBS as well. There are some changes going on. Rick Blackburn at CBS just told Billy Joe Shaver to go make an album that sounds like Billy Joe, keeping the honesty and integrity of the music intact. That's not the way we traditionally think of record labels. I think you're in a real good place right now to make some things happen.

McMurtry: My song about a small town was inspired by a sign on the door of a general store in southeast Virginia. In one of those little towns—they've got millions of them—it was a cardboard sign that said, "Positively, no loafin', bare feet, or foul language in this store." So, I just remembered that. It's probably been seven or eight years since I've seen that sign. I needed a song so I wrote that.

Hudson: Was that song a fragment for a long time?

McMurtry: It was just that first little line. I didn't really take it very far. I had written that first line, "No shoes, no shirt, no service," and it sat around for a couple of years. I kept trying different things with it that didn't work. Then I wrote a second bit about using up credit and added it. Then I added some instrumental stuff.

Hudson: You mentioned another song that was Archer City in song.

McMurtry: I'll play it for you. I wrote it the winter I was up there painting on the house. It was the first time in my so-called adult life that I spent more than a month there. I used to go up a lot for summers when I was a kid. I lived with my grandfather one summer. That was the year he died. The next year I spent with my grandmother but not in the same house. After being married forty years, Granny finally got up enough nerve to leave. She moved out to Wichita Falls. She just left. They didn't get a divorce or anything. She couldn't stand living with the old guy anymore. She'd come back every so often. She'd come back to get into a good fight. That was one thing they lived for—to yell at one another. When he died she came back one summer and yelled at me. I'd never been yelled at in my entire life. I wasn't used to it, but I got where I could yell back.

Hudson: Any specific influences on your writing?

McMurtry: I like John Prine a lot. I like Steve Goodman. I'm sure they've all had some kind of influence. I can't point to a line and say where. A guitar player once told me that one of the ways you develop your style is by stealing from other people. When all these stolen parts come together, they become your style. [He plays "It's a Small Town," not to be confused with Mellencamp's "Small Town." Ironically, two years later Mellencamp produced McMurtry's first album.]

Hudson: Do you have any procedure to your songwriting? Is there any discipline to your day?

McMurtry: Very little. I feel like that's something I need to work on. The songs get written when they absolutely have to be written. When I cannot avoid sitting down and working on the songs. That's when they get finished. Lately, I've been getting more inspiration than I have in the last couple of years. I get where I want to sit down and write songs. But there's always something else to do. I feel like if I sit down to write, I'm missing something that's happening down the street. So I go out and think about writing songs. Then when I get back I'm tired. I used to worry about losing things. But I don't think you really lose them; they come back. They come back differently, but they do come back.

Hudson: Do you ever just try to save things you're writing on napkins?

McMurtry: No, I always lose the napkins.

Hudson: Do you notice a common thread in all your writing?

McMurtry: The only thing common to all of them is that they're written on yellow legal paper.

Hudson: Did your stuff start off as songs? Or did you write poetry and put music to it?

McMurtry: It always started off as songs. The thing about songs is that you can add depth with music. It will not come straight off the page—usually. You can do things with inflections and chord changes. I also don't think good poetry necessarily makes good songs. A lot of Dylan's stuff is better poetry than song.

Hudson: What are your plans for the future?

McMurtry: I'd like to play a lot more and write a lot more. I haven't been very prolific. I haven't been hustling out there and trying to get as many jobs as I could. I've been sort of sitting back, checking the situation out and talking myself out of things, for one reason or another. I'm bored with that. I want to go out there and play. Even if I have to stand on the street corner. I want to work on the business aspect of it. I didn't think that was interesting, but I do now. It's a challenge. It's sort of stretching your consciousness to go from the dream world of the artist to the real world and still come up with a little of the art left. Making some money would be nice, too. I hear people preaching all the time about how they do it just for the love of it. I do love the music. I like songs, and I like the works of good songwriters. I like to perform too. But performance doesn't last. Performance gives you an instant high which the writer doesn't get. My father complains about that. He tells me I'm lucky because I get instant response when I'm out there. He claims that even if the written work is a great piece, the satisfaction doesn't last. When he finishes a book, he's done with it. As soon as he's finished writing he loses contact with the characters and basically forgets what he's written. In the case of *Lonesome Dove*, he got all those prizes, which was really neat. But it got old because he was starting to lose contact with what he had written. With performance, you do get that instant recognition. That's the goal. I want to write a few good songs that people are always going to remember. Immortality, that's what it is.

Hudson: In graduate school we studied language as a chisel that creates at the moment that it's working.

McMurtry: It's also in the oral tradition. The last vestiges of the oral tradition. I hadn't thought of it that way.

Hudson: James, sing another song. I want to hear some more of your music.

McMurtry: [He tunes his guitar and begins.] "Crazy Winds and Flashing Yellow Lights," a song about a woman who becomes disillusioned with her life and finally leaves. The wind makes her crazy and blue. "It's a restless feeling and it's nothing new."

Hudson: I like that.

McMurtry: Good. That's my current masterpiece. The best I have to offer right now. I worked on that one longer than any of the other five. I think it took about three months of writing every day. I would sit down every evening and try to make it work.

Hudson: Do you do a lot of rewriting?

McMurtry: I start messing with things; the page gets all jumbled up and I tear it off and set it aside. Don't throw it away yet. So if I want to look back, I can. Then I'll end up with a stack of pages. Finally, I come up with a song. My favorite songwriters have written a lot of mediocre songs, some of which even got cut. Robbie Robertson, one of my favorites, is very prolific. Some of his songs are incredible and some are just okay.

Hudson: What magic moments have you experienced in the process?

McMurtry: You calling me up wanting to interview me. That was a bolt from the blue. Having written only six songs and being interviewed was a real turning point.

Hudson: That's going to happen even more, I guarantee you.

McMurtry: One moment that comes to mind was when I did an open mike in Tucson a while back. I got up and the first two or three songs I was on the verge of losing it. I was so nervous. I was standing up, I play standing up. That way I won't slouch. If I sit down, I slouch. Better overall if I'm on my feet. Also you're at a better vantage point to dodge flying objects if you're on your feet already. Makes me feel a lot better. I was so nervous I almost didn't stand. It was a place I had played as a student. I came by for this open stage, down in the basement. When I played there before it was an outdoor place. People came and didn't really listen. This time, they all came to the open mike to listen. I wasn't used to that. They were all tuned in. I got through the first song, and I thought I was going to fall on to the floor. I got past that. It was finally okay. People were really getting into it. When I got past that, I felt like I could fly. That was magic, and it's not something that has to do solely with the performer. It's also the audience. It's energy that's happening. That's what I look for.

That's my goal in performance. To find the magic. I saw this happen in Madrid. I was eighteen. I had gone over as a teacher's aide. I was just out of prep school, and the school was sending over students to live with families and do some intensive study. Just about every night I would go down to the Plaza Mayor and hit all the bars. I was there one night, about three in the morning. There were all these street musicians in the plaza. Some of them were pretty good. Some of them were more or less polite beggars. I remember this guy who used to sleep with his hand permanently out. He might wake up and find a coin. Another guy had a gut-strung violin, and he had this drum with him. It had a fiberglass body with a skin head. The body came out in a bell shape. He would put one hand inside the drum and do all this beating on it. He could get different tones by moving his hand.

I came out and sat down with this circle of drunks under this streetlamp. These guys were way out in the middle of some drunks gathered around them. The music was kind of halfway working. I just sat down. All the bars were closed, and I was drunk anyway. I was trying to figure out what to do. A little crowd of people came out on their way back from the bars. They were well-dressed, uptown Castilian folks. Suddenly these two musicians just snapped into line. The fiddler was really heavyset. He didn't look Spanish at all. Russian, or something. He had real thick glasses on. He had a case full of sheet music that he wasn't bothering to read. The drummer was from southern Spain. He looked kind of Arabic. Something happened. All the women began dancing; the men just stood there awed. I did too. I couldn't believe this. They were all in fine evening dresses, and they were dancing like crazed Gypsies. It got very intense. They kept at it as long as they could, as long as they could keep that magic. Then they just gradually slipped away. The dancers slowed down and sort of spiraled out to the edge of the circle. The crowd drifted off. Finally, I drifted off too. I want to capture that. But I think you have to go for something else in a studio. There are studio recordings that I really love, but it's a different skill. I don't know how that works. I have a real problem recording on this machine here at home, alone. It's always real laid back because the room is empty.

Hudson: Texas music is . . .

McMurtry: Texas music is music for people that know this stuff on some level or another. I don't guess you could do it if you haven't really been here. You can't copy it. I've heard that Asleep at the Wheel is from Pennsylvania and they do great Bob Wills type stuff. You were asking about influences a while ago. I guess what influences me are Hank Williams on the radio when I was four years old and mediocre bluegrass at the fire station in Virginia, which I used to go listen to from time to time. One of the great things is to go back to Waterford and visit and hear that bluegrass. I never played bluegrass much, but I did listen to a lot of it. I didn't think much of it at that time. But it sunk in somehow. Then when I got to Arizona, people were listening to that stuff out there. I never really considered myself a Texas musician. I guess from the time I was fifteen or sixteen and started thinking about it, I considered the foundation for my music to be bluegrass. I hadn't heard a lot of Texas music live until I started coming down here to San Antonio. I'd go and hear Gary P. Nunn or Joe Ely. I didn't know anything about it until a couple of years ago.

Hudson: The diversity and eclectic nature of it, from Joe Ely to Joe Paul Nichols.

McMurtry: At the Celebrate Austin Music Festival in 1985, Dave Bromberg played with Jerry Jeff Walker. That was the best concert I've ever seen anywhere. There were a hundred people in the audience, and nobody cared that it was raining. The musicians were all up, and that magic was happening. Even Kennedy was funny. First time I've ever seen Rod Kennedy funny. I saw Joe Ely there. First time I ever saw or heard of him.

Hudson: He rocked the crowd in Cannes, France, this year.

McMurtry: First time I saw Terry Allen was at the Southwest Crafts center in San Antonio. Lubbock has produced some good ones. Maybe I should move there.

Hudson: Joe Ely told me that the wind blowing created much of the rhythm in his music.

McMurtry: The wind blows in Archer County, and it doesn't create much of anything, except insanity.

Hudson: You got that blues in your music from somewhere. We're in San Antonio, Texas, we're out of wine, and we'll continue this some other day.

McMurtry: Couldn't think of a much better way to spend the day.

James and I kept up our conversations on a regular basis. He signed a three-album deal with Columbia Records after his dad gave John Mellencamp a tape of songs. He went out to Archer City and stared at the bullet holes in the mailbox before writing "Too Long in the Wasteland."

Hudson: You said the writing was not the fun part and the recording was.

McMurtry: No, it's never been the fun part. I never wrote an album's worth of songs until I had a record deal already.

Hudson: Personally I think those are really great songs on that album. You said you scratched some more songs for it.

McMurtry: Some of them were rewritten on the spot. I'd get in there and find out it wasn't working, or it would need a bridge or something. I'd have to tell the guys to go play basketball while I fixed it. It was a scary process. It was something I put myself up to then to see if I could work under pressure. Don't much wanna do it that way anymore. I think a couple of the songs suffered some minor damage from that process. There's a couple of lines here and there that just don't work.

Hudson: The one I heard driving into town Friday—"Vague Directions"—just absolutely takes my breath away. As the writer of the song, why don't you speculate on why it would have that impact.

McMurtry: I was just scratching for material at that time. I think I started it in Dallas. I went up there for a week and holed up in a La Quinta Hotel on Central Expressway there next to the Denny's. I used to like that place. I stayed there a couple of times while I was touring. At the time I liked the hotels that were next to Denny's because you could get up in the middle of the night and go eat steak and eggs. I started *Candyland* there.

Hudson: You're going into the third album now. Is it anything like you would've expected?

McMurtry: I think I would've expected to make more money at it. But I'm learning a little bit about the business after two records. It's not much job security, because they can turn around and drop you anytime they want to.

Hudson: How is the label marketing you?

McMurtry: I don't think they really know what to do with me. When I started out with Mellencamp the whole idea was to get AOR radio play because he thought that was the best way to market a record. At that time it was. But very shortly AOR began to change to more of a classic rock format. So even if you get asked, you're still not going to get as heavy rotation as stuff that was made twenty years ago. You're competing with the Rolling Stones and all those people. It's not going to break the record that way—it's not going to get played, so it's back to where the only surefire way to break a record is to tour nonstop. I can't do that now.

Hudson: How do you feel about your body of work right now?

McMurtry: It's pretty solid. It was put together well. There's not enough fun songs in there though.

Hudson: Is there a reason for that?

McMurtry: Too many words. You notice guys like Robert Keen and Guy Clark—they always have a couple of funny songs to lighten it up. Because they play those roadhouses year in and year out—they got to get through the set. I'm just now figuring it out—every time I don't write steadily, it's like learning to walk again. You learn to walk different each time. Now I listen to more music than I do words these days.

Hudson: Have you found yourself getting baffled or confused by feedback in the last couple of years? I mean from the critics who say there's a lot of dark songs in this album.

McMurtry: I figure they don't know anything. You're always going to deal with somebody else's idea of who you are and how best to get it to people. When I turned in the second record, the record company was completely baffled. It didn't sound like the first record. You're always marked by what you did to start with.

Hudson: How are you going to counteract that for the third album?

McMurtry: We're not going to worry about it.

Hudson: Do your songs come out of your experiences?

McMurtry: Imagination mostly. I write mostly fiction just because there's more of it out there.

Hudson: Imagine yourself twenty years from now. Describe what that's going to look like.

McMurtry: I can't see that far. But I'd like to be able to generate enough revenue to take a bus on the road and a band. I took a band on the "Wasteland" tour. I went through about seventy thousand dollars in tour support, and they're not just handing that money out like they used to.

Hudson: Whose writing do you really like?

McMurtry: Leonard Cohen. He just keeps getting better. You've got to get *The Future*. He is one of my all-time favorites. Absolutely. He's gotten better because after he learned how to record, he really found his sound. Where he could make that whisper just be a giant whisper, a ten-story whisper.

Hudson: What do you do that's totally separate from music?

McMurtry: I'm going fishing tomorrow. I haven't been fishing in forever. I wrestle my kid a lot—that's totally different from music. I can't disappear anymore and that's the hard part. I've always got to check in somewhere.

In October 1996, James and I talked on the phone before he played Cibolo Creek Country Club. He had been dropped by his label after three albums. He's touring and looking for a label. And standing on a firm foundation of strong writing.

Hudson: You play with a trio now. Could you come do a solo gig at Schreiner?

McMurtry: I've done enough of that. Actually, I just did a solo gig when I went back to my old boarding school and played. They beat my highest ever guarantee by a hundred bucks. But it was sure weird. It was actually better than I expected, but it had this nightmarish quality about it. Saw lots of teachers and people I knew.

Hudson: What would you say is the biggest change that has occurred for you as you've been writing and performing?

McMurtry: Probably that I just don't listen to music anymore. I used to go around and listen to a lot of other artists, but I don't anymore. It's like work to listen to music.

Hudson: Which part of your creative life do you find you enjoy the most?

McMurtry: Mostly I enjoy the guitars, just messing with different kinds of guitars, amps and tones and different tunings. There are all kinds of weird tunings that nobody's come up with yet, and there are some that aren't so weird that just aren't used. It's kind of cumbersome to carry so many guitars around or to stand there and twist them up and down, and I have some I keep a half step down from the rest, and I've got a baritone guitar that's tuned to a low A, which is kind of cool. It makes it a completely different instrument. David Grissom's got one that he tuned to a C sharp, which is unique. He had to set it up with a very heavy string gauge.

It is getting harder to write all the time. I get less and less impressed with what I can write. I'm more inclined to leave stupid lines in a song now just to see what will happen. I don't mind if this complete non sequitur is in a song, if it sounds cool. I think I sort of learned that from Prine. I just get a little more irascible all the time, and at performances I get louder and more obnoxious as I go. I really prefer to play in rock clubs for rock crowds because they just have a better time. A lot of times I have to bludgeon promoters into believing that. A lot of times I'll show up and they'll have seats right up against the apron of the stage, to seat the whole thing and not leave any room for anybody to move. That makes my job harder because if I get even one person dancing, it's so much better. It gives an emotional lift to the whole thing because you know at least that guy is having a good time.

Hudson: You don't see yourself as the ultimate folksinger?

McMurtry: I'm trying to get out of that box.

Hudson: You ought to find some outrageous rock band you could open for.

McMurtry: Or even some not so outrageous.

Hudson: How do you see your writing and your life right now?

McMurtry: My writing reflects my life. I mean, it's fiction basically.

Hudson: I think of you and Tish playing at a restaurant in Kerrville. You both went your separate ways.

McMurtry: She's kind of stuck in her own box; she's trying to get out of the ethnic thing. Her husband was over here yesterday and he said that everywhere she goes, they want her to stick a flower in her hair and sing in Spanish. Everybody pretty much gets pegged by what they start out doing.

Hudson: Who is a hero of yours, a role model who gets out of boxes?

McMurtry: Dylan broke it years ago. He went ahead and got booed off the stage at Newport, but nobody's booing him off the stage now. Even if he plays horrendously badly, they'll come back and see him.

A Harder Edge
Steve Earle

I listen to a lot of different kinds of music. I just like good music, music that means something to whoever made it. If music is deeply felt and means something to the person who made it, then other people will get involved in that.

We met at the Inn of the Hills in Kerrville, during the Kerrville Folk Festival. Even though Steve Earle had hits on Top Forty radio with his band, the Dukes, he arrived alone to perform an acoustic set.

I had already talked with him once at Gruene Hall, a hurried conversation standing at the back of his car. He had just entertained some old San Antonio buddies on the bus after the show.

His show that night had been powerful, containing his hard-edged country accented with rock and roll rhythm. The packed crowd stomped the wooden floor for more. Steve, dressed in jeans, a tee shirt without sleeves, headband to keep his long Indian-straight hair out of his eyes, commanded the stage. Often turning his back to the audience, he dropped to one knee in a pose that reminded me of Elvis Presley.

Later, I asked about the influence of Presley. He answered, "I have a video that we watch all the time on the bus, but I'm not sure there's a direct influence."

I had been frustrated after the show, awaiting the conversation. But it gradually dawned on me that watching them reminisce about all the joints they had covered while running the streets of San Antonio gave me additional insight into this man. So I just watched.

Our Kerrville meeting was different. He was alone in his hotel room when I arrived. He had some time before the show. Somehow we started talking about motorcycles, before the "official" interview started. His interesting and colorful past is reflected in his music.

He moved quickly about the room, setting up a table for us. He talked quickly, creating a sense of urgency.

First, the conversation at Gruene Hall:

Hudson: We'll talk for just a few minutes because it's the end of a long night and a long tour.

Earle: We've been out for a while and are headed back to Nashville. We've been out since May 5th. It's about over with.

Hudson: What is the most important thing you learned from Guy Clark?

Earle: Guy has probably been the biggest influence on me as a writer because Guy writes story songs. What he's doing is more prose set to music than poetry set to music. I was real lucky to have Guy's support. When I first got to Nashville, he took an interest in my writing and got me my first publishing deal. So I learned to always put the cap back on the bottle because if you don't, somebody will probably kick it over. Guy's big thing, which I never learned, was not to become emotionally attached to guitars. They're only tools.

Hudson: You have a lot of tools. I'm not sure I've seen any performer bring out that many guitars in one evening.

Earle: I break a lot of strings. That's the only reason for that. I'm not being pretentious. Most of them are fairly new. The older ones don't go out on the road.

Hudson: Your singing makes a statement. Is it possible to summarize that statement?

Earle: Not in general. Music ought to say something. I feel like songwriting was elevated to the level of literature a long time ago, and I feel like it ought to be kept that way.

Hudson: The energy in the performance and the traveling on the road is immense. When do you find time to write?

Earle: I have to do different things. Last year I needed a couple more songs on the album, and we were doing the Tonight Show, and I couldn't really go home. It's hard for me to write around the house, anyway. I've got three kids. So, I just stayed in L.A., checked into a motel and wrote for three days. I can write pretty much anywhere. Every once in a while I'll get behind and have to create a little different situation so I can write. I like situations where there is something going on outside the window. I don't write very well in the woods. I write real well in L.A., New York, and Nashville. I like to work two or three hours and then go for a walk where there's something going on outside.

Hudson: Do you have a favorite song of yours?

Earle: It's hard to say. Probably, "My Old Friend the Blues."

Hudson: That's one of my favorites, too. What about plans for the future?

Earle: I'm hoping that every record will take another step. I'm just trying to make '80s hillbilly records. I'm trying to make records of songs that are good. There's a lot of talk about the labels country and rock. I've even been accused of trying to get to a rock station by way of country. But I'm always going to be a hillbilly singer, because I'm always going to talk like this. This is a rock 'n' roll band, but country and rock have always had a common ground.

Hudson: That's basic to Texas music, isn't it?

Earle: No doubt about it. It's basic to music in general. Rock 'n' roll was invented by two guys in a western swing band in Memphis; they backed up Elvis Presley. So I don't understand what everybody gets upset about.

Hudson: I loved the talk you gave onstage tonight when you explained what your music meant to you and made a comment about labels. Much of it defies labels, and you're successful at what you do. You're doing what you love.

Earle: You're right. I listen to a lot of different kinds of music. I just like good music, music that means something to whoever made it. Generally, if music is deeply felt and means something to the person that made it, then other people will get involved in that.

Hudson: I kept feeling reminders of Elvis in your performance tonight. Do you hear that a lot?

Earle: I haven't been told that in a long time. It was more obvious when I had the rockabilly band.

Hudson: Maybe it's the energy.

Earle: You can't grow up here and not be affected by him as a performer. I've got a tape on the bus that's all the TV appearances from the '50s, when he was first starting out. It's a great tape to watch. I think there are a lot of people that are strongly affected by him as a performer. He was the first rock performer. Everybody steals a lot from him.

Hudson: The crowd really enjoyed you tonight. They packed in close around the stage.

Earle: I'm glad. This is the first really great gig we've had in South Texas. Times are hard down here. Everybody's having a tough time selling tickets. I needed this to happen this time. I love this place. I played here once, about six years ago, with the rockabilly band. It was a good gig. I've seen a couple of legendary Joe Ely gigs here. This is a great place.

We did follow up that quick conversation at Gruene Hall with a longer one in Kerrville.

Hudson: Last week I talked to Guy Clark about his influences. One of the people we talked about was Townes Van Zandt. I'd like to talk to you again about the influences on your music.

Earle: When I started out, I probably listened to more rock 'n' roll than anything. I grew up in San Antonio, so I was exposed to a lot of dance-hall variety country music, too. Because I had an acoustic guitar, and I couldn't make my guitar sound like the Beatles or Credence Clearwater, I started gravitating toward folk music. When I first began in San Antonio, going out and playing, around '68 or '69, I was real young, like fourteen. I wasn't old enough to play places that served liquor, so there was a coffeehouse called the Gatehouse on Fourth Avenue. I'd go down there and play. The local underground newspaper was published there, called the *Eaglebone Whistle*. It was one of those places that all the waitresses were braless and reeked of Patchouli oil. They had banana bread and tea. People sat out back and smoked joints. Pretty much the local characters. It was sort of right on the edge of downtown, near where the Greyhound bus station is. There was a guy named Mark Johnson who played there. And a guy named Will Beely.

Will had made a couple of records for an independent label in Nashville. He was sort of a Neil Youngish kind of folkie. In fact, he sounded like his mother had been very badly scared by Neil Young during her pregnancy. Those guys were some of the first people I had met who made records. There was also this guy named Don Harding, and Rex Foster, who originally had a rock band called Rachel's Children in San Antonio when I was growing up. These guys were my heroes when I was growing up.

I was looking for a club outside of San Antonio to play. Mark told me about a place in Houston called the Old Quarter. By that time the folk scene was kind of dying down. Guy was in California in the process of moving to Nashville. He had already signed a deal with a label on the West Coast and they were moving him to Nashville. He'd been out there making dobros. He had recently gone out there with a guy named Miner Wilson. They had a guitar shop together, making classical guitars.

Townes was sort of a migratory beast in those days. He spent winters in Texas and summers in Crested Butte, Colorado. He had a horse in those days he boarded in Boulder. He'd go in every year and get his horse, named Amigo. And he'd ride over the mountain from Aspen to Crested Butte every year and spend some time camping in that wilderness area in between. In the winter he was usually in Texas. And he'd spend a month of the year in Nashville. When I met Townes, I was playing at the Old Quarter in Houston. Basically, he was heckling me. He yelled at me to play "The Wabash Cannonball." I knew who he was, and I just sort of ignored him. But he kept yelling that. I finally just turned to him and said, "Man, I don't know 'The Wabash Cannonball.'" He said, "You call yourself a folksinger and you don't know that song?" I did know "Mr. Mudd and Mr. Gold," a song of his with about a million words. That shut him up. I played the Old Quarter quite a bit and Sand Mountain, which was on its last leg. The club had gotten sort of run-down. They didn't serve liquor and couldn't compete with the other clubs in the Montrose area. It was right at Richmond and Montrose. I played those two places for a while and got to know Townes.

I moved to Nashville in '74 because of an invitation from a guy named Richard Dobson, who's one of the best songwriters I know. He came down when I was opening for Eric Taylor at the University of Houston Coffee House and did a guest set. I was about eighteen at the time. He told me to look him up if I was ever in Nashville. I hitchhiked up to Nashville just to check it out in September of '74. I was looking for a place where I could play for tips. I walked into a place called Bishop's Pub, and Richard Dobson was behind the bar. I hung out for a few days and slept on Richard's couch. Then I came back to Houston, got my stuff, and moved to Nashville in November. I had a lot of real good teachers. Most of my influences by that time were people that I knew rather than . . . I was listening to a lot of Bob Dylan at that time and a lot of rock 'n' roll records. But most of the people that really had a profound effect on what I was doing, the way I wrote, and the fact that I started writing so young were people like Guy and Townes, Richard and Mickey Newbury, Keith Sykes. There were a lot of people that I had access to.

Hudson: Very impressive list of songwriters you just went through. A list that is probably at the heart of Texas music.

Earle: Yeah, there's something in the water. A lot of great songwriters come from here and always have.

Hudson: Are you aware of a specific moment in your career when you said, "By God, I'm going to do it my way"? Everybody else seems to be doing what Nashville wants, what the label wants. How do you handle all those pressures?

Earle: I was sort of lucky. Basically I came here under Guy's wing. I was playing bass in his band. It became real apparent to me very early on that making money really didn't make that much difference. Art has been subsidized since the beginning of time. As long as I had enough money to eat without taking a day job, I was basically happy. A lot of women that I was involved with probably didn't agree with me. As long as I could get a draw from a publishing company I was okay. They were paying us because they saw we had talent as writers. I got a cut here and there, just enough to keep everybody interested.

In the early '80s I went into a period where I did go into the office and try to write songs that would get cut. I finally got a Johnny Lee cut on a song that I had co-written with someone else. I was co-writing a lot. I had to be concerned about the money. I made some money on the one record, and it was a real unfulfilling experience. I went through a period after that where I sort of lost confidence in myself as a writer. So I went real hard the other direction. I put together a rockabilly band. The songs that I was writing at that time weren't story songs, the kind of thing I was brought up to write, but it was fun.

I developed a lot as a performer in that period. I ended up on an independent label, and CBS picked it up. I was on CBS for a few singles, but they never released the album. That's the record CBS later released after *Guitar Town* came out. By the time '85 rolled around, I was out of my CBS deal. I had learned a whole lot about being concise and about craftsmanship when I was going to the office and writing eight hours a day. I just applied the old things I knew to the new ones I had learned being a staff writer. I found out that I could say things a little clearer in a way that was easier for most people to understand. I think my work became much more accessible.

"Guitar Town" was the first song I wrote when I went back to write for me. *Guitar Town* was written to be an album. I decided if I was even going to look for another record deal, I'd cut a few demos and go around. If somebody wanted to put it out, then fine. If not, I really didn't know what I was going to do after that. But I didn't really worry about it that much. Actually MCA was interested in putting it out before I had even finished writing the songs. Emory Gordy had cut my last songs for CBS and he had moved to MCA by that time. We went to Tony Brown and Jimmy Bowen and cut a demo. That's what got the MCA deal.

Hudson: And then *Exit Zero* came along.

Earle: *Exit Zero* was just the next step. It was designed to be a Steve Earle and the Dukes record, to be a band record. We came straight in off the road. We had played most of the songs out live. We overdubbed it only where necessary for sound quality. It was a better representation of what the band had come to sound like live.

Hudson: Let's talk about what you are doing now. I know you came into Kerrville from Memphis, by way of San Antonio.

Earle: I've been in Memphis for two months, working on the new record, which is called *Copperhead Road*. It's a rock 'n' roll record in the sense that I didn't stop myself from doing some things that I probably stopped myself from doing before. Concession on my producer's part for country radio. This time I co-produced the record with Tony Brown. It's the first time I've been a producer in name on my records, although I did all the preproduction on the previous two records. But it's got more edge. Song-wise, it's the strongest thing I've done. It's a little more of a Steve Earle album and less of a Dukes album.

There have been some changes in the band. There's going to be a seven-piece band this year. I've added one more piece. A couple of guys are gone, the drummer and bass player. There's a new guitar player in addition to Michael McAdam, a guy named Donnie Roberts. He's been with Webb Wilder for the last few years. We used John Jarvis on acoustic piano, who we've always used on the records. Then Ken Moore, our regular keyboard player on the road, did all the electronics. We did seven tracks with that band. I did one track with the Pogues from London. The rest of it we did in Memphis. I did one track with a drum machine and a bunch of acoustic guitars. It's a little more diverse. I stretched out a little more. It's a little more of a solo album as opposed to a Dukes album.

Hudson: Does that feel like a risk to you?

Earle: I think it's a risk. But others involved see it more as a risk than I do. I think there are about 300,000 people that buy Steve Earle albums, and I don't think it's going to put them off at all. They've seen the band live. I think we've got a real strong base out there. It's going to bring in some new listeners as well, and I don't think we're going to lose anyone. It may put off the people that only know me from hearing the song "Guitar Town." It's probably not as much of a risk as it looks like on the surface.

Hudson: There's a group of young Texas songwriters who are stretching out. Lyle Lovett has crossed a lot of boundaries. And Nanci Griffith has done some innovative things. You hear two opinions of all this. I think it's real interesting that performers this young, at this growing time in their careers, are ready and willing to try new things.

Earle: To me, *Guitar Town* to *Exit Zero* to *Copperhead Road* are real logical steps. *Copperhead Road* is a much harder edged record. We're still using steel guitar, we're still using mandolin and a lot of acoustic guitars. Probably more use of acoustic guitars than ever before. We're still using six-string bass and a twangy guitar sound. But there are some bigger, kind of crunchier guitar sounds on this record. Like almost hard rock type guitar sounds. A lot of the younger audience that I run into are in smaller towns, probably listen to more heavy metal and hard rock than anything else.

Hudson: It sounds like growth and progression for you. The *Rolling Stone* review on one of your albums was talking about the edge and energy. I've done about 150 interviews so far, and one word that those interviews keep revealing is that Texas music has an edge.

Earle: There never has been that much concern in Texas about what was rock and what was country. Austin has always been a very diverse musical community. I didn't stay here because I'm ambitious. If you stay in Austin, things just get out of hand. It's too close to the border. The dope's too cheap, the girls are too pretty, and the weather's too good. You can't get anything done.

Hudson: So you got serious about your music and left.

Earle: You have to realize that when I moved to Nashville, everybody was saying it's going to happen right here. I moved there in '74. A lot of the folks in Austin had already been to Nashville and been chewed up and spit out. They were telling me that Austin was the scene. Nashville is still very conservative. It's a good place to live on the whole. It's full of some excellent songwriters, although not all of them are writing up to their potential. There is probably more raw talent there than in any other city in the world. At least there's a shot at getting on a draw at a publishing company and making some sort of living out of writing songs. That's not unusual for artists. Painters have painted portraits for a living while continuing to work on other things. As long as you're still working on your craft, you're still learning something. Then again, it's dangerous. It's hard to keep your perspective at some times, keep your own voice, keep your stamp on everything. I've been pretty lucky in that respect. I've been able to make every record on my own terms. Tony Brown has had a lot of confidence in me. I've had to fight a little bit, and I've had to fight Tony a little bit. This time he stood back and let me go for it. I definitely had the most control over this record than any other. It was a natural progression. I wasn't ready earlier. I didn't have enough confidence in myself to insist on that when I made the first two. They still turned out well. Tony had pretty good instincts about what I was doing. By the time this record came along, I had produced some other acts. I had produced an album called *The Bible* for Crysalis in England. I did a couple of sides on Charlie Sexton. Producing the two outside projects really helped my perspective on my own.

Hudson: What do you do when it's time to write? Let's talk briefly about your writing process.

Earle: That's hard. I don't have a particular process. I'm trying to establish some semblance of routine. I don't start out writing lyrics first . . . or music first. Sometimes it's just a guitar lick. Other things start with an idea, or with a line. There really aren't any rules. Just whatever gets the song written.

Hudson: Is there a particular discipline involved in your writing process?

Earle: When I am writing, as it gets down toward album time, a deadline imposes itself. I didn't want to miss the May 2 deadline for recording. Toward the end of March, I had to sit down and set aside some time for writing. That's hard to do. When I am in this mode, I generally get up in the morning and try to write about three hours first thing. That's when most of it takes place. I may spend time later in the day looking over what I have done, editing. The best times for me are in the morning before the phone starts ringing and people start putting other things into my head. I'm probably the most lucid first thing in the morning.

Hudson: When I talked to Kim Wilson, he told me that he liked the busy atmosphere of a city while writing.

Earle: I do, too. I wrote "I Ain't Ever Satisfied" in L.A. We were doing the *Tonight Show*, and I stayed behind to write. Sometimes it's easier when there is something going on outside. You end up staying inside to write. But I write real well in New York and L.A. I'm probably going to start living in New York part-time and Nashville part-time. I've been commuting between L.A. and Nashville the last six months. I like big cities. I think New Orleans would be a good place to write. You draw from the energy of what's going on outside, whether you're out in the middle of it or not. It's just the idea that you can work a few hours then go out in it for a while and get away from the work. Then come back and sort of clean things up.

Hudson: That's a different approach from the songwriter who isolates himself in a natural setting, like Ian Tyson, to write. He goes to a log cabin in Canada, takes himself away from everything, and writes. He needs that solitude.

Earle: Ian is like that anyway. He lives on a large ranch in Alberta. I'm a little more people-oriented. I don't do anything in the woods but hunt and fish. It's not a good place for me to write.

Hudson: I teach a writing course in San Miguel de Allende each January. I understand you spent some time there.

Earle: I commuted between Nashville and San Miguel for a couple of years. I'd come back to Nashville every three or four months. I basically was waiting for a publishing deal to expire. They were paying me a draw, but there wasn't an office in Nashville anymore. I could live better in San Miguel on $150 a week than I could here. The town has always been an American artists' colony. Back then there were really a lot more writers and painters in town than now. The Instituto de Allende was open and fully accredited. There were also a lot of college-aged kids in town, which put a little more energy into the scene. I think it's largely retired people and older expatriates now. I still go to San Miguel. The last time was April. I wrote a little bit of this album there. I write real well in San Miguel. It's a pretty concentrated scene, even though Mexico is pretty laid back. You can walk from one end of town to the other. The town's like a labyrinth, I find something new each time I go there. They're not only used to Americans; they're used to crazy Americans. Neal Cassady died there, you know. He finally made it to Mexico and ended up in San Miguel. Eric Von Schmidt lived there when he was painting "Custer's Last Stand," and the "Alamo." He was also a folksinger.

Hudson: Did you hang out at La Perla Bar?

Earle: La Perla was my favorite bar. The difference culturally between a bar and a cantina is that women are allowed in bars. Well, women are "tolerated" at La Perla, but only at certain times of the day. The old-style cantinas don't have restrooms. They have a trough along the bar so it's not practical to allow women in. La Perla is where the 16th of September Revolution, the one that failed with Father Hidalgo leading it, was planned. That's why San Miguel is a national monument with only colonial architecture. It's illegal to build anything else. The planning meetings for the revolution took place in that bar. It was an inn and a whorehouse. It's also the only place you can see the Cowboys playing in San Miguel. So all the Americans hung out there. The Mexicans would come in and watch the soccer games in the morning and then watch us watch American football in the afternoon. It was real weird because it came from San Antonio. They would beam it to Mexico City. You could hear the American announcers in the background, and there would be these two guys in Mexico City calling the game in Spanish.

Hudson: Let's talk a little bit about Buddy Holly.

Earle: I don't think there's anybody in music, period, who hasn't been influenced by Buddy Holly. The Beatles were very heavily influenced by Buddy Holly, both melodically and lyrically. Either directly or indirectly you're going to be influenced. For the Texas musicians, that influence is even stronger. The West Texas guys have always been one of the stronger suits in town.

I'm looking forward to seeing David Halley tonight. I don't understand why he doesn't have a record deal. He's probably the best of the West Texas guys. He's probably even better than Butch. [Earle is talking of the Lubbock mafia—Butch Hancock, Joe Ely, Jimmie Gilmore, David Halley, Tommy Hancock, Terry Allen, and others.] I never have understood why Halley has not even come close. Some of those guys can be their own worst enemies. He must have shied away from this kind of success at critical points in his career. I plan to take that up with him tonight.

Hudson: Good. One of my favorite Halley lines, "The rain doesn't fall for the flowers when it falls, the rain just falls." That was the first David Halley song I ever heard.

Earle: He's a great writer, a really great writer.

JULY 25, 1996, AUSTIN. I'm taking Steve's advice and holing up in a motel outside of my own town of Kerrville, to write. Last night I saw Steve perform at the Backyard, an outdoor classic Texas venue owned and operated by Tim O'Connor, a Texas legend in his own right. Steve's 1996 performance only enhanced what I already knew about him. No surprises. Just a reminder that he really has something to say, and he's willing to say it. No catering to the audience. Just Steve being Steve.

When I met his manager and friend, John Dodson, I saw the kind of love that surrounds this man. John said, "I was his agent for eleven years. I've been his manager for the last three. I've had a ringside seat to a lot of events and changes in his life." The understanding smile on his face testified to the task of managing Steve. Like me, he too wanted the world to see and hear what Steve has to offer. Stories of the road, the pitfalls, the energy, the outlaws. From the stage Steve told stories: "I remember my dad telling me of the college boys who would go buy beer then gather at the wall in Huntsville. When the lights would dim due to the electricity drawn by the electric chair, the college boys would cheer." This was the seed for his song "Billy Austin." He recommended that every Texan see "Dead Man Walking." He performed his songs as if he were talking to each individual in the audience. Wearing black glasses, black tee shirt, and a black band of tattoo art on his left arm, Steve stepped to the edge of the stage. "Here I am," or "This is a love story, a fucked up love story," or "This state thinks it's running a large animal practice in Huntsville," or "I ain't never satisfied," or "I just want to let you know it's more than I can do." Or, as he began the show with the tour and album title: "I Feel Alright." Steve has been back on the road since 1996, carving out his own niche in the heritage of Texas music.

The Storyteller
Guy Clark

In the process of writing, I'll have it turn around on me and have the whole meaning of the song change. But that's just because it wasn't finished. That's just part of the process. I don't know how they work until I've played them onstage ten or fifteen times for an audience. To me, that's finishing the song. Not just having it down on paper and singing it into a tape recorder. It's the performance. It's just as much a part of the writing process as the rest of it.

Guy Clark has been singing at the Kerrville Folk Festival as many years as I have been attending. When I interviewed him the first time, on June 1, 1987, I had been absorbing his music for a long time.

He captures the essence of Texas mystique in his song, "Desperadoes Waiting for a Train." Everyone has an "old man" in his or her life, an older person who leads the child in us by the hand. My old man was Big Mac, my grandfather. He told me stories growing up. He took me places and showed me things. Guy's old man was a real person in his life. Jack Prigg was an old well driller who lived at his grandma's hotel in Monahans. Guy remembers Jack on the front porch of the hotel in this West Texas town. He remembers Jack as his grandma's "sometime" boyfriend. Memories like these become songs for those who are inclined to express themselves this way.

Guy began to take his songwriting seriously after spending some time with Townes Van Zandt in Houston. Guy said, "I heard Townes sing at a local folk club one night and it hit me. I realized that I, too, wanted to tell my stories in song." Rather than be intimidated by someone he admired, Guy used this inspiration to serve as fuel for the fire within him. He began to write seriously.

Nashville has taken Guy Clark seriously. His songs have been recorded by Ricky Scaggs, George Strait, Earl Scruggs, Rita Coolidge, Slim Pickens, Bobby Bare, David Allen Coe, Rodney Crowell, the Whites, Gary Stewart, and others.

Guy's own album catalogue is not just a significant body of work, it is a documentation of his life as well. It is a life worth living.

A concert review from Washington, D.C., said Clark "captured modern Texas as well as any book Larry McMurtry has ever written." The comparison is even more revealing when it is known that Larry's son, James McMurtry, sent a tape of his songs to Clark after winning the 1988 New Folk songwriters contest at the Kerrville Folk Festival. Clark reported, "I really like the few songs I heard. He can write."

Guy lives near Nashville now. He had to leave Texas, the source of his music, in order to take care of the business of music. His album on Sugar Hill Records, *Old Friends,* is a collection of diamonds. But, for unexplainable reasons, Guy's versions of his own songs do not make Top Forty radio. Kathy Mattea recently had a hit with a song written by Guy's wife, Susanna. The chorus sums up a driving force for many writers. "You've got to sing like you don't need the money, Love like you'll never get hurt, Dance like nobody's watching, It's gotta come from the heart if you want it to work." Guy's music comes from the heart.

My favorite Clark song happens also to be his favorite. Containing lines like, "She's standing on the gone side of leaving. . . . She ain't going nowhere, she's just leaving. She ain't going nowhere she can't breathe in. She ain't going nowhere, that's for sure." Guy explained, "That song is about ten seconds in a woman's life. It took me thirty minutes to write it, and it takes me three minutes to sing it."

He writes out of his life, his feelings. As Casey Monahan put it in the October 21, 1988, *Austin American-Statesman:* "Guy Clark has lived not only through his songs but within them."

Some of my other favorite Guy Clark lines include "Calling him out to the lunatic fringe," "Laughing just to keep from crying is no way to grow old," "Tell them the difference between caring and not. It's all done with mirrors, lest they forgot," and "Backslidin', barrel ridin', Rita Ballou, Ain't a cowboy in Texas would not ride a bull for you," "Look out here she comes, she's coming. Look out there she goes, she's gone. Screamin' straight through Texas like a mad dog cyclone," he describes the train that ran through Monahans.

Guy usually includes in each set the first song he learned, a Jimmie Rodgers tune, "He's in the Jailhouse Now." And he always includes songs by Townes Van Zandt and Susanna, his wife, a strong writer herself.

His son Travis has toured with him, playing an acoustic bass. He often takes the lead on guitar, and he harmonizes on all of the songs. "I've never enjoyed touring as much as I do now," Guy explained in September 1993. By 1995 Guy had released *Dublin Blues,* his second album on Asylum Records. In the liner notes he said, "Writing is not magic. It doesn't just happen. There's a certain amount of discipline involved with it, as loose as it might be. One of the first disciplines I learned about songwriting is when you have a little snippet of an idea, write it down. No matter how good you think it is. No matter how sure you are, 'I'll never forget this,' in five minutes, it's gonna be gone if you don't write it down." Our first conversation took place in Kerrville in 1987.

Hudson: Modern composition theory divides the writing process into three areas: invention, structure, and style. Let's talk about invention, the generation of ideas, your sources for writing.

Clark: I don't have any formulas. Purposely. Over the years I had opportunities to apply formulas and didn't. No patterns. Sometimes when I would sit down to write, I'd sit and look out a window for two days. Just trying to get in a serene place. Sometimes lines come to me in the oddest situations. If it strikes me as good, I'd try to write it down. Sometimes I wouldn't do anything with it for a while. Like at four in the morning riding back to San Diego from L.A., after a gig. Riding in the back of this car, I turned to Susanna and said, "Man, if I could just get off this freeway without getting killed or caught." I heard it. I didn't say it as a line, but when it came out of my mouth, I heard it. So I got a piece of paper right then and stuck it in my wallet. The next day I wrote it down in a journal I keep. Then I didn't even approach the song for another year. It just sat there and festered. Weird word, but I didn't even try to write it. But I knew it was really good. I was in the middle of the song, and I didn't have any perspective. I was in the middle of what the song was about. I had to get out of that to be able to look back at it, for that line to make any sense.

Hudson: You heard it when you said it? That's a special kind of awareness.

Clark: Seventy-five percent of the time I don't even write it down. I think, "Boy, I ought to write that down," and then I don't. I have a couple of hardbound journal books that I write in. But a couple of years ago they became too important, too precious. I wouldn't write in them until it became just right. So I started writing on paper.

Hudson: Do you ever look back and notice themes, recurring images?

Clark: I look back through them all the time. There's still a wealth of material written in them. About two or three years ago all the work on every song was in those books, those journals that became too holy.

Hudson: Do you ever say, "Time to come up with some new ideas?"

Clark: More now than I used to. When I first started writing, it was like being on fire. You're just driven. The longer I've done it, the harder it gets to do.

Hudson: I would think you would constantly have to fight formalization of what you do.

Clark: I never thought about that entering into it. Sometimes, I just have better taste and more knowledge. I don't write as much bullshit. I'm more discerning when I put pen to paper. That's pretty easy to talk about, perhaps a substitute for just being lazy. [His short laugh punctuates these statements.] Or just being uninspired. It gets harder all the time.

Hudson: What does inspire you?

Clark: I always have to create a little nest, whether it's a room in the house or whatever. The last thing I did was go out and buy a little used-car office, a portable building, and set it out in the yard. If I'm working on a song, and I think somebody can hear me, I'm real intimidated. I've got to really be alone. Unlike prose writing—this involves playing the guitar and singing, making mistakes, trying out things. I don't like people hearing that.

Hudson: Do you see your writing coming from those times of peace and serenity? Or does activity inspire you?

Clark: Both. It's never the same. Sometimes just sitting in a room two days by myself is the answer.

Hudson: I know that lots of activity inspires me. I was in a tattoo parlor in

Fort Worth while working on my Ph.D. I asked the owner, who had just showed me the tattoo on her lip, if it hurt. "You're not going to start me to lying," she answered. I quickly wrote down that phrase on an old deposit slip. I collect language.

Clark: [laughing] I've got some of those old deposit slips myself.

Hudson: When did you start writing?

Clark: There was a point. I don't remember the date exactly, but the first time I sat down and listened to Townes Van Zandt. I had never really seriously approached it until I heard Townes. First time I ever did it at a real serious level. We've been friends since '64. He had just started writing. He played the Sand Mountain Coffee House in Houston. We were hanging out together, and one night I was sitting there listening. It just hit me. Jerry Jeff was an inspiration, too, but it was different. Townes is a real serious, serious writer.

I like Robert Frost, too. I have a literary background. I studied English, and I like a number of writers. I've grown up with poetry in the house, reading. I went to a bunch of schools, but never got a real degree. Texas A&I, University of Houston, University of Texas, Del Mar. I really cared for the language. Also, the real madness of it. Coming from what people call the Alpha state. Where does that come from? That all just took my breath away. Still does. The amazing thing about it, as crazy as Townes is [long pause], probably 90 percent of his writing was stone cold straight. He made it a point to write straight.

Hudson: Let's talk a bit more about your writing habits.

Clark: I like to do it in the morning. Always best in the morning. Sometimes I really discipline myself and follow a schedule. There really is hard work involved.

Hudson: What writers have influenced you, other than Townes? Writers, poets, novelists?

Clark: As a kid, Robert Service, Stephen Vincent Benet, and Robert Frost. I was always a great fan of Shakespeare. Robert Frost, especially in his narrative poems, like "Death of a Hired Hand." That's the stuff I grew up with reading as a kid.

Hudson: Any writers you turn to now?

Clark: I enjoy Kurt Vonnegut's works and John Le Carre. He writes those real involved spy novels, a brilliant writer.

Hudson: Other areas in your life that influence you. Art?

Clark: I used to be the art director for the CBS affiliate in Houston. That was something that came real easy for me. Writing and music don't. [Check out his self-portrait on the *Old Friends* album on Sugar Hill.] I have to work at that. The art is perfectly natural to me. I still paint some.

Hudson: Do you see a correlation between the interest in art and in music?

Clark: They're both artistic endeavors, both urge me to express something. I've got one painting I'm working on. But several years ago I decided that I was going to devote my time to writing and singing. I had so many interests that appealed to me—building guitars, painting, photography. It's hard to wear all those different hats. I decided to just do this for a while. You can spread your energies in just so many different directions. And this inspires people. I may go back to some of these other interests. You have to devote your life to something to get the most out of it.

Hudson: If students observed professional writers, what would they learn?

Clark: [laughing] How not to do it. Everybody has their different bags of tricks to use—to fool yourself into doing it. Steinbeck, I think, in setting up his little nest, had to have like twelve No. 2 pencils freshly sharpened, and a legal pad. He wrote everything out longhand. He couldn't start unless he sharpened all his pencils. Rituals become real important.

Hudson: What do you like best about your writing?

Clark: The visual pictures that I paint. Being able to capture and evoke a feeling or emotion out of a word painting. I paint a picture of Jack Prigg in "Desperado Waiting on a Train." Make you feel something. That's the thing I try to do.

Hudson: What do you hear over and over from others?

Clark: People always say about "Desperadoes," "Hey, that's my grandfather. You said what I feel, what I wanted to say." "That song changed my life." Those are the kinds of things that are nice to hear.

Hudson: What do you like least about your writing?

Clark: It gets a little too convoluted, too wordy sometimes. Too intellectual.

Hudson: Do you ever consciously try to simplify?

Clark: When I sit down to write, I do. But then I just go ahead and do what I do. I may think about it ahead of time or afterwards, but in the actual process I don't have any control over it. If I'm thinking about that, I'm not writing the song. You kind of have to give up, turn yourself over to it, whatever it is.

Hudson: What advice would you give young writers?

Clark: Write what you know about. Don't make something up. Personal experience is important. This can be intimidating and painful, but it is the only way it can ring true. Of course, some of it has got to be made up, but it needs to be based on something that you experienced, something that you know.

Hudson: Any advice on how much to write?

Clark: As much as you can.

Hudson: Would you recommend writing even when you don't feel like it?

Clark: Sure, but I can't do it. Sometimes I have a headache or a hangover, then I don't want to, but I do. Other times I really don't want to write. So I don't.

Hudson: Some writers sit at the typewriter from eight to twelve, whether they feel like it or not. And they reason, "I'm writing a lot of junk, but when that good stuff comes, I'll be there to catch it."

Clark: That's really true. Especially if you're writing prose. I think it might be different in songwriting.

Hudson: Do you think that songwriters are any more aware of audience than other writers?

Clark: Sure. In a different context. You've got to play them for the folks. You get an immediate reaction.

Hudson: Does the conscious awareness of audience enter in your writing process?

Clark: It's a built-in thing from the beginning. I think about it with every song. There are certain things that have to work. It's not like a poem, where you have the book of poetry to read it over and over, contemplate it. A song has to hit you at the moment you listen to it. Whether it's on the radio or in front of an audience. You've got to communicate in that one moment. Repeated listenings are even more enlightening. But it needs to hit you the first time.

Hudson: Is there any particular way you start a piece?

Clark: Sometimes I'll hear a line. Or I might be playing something on the guitar and hear a groovy little lick that stays with me. And you've got to have a real genuine love for the language. You have to care for it—not just the grammar—but you have to want to use the language in a way that is correct and makes sense. Try to avoid mixed metaphors. Writing from personal experience will produce writing that is strong. The honesty comes through.

Hudson: My enjoyment of Dylan Thomas has to do with what he does with language. And Shakespeare.

Clark: Shakespeare was writing for the common man. He wasn't writing for the intellectuals. One of my favorite songwriters of all time is Chuck Berry. His use of the language paints pictures. His songs work on two levels. Songs that make you want to dance. You don't care what it says, but if you want to sit down and listen, they're really good.

Hudson: I'm interested in the kind of things that you like.

Clark: The best thing I've heard lately is Lyle Lovett.

Hudson: Did you hear him last night at the Kerrville Folk Festival?

Clark: I got a tape of his about a year ago. I had never met him. The first time I put it on, my mouth just dropped open. He really can put words together in a wonderful way.

Hudson: Any other writers that come to mind?

Clark: Dolly Parton is a good writer. And Roseanne Cash.

Hudson: What a set that was last year at the Folk Festival. You, Rodney, Roseanne, and the moon up above. I've been coming to the festival nine years, listening to you. I brought an artist friend of mine to the festival, and he was blown away by Townes. Decided he wanted to do a full-length statue of a musician.

Clark: Townes has the highest IQ of anybody I've ever met. He's well-bred too. Van Zandt County in Texas is his family. Van Zandt museum in New York is in his family.

Amidst the clink of silverware and coffee cups at the YO Ranch Hotel, we ended our conversation on songwriting.

We talked many times after that. He came to my writing class at Schreiner College in 1993 after playing the tribute to Jimmie Rodgers that I produce on the college campus each September.

Clark: What do you want me to do?

Hudson: Play a song for us that you really like.

Clark: Usually in the writing process, I find that I like best the last one I've written. Here's a new one called "The Cape." It's been in progress for two years. It's co-written with two other people, and it's evolved over a couple of years.

Hudson: I keep hearing a similar thread in many of your songs: trust yourself, take risks, be yourself. I hear that in "Picasso's Mandolin," and in "Boats To Build."

Clark: This whole thing I do embodies that. This is not a secure vocation. Everyday you wake up going, "God, can I do this again? What am I doing?" It's living pretty close to the edge, and the edge keeps creeping closer to you.

Hudson: What came out of your background in Monahans, Texas?

Clark: When you're a kid, things are bigger than life, and when you're remembering and conjuring up those memories, they're even bigger. But, Monahans, Texas, that's some pretty serious hard country in West Texas. It took a certain breed of people to even be able to survive there. For example, my grandmother, she had her leg amputated on the kitchen table when she was twelve years old with no anesthetic. Her husband left her with my father, when he was only seven years old. She started a hotel and bootlegged whiskey. The wildest stuff you can imagine. To me, it was living in the West. It was growing up there. There's some pretty incredible characters who influenced my life forever, but I don't think my experience is unique. I think that's happened to everybody. All you want to do is express it or write about it. Or lie about it.

Hudson: Let's talk about your background in writing.

Clark: My father is an attorney, and that's a fairly educated upbringing. But it was pre-television. I'm fifty-one. We didn't have television till I was sixteen. Our entertainment, aside from the radio, was sitting around reading poetry after dinner. I grew up with this love of the rhymed word. It's always held a fascination for me.

Hudson: Do you have a particular reading interest right now?

Clark: I like Cormac McCarthy. And Larry McMurtry, of course.

Hudson: Advice to young writers?

Clark: Write with a pencil and a big eraser.

Hudson: You write what you feel, and you write on demand for a publishing company. Is that a difficult balance?

Clark: I have a publishing company that publishes my songs, and whatever I give them is what they get. I don't write on demand or assignment. You still have to produce quality work.

Hudson: When did you decide you could do that?

Clark: I started trying to do that in about 1966, and I didn't write a song that I actually kept until 1971. But I knew immediately when I finished that it was good. It's called "That Old Time Feeling."

Hudson: A lot of what you write connects with memories I have.

Clark: That's on purpose. That's part of what writing and communicating with people is all about, allowing people into the work so they can make it their own, rather than you making it so tidy that nobody can get into it. It's like good guitar players. It's not what you play; it's the holes you leave. And it's the same with writing. You have to allow people to project themselves into it and to become part of it and become emotionally involved with their own imagination, and that's what makes good work.

Hudson: I love the line "Paint me a hole in the light of day." Where did that come from?

Clark: I'm a big fan of negative space like in a Japanese painting. I paint as well. I find that becomes a great yin-yang thing to do with the cerebral part of writing. It's what you leave out, so you focus on the important part rather than the clutter. I'm very bad about that. My songs have so many words in them. I can't sing 'em, I can't learn 'em.

Hudson: Let these students know what songs of yours they would have heard on the radio.

Clark: Ricky Scaggs did a song called "Heartbreak." Foster and Lloyd did "Fair Shake." Rodney Crowell just had a song out called "She's Crazy for Leaving." Vince Gill and I have worked on some songs together, one for his little girl.

Hudson: Why did you decide to go to Nashville? Many Texas writers stay home.

Clark: If you're going to be in the songwriting business, there's three places, L.A., New York, or Nashville. I was living in L.A. when I made the decision. I didn't particularly like that, and I knew I didn't want to live in New York. Nashville was the obvious place even though what I do is not really country music. I mean it's pretty left of center, but there's the odd time that somebody connects with it. That's how the majority of my living is made, with other people doing the songs. The business of getting songs recorded by artists is so immediate that it's very difficult to do it long distance. It's like Paris in the '20s. It's on fire with good writers and players. If I could find that combination where I could live in Texas and still keep the immediate contact, I would.

Hudson: When you collaborate with other writers, what sort of compromises do you have to make?

Clark: It's different every time. It's always a new experience for me. I never did it until about four years ago. In the case where I'm writing with someone like Vince Gill, for example, it's a question of finding out what he wants to do and what he wants to say and try to help him do it. It's kind of evolved for me where I'll sit down and then it happens. It happened with "Picasso's Mandolin," with "Too Much." It happened with several songs lately. I would start a song with a co-writer, and we'd have the kernel of the idea and sit down and get it figured out. At the end of the day we'd split up, maybe we couldn't get back together for a month or so. I would sit down and finish it myself—the way I wanted to hear it and just call him up and say, "Hey man, it's finished." I worked with Radney Foster and Bill Lloyd on "Picasso's Mandolin." I'd gotten real taken with the mandolin and always wanted to play it, so I bought the cheapest Korean-made mandolin, the real fancy ones with the big curls and the fancy headstock. It was an approximation of that and the three of us were together in my office one day. We got to looking at this mandolin and laughing because the more we looked at it, the more cartoony it looked. Finally we decided these Korean guys must have gotten a painting of a mandolin by Picasso and taken it as the plans, and that's how the song came about. Then the obvious metaphor was there: "Play it on Picasso's mandolin."

Ultimate Tales

Townes Van Zandt

I'll tell you what it takes, darlin'. It takes like driving eight hundred miles, throwing away your whole family, your whole life, your liver, anything you've ever dreamt of except playing guitar and singing. You've ruined your whole life, and you get all the way up, and then you hit that one note, and everything is okay.

When I was working at a Jewish summer camp in Canada, my son, age eight at the time, insisted that I come to his cabin each evening and sing "Pancho and Lefty" by Townes Van Zandt. The boys in his cabin had already become fans of this legendary songwriter from Texas. Merle Haggard and Willie Nelson made the song famous for the rest of the world.

When Townes was living in Nashville, he made regular treks to Texas. His albums are now out on Sugar Hill Records, a strong independent label that also houses Guy Clark, Butch Hancock, Terry Allen, Robert Earl Keen (pre-Arista), and other Texas songwriters. Townes writes of life and love. Always projecting the lure of the road, the lure of moving on, his songs also focus on the hold women can have over men.

He juxtaposes opposites in lines like "You're soft as glass, and I'm a gentle man." His writing is like broken colored glass. When the sun hits the mountain of glass, rays of many colors flash. Many sharp edges. Be careful, beware. You could get cut. You could bleed.

A master of the blues, Townes knew Texas bluesman Lightnin' Hopkins when they hung out together in Houston in the early 1970s. His friendship with Guy Clark also started there.

Townes's name comes up in many conversations with songwriters. Guy Clark hails him as a primary influence. Steve Earle said, "Townes Van Zandt is the best songwriter in the whole world, and I'll stand on Bob Dylan's coffee table in my cowboy boots and say that." Rumor has it that one time Dylan wanted to team up with Townes for some writing. I was at a Dylan show in Austin and heard Dylan say, "I'm going to sing a song by one of your great songwriters," and he started "Pancho and Lefty."

Everyone who knows Townes has a "Townes" story. Harold Eggars has been helping him with his career for years. He's truly been on the road with Townes. And Townes says, "Living on the road, my friend, was gonna keep you free and clean." C. J. Berkman, teacher and writer in San Antonio, has gambled away many a hat with Townes. George and Ingrid Dolis have produced years of documentary video on Townes. This man inspires others to just stay around and hear the stories. Or maybe we all just stay around and become the story. Guy Clark told me my favorite story as he shared memories with John Lomax III one gray day in Cannes, France:

> Townes was in elementary school, and he started a science class. The teacher told them that the sun was the center of their solar system. The teacher added that the sun was burning out. Townes said, "Wait a minute! You mean to tell me that the sun is going to disappear? It's burning out?" The teacher replied, "Yes." From that day on, whenever Townes was confronted with a responsibility, a deadline (homework), he said, "Hey man, did you know the sun is burning out?"

Townes asks in one song, "Why does she sing her sad songs for me, I'm not the one. . . . Maybe she just has to sing for the sake of the song." He is the maestro of simplicity when he says, "If I needed you, would you come to me? Would you come to me for to ease my pain? If you needed me, I would come to you. I would come to you for to ease your pain." Emmylou Harris took that to the top of the charts.

Talking to Townes is like hopping a freight train; you wait until just the right moment and jump, hoping you guessed accurately on momentum. Maybe you did and maybe you didn't. We talked for three days once in Nashville. He played the annual tribute to Jimmie Rodgers in Kerrville with Guy Clark one year. We taped a conversation he had with Glen Alyn on Mance Lipscomb. Townes has played the Kerrville Folk Festival for years. The following is a combination of several interviews over a ten-year period.

We talked first at a Mexican restaurant in Kerrville in the late 1980s.

Hudson: Let's talk about songwriting.

Van Zandt: "Delta Momma Blues" may be the easiest song I've written. It just came to me in a hurry. I have to wait for inspiration. I'm not going to churn out albums. I'm in competition with Mozart, Beethoven, Lightnin' Hopkins, the Rolling Stones, and the Lord. I can't just make up some silly song and put it out there. Songs appear in mysterious ways to me. Sometimes in a dream, sometimes in the voices in my head. Some take craftsmanship; others just hit you on top of the head. Some take a year; some take thirty minutes. It comes from elsewhere. They can come straight through you, and you don't know what they're about or where they're coming from. You just write 'em down and play 'em.

Hudson: Who were your major influences?

Van Zandt: It was a combination of Lightnin' Hopkins and "The Times They Are a-Changin'" that did it to me. I realized, man, you can write songs that really do make a difference. Also Mickey White and Donnie Silverman [two-thirds of his trio that night in Kerrville]. Stuff like that. In the hum of the wheels, you know, in the highway. That's a big part of it. Everybody forgets that part, you know. That's a big part.

Hudson: How did you feel when Willie and Merle recorded "Pancho and Lefty"?

Van Zandt: There's nothing better for a songwriter than to have a song recorded by somebody and have it do good. If it had been recorded by a little Austrian girl way over across the ocean, that would mean as much. But she probably couldn't have come up with the money Willie Nelson did. But it's still the same thing just to hear it performed by somebody else. It's a way of passing it on.

Hudson: Songwriters have a lot of special musical moments in their lives. Tell us about a magical moment.

Van Zandt: When I split Houston with that forty bucks. That was like cool, heavy, and adios for Townes.

Hudson: Tell me the story about writing "Pancho and Lefty."

Van Zandt: I had a three-day gig at the old Rubaiyat Club in Dallas. During those three days Billy Graham and the guru who worked with the Beatles also had three-day gigs in the area. All the hotels were full for a hundred-mile radius. Billy Graham drew 500,000 young Christians and the guru drew like 300,000 young gurus. I had about nine winos at the Rubaiyat.

Because of all this religiosity in Dallas, me and my friend Daniel had to go about fifty miles north of Denton to find a room. There was no TV, no telephone, no nothing. The second night we got back I said, "I'm gonna sit here in this chair until I write a song. I don't care if it's a stupid song, a smart song, a long song, a short song." I sat there for four or five hours and "Pancho and Lefty" just sort of drifted through the window. The next day on the road to Dallas, Daniel is swerving to avoid hitting all these young Christians hitchhiking to see Billy Graham. A cop pulls us over, naturally. Daniel's hair is real long, and I looked like a wild Indian. Daniel handed him this fourteen-year-old expired Georgia license. All I had for an I.D. was a record album with my picture on it. This cop is looking at this driver's license, and it's dawning on him that it's been expired for fourteen years. About this time Daniel looks up and says, "Excuse me, sir, do you know Jesus?"

The cop hands Daniel back his driver's license, gives me back my record album and says, "You boys be careful." Since that time, I've always regarded "Pancho and Lefty" as one of my favorite songs.

Hudson: Do you have anything special you're trying to create with your songs?

Van Zandt: Money. Actually, there's a certain moment when Mickey's playing exactly right, and I'm playing exactly right. We're exactly in tune, and there's a certain note . . . BOOM . . . that hits. It may go away, and it may come back, and we keep playing. Nobody can have it there always. Tonight was real nice, real nice people. There's a certain time . . . BOOM . . . and we don't even slow down. It's so fast that we might not even notice it. Harmony—all of a sudden everything, all of our instruments, my voice, all of our instruments—even for one note—BOOM. I mean, there's nothing better. Occasionally we get a couple or three notes even.

I'll tell you what it takes, darlin'. It takes like driving eight hundred miles, throwing away your whole family, your whole life, your liver, anything you've ever dreamt of except playing guitar and singing. You've ruined your whole life, and you get all the way up and then you hit that one note, and everything is okay.

Hudson: Does one song represent that to you?

Van Zandt: There's no particular song. We have like 150 songs. I have a song called "Snow Don't Fall" that I like a lot, but I never play it.

Hudson: How do you know when you're ready to write?

Van Zandt: Just whenever you start writing. It ain't complicated. You just put down a piece of paper and write. Anybody can write, anybody.

Hudson: Do you have any particular writing habits?

Van Zandt: I get up in the morning and start drinking. Then I feed the dogs and the birds. Then I feed the birds to the dogs, and when the dogs go to the bathroom, I feed that to the cat. I lay down, take a shower, get in there and hit the typewriter.

Hudson: Do you write every day?

Van Zandt: No. I write when I feel like it. There's a lot of people who think writing is some kind of hard deal. I say some people like to pump gas. Some people like to drive trucks. Some people like to sell insurance. But the lazy ones write songs. It's not hard. You write everyday. Mick writes everyday. I write everyday. I write tons of songs. The only difference in writing them down and getting them published is a lot of work. I could write a song right now, so could Mickey, so could you.

Hudson: But you know you have something special going on.

Van Zandt: I've been fortunate enough to know what I wanted to do. I decided early on that's what I wanted, to play the guitar and sing songs. So, I wrote them down, and this, that, and the other came along. My little brother never played the guitar at all. I'm sure he could write songs as good as I could. Maybe they wouldn't be songs, because he doesn't play the guitar.

Hudson: How do you describe your music?

Van Zandt: Dismal.

Hudson: Does location have an impact on your writing?

Van Zandt: Yeah, I started in Houston. It was real heavy, dark, and murky. If you can't catch the blues in Houston, man, you can't catch them anywhere. I figure there's heaven, hell, purgatory, and the blues. I've always been in the blues just reaching up for hell.

Hudson: What effect has Austin had?

Van Zandt: I moved here because I was thrown out of Nashville. We didn't have any money and someone was either going to get us a plane ticket or have his house bombed. We ended up here. The Hole in the Wall, in particular. If you need to get thrown into jail, if you need a place to sleep, go to the Hole in the Wall. Just don't act right, and they'll take care of you.

Hudson: What about Kerrville?

Van Zandt: I've been in the hospital in Kerrville about four or five times. I even played there.

Hudson: And you play the folk festival.

Van Zandt: Yeah, it's almost even. If I can make a couple of more stays in the hospital, I can even up the time.

Townes and I met for three days during the summer of 1995 at his cabin in Mount Juliet, Tennessee (a cabin formerly owned by Guy and Susanna Clark). In between conversations, we took a canoe ride, and we looked over the artifacts he's collected in his house. He really liked living in the spot formerly occupied by Guy and Susanna. He really enjoyed telling me his stories. At a heart level, many of these Texas songwriters are storytellers first.

Roxy and Judy Gordon had a house in Dallas on Oram, just blocks from Poor David's Pub, the songwriters' haven in Dallas. When Townes came to town, he stayed at Roxy's. And the stories spill out night after night. Ah, the stories that house could tell. Bones and paintings adorn the front porch. The house, once featured in the Dallas paper, is a small museum to Texas culture. Books, recordings, and art by the owners adorn the walls and ceilings. Roxy and Judy are truly living a creative life one day at a time. They do make it up as they go along. They've created an atmosphere conducive to storytelling.

Locations do have an effect on the kind of stories we tell. Houses, folk festivals, motel rooms, backstage at clubs, front seats of cars—all affect the way we tell our stories.

And this is the way Townes told his story one hot summer afternoon in July 1995. I was passing through Tennessee on my way home from New York City. Townes gave me a tour of the house, drank some vodka, showed me some of his "important" artifacts, sang songs for me, drank more vodka, quoted his songs as poetry, showed me manuscripts, took me for a canoe ride, and drank some vodka. The reader can fill in the spaces of the conversation—just like we, as an audience, fill in the spaces of a Van Zandt performance. When he says, "Sunrise comes, and I don't know why," I'm reminded of the story where Townes realized the sun was burning out. One evening at La Zona Rosa in Austin, many performers joined to pay tribute to Townes by singing his songs. Bob Dylan showed up in the restaurant and disappeared just as quickly once people began to barrage him with requests.

Hudson: Let's talk about your friendship with Lightnin' Hopkins.

Van Zandt: I considered it a privilege to play with Lightnin' Hopkins, the last of the great blues players. The first marijuana I ever smoked was given to me by Lightnin'. Spider, the drummer, used to bring a couple of sandwiches in a brown paper bag to the gig. And Billy was the harp player. I knew those guys. They taught me this [he picks up the guitar and begins strumming Hank Williams]. I used to play guitar like that. Then I went to see Lightnin'. The first time I saw him, he fell flat back over the stool into the drum sets. Spider had already left. Billy reached over and picked up his Gibson. I walked over and said, "Sir, I'd like to introduce myself." Lightnin' always liked being called "Sir." "Have a seat, son," he said. Which I did. Did you know Lightnin' is Keith Richards' favorite guitar player?

I did once have a band called Townes Van Zandt and the Hemoridge Mountain boys. We had to get out of town after playing a Rex Bell song, "Baby's Face."

Back to Lightnin'. Yes, Rocky Hill played at his funeral. He is one of the best players I've ever heard. His specialty is blues, for sure. He told me it was the most nervous he's ever been. He's a blue-eyed blond. He wouldn't see that my grave is kept clean. He told me later there were lots of cousins, lots of family. Lightnin' Hopkins was a real driving force in the Houston scene. There were a whole bunch of "little" guys, me included. Even though we didn't think we were important, it takes mud below the dirt to grow flowers.

Hudson: Tell me about blues and hair. I keep hearing these songs about wigs, short hair, and haircuts.

Van Zandt: Lightnin's wife got her hair all cut off. And Lightnin', he said,

"I don't want no woman whose hair's no longer than mine." I think hair is a woman's crowning glory. Now mine's real short. Let me tell you about that. I got real sick last year. Harold [Eggars] and I were booked in Europe for forty nights and forty-three days. Jeanene said, "Don't do it; you're going to die. It's gonna kill you." It didn't. But, I came this far from croaking. Roxy told me I needed long hair. Hair is your strength. I went over all of Europe and almost died. I fell down, no, I laid down in the Minnihopeless airport and screamed. The cops and paramedics came. Harold told them I was on medication. The cops said, "He'd better be out of there in one minute or he's going to jail, shithead."

Hudson: But you said you wanted to go on this tour. Why the screaming?

Van Zandt: I was in the hospital dying, big time. Then I slid out, big time. Harold took me to an airport hotel. I woke up in the morning asking Harold, "Where are we?" He said, "Minneapolis," and I said, "Jesus, we're supposed to be in Amsterdam. What the hell's going on?" I went, and we did forty days and forty-three nights. Many standing ovations. Each day I ate breakfast, took a few shots of hootie. Just did it.

Hudson: When did you cut your hair?

Van Zandt: I got back here and called my friend Jimmy, a blood brother of mine. I said, "I've been sick. I got long hair, and I get into too much trouble. I want to cut it off." He came to visit. It was a gamble. I told him I wanted to go buy a suit and get a haircut. I told him I have to go to a funeral. He asked, "Whose funeral?" And I told him, "I'm not sure yet, but it's going to be before long." He said, "You shouldn't think that way." We went out to get the suit and get the haircut. When I got back I told Jeanene, "I know you're going to laugh, but try not to."

Hudson: It's a good haircut, Townes.

Van Zandt: I got a good line out of it. On stage, I'll be introduced. I sit down with the guitar and say, "This haircut is for sale."

Hudson: Tell me a hunting story.

Van Zandt: I was thirteen. My dad bought me a 308 Savage, which is a beautiful rifle, top of the line. I'd grown up from the age of three knowing about and not caring about guns. In Texas on a ranch, you just think "no big deal." On my thirteenth birthday, I got this beautiful gun. We were up in Montana going up this real deep canyon in a jeep. I'm in the back seat, it's snowing, I'm looking down. About a hundred yards up ahead in the fork of this tree stands a doe. I was encouraged to shoot her. The guy stops the jeep. I took my new rifle, which had been sighted in Wyoming with my dad's help, and shot this deer right through the adam's apple. It dropped just like that. The guide looks around at me, saying, "Where did you learn to do that?" We walked up the hill; it was a long way. I was carrying the gun properly. We got there and behind the tree the deer lay, hot blood still steaming in the snow. I looked at it. It was like Robin Hood . . . the arrow. I turned around to my dad, and said, "Sir, I never ever want to shoot anything alive again unless I have to." And handed him back the beautiful new rifle. He said, "Good, you've learned a lot." We took the deer back to the jeep. My dad and the guide sat in the front seats. I sat in the back with the deer, just looking at it. And I've still got buck fever. We're coming out of this canyon down a fence line when up ahead we see a huge elk with about five cows and calves. "Wow, that's a record elk," says our guide. We were close. He could have spun around and killed him. The elk was just cruising. My dad shot about six times and missed him. I said, "Dad, you could have shot him in the eyeball, or anywhere; he was as big as a car." Dad looked at the guide, turned around and handed me the gun and said, "I've just missed him, I guess." How could he possibly have missed him? In about two years I figured out what really happened. I personally delivered my deer to an orphanage.

Hudson: You would enjoy talking to my dad about hunting. He has a real primitive appreciation for the stalking.

Van Zandt: Let me tell you this. Guy used to sit on this porch and shoot bumblebees with a Daisy Red Rider BB gun. He doesn't like pellet guns because he can't see the BB's. He used to sit on the porch of this cabin, drink mint juleps, and shoot bumblebees.

Hudson: When is a performance perfect for you?

Van Zandt: I love to play when the sound system's good, when I'm singing good, and my voice matches my guitar. It's comparable to having a fine meal, or having fine sex, or helping a little kid throw a Frisbee. There's certain times that you don't think about nothing. You're just being carried on the flow of life . . . the blues. You're not thinking about your friends dying.

Hudson: Why are you so drawn to the blues?

Van Zandt: Blues is happy music. Plus, people have the wrong idea about the blues. They think it's all "down." If somebody tells you Hank Williams didn't play the blues, they're wrong. If somebody tells you Duke

Ellington didn't play them, they're wrong. Whoever—Elvis? Wrong! You don't have to be some old black guy to play the blues. The blues is everywhere. It gets us through. I look at everything as the blues.

Hudson: Some say the blues is just a good gal gone wrong. Others say country music is the white man's blues.

Van Zandt: Job had the blues—for sure. I asked Lightnin' one time what the blues were, and he said, real slowly, letting me hang on every word, "Well, son, I think they're a cross . . . between the . . . greens and the yellows." The way he delivered it! Mickey Newbury told me a long time ago, "If you can't make yourself at home, go home." So, make yourself at home.

Hudson: Tell me about that picture of Woody Guthrie on that chest.

Van Zandt: Harold and I were driving down the freeway in Oklahoma. I like to drive a lot. Sometimes to the point where it just amazes Keith [of Case Management]. "You mean you're going to drive to San Francisco?" he asks after booking me. I like being in the car—in the back, in the death seat, in the driver's seat. I like the hum of the wheels. I started when I was eight years old on the ranch driving all those cow paths outside of Houston. I lived in Fort Worth about ten years. Then we moved to Midland for two or three years, then Billings, Montana, for a couple or three, then Colorado, then Illinois, a school in Minnesota, then back to Texas. After that I hit the road. The road has always been a big part of my life.

Hudson: I like the article Keith Case sent me entitled, "Townes Van Zandt: Road Scholar."

Van Zandt: We were driving down the slab, Harold was driving. I look up and see Okemah, Oklahoma. That's where Woody Guthrie was born. Wow. "Pull off," I yell. Harold says, "You sick? Got to use the John?" "Nothing, just pull off." We pull off the interstate and Harold's saying, "What happened?" I say, "This is where Woody Guthrie was born." He'd heard of Woody but not with the same inclination I had. So we drove up to this store. He reminds me we have Cokes in the back. This trip is not about getting a drink. There's this old man and woman in the store. I said, "Sir, how are you doin'?" Then I tell him how much I appreciate Woody Guthrie, and I offer to buy the picture I see in the corner of the store. He took me outside where Woody—Woodrow Wilson Guthrie—had carved his name. It was a one-horse, one-mule kind of place. Woodrow Wilson Guthrie, right there. So, I packed up all the stuff we bought. "Son, I'm going to give you a picture in a frame for the same price as that photograph," the owner said. Then I told him, "I appreciate that, sir. I'll keep it where I can see it as long as I'm alive. Adios."

Back on the slab, another thousand miles behind the wheel. I put that picture here in the house in a place where there's nothing else. [He continues the tour of his room.] I have all the mirrors angled so I can't look in them; I don't like mirrors. Shakespeare's looking that way. Woody's looking that way. Susie did the parrot head up there. An old man did that one, the boar, over there. There's a picture of three of my best friends. Blaze is no longer with us. That's Rex Bell on the right and me in the middle. And that's a pearl-handled machete I'm wielding.

Hudson: Who did you really love?

Van Zandt: Lightnin' and Muddy Waters. First was Elvis and Dave Brubeck, Mozart and Peter LaFarge. Kate, instead of the music, it was more the attitude of "I can do this if I decide it. I think I can do it." That attitude! But there's so many musicians. You have to pick your own trail to follow. There's Indian chants. I've seen kids sing and dance around a circle. There was enough feeling and love generated in the air that you could write a song.

Hudson: You talked about the joy you felt in the presence of Richie Havens. Tell me about meeting him.

Van Zandt: I met him in Minnihopeless a week ago at a folk festival. Of course, I've known about him forever. I was close to "overwhelmed" by the good vibrations. He put out stunning karma. He had on a blue African-style robe, beads and bracelets and rings and the biggest smile—not a grin—I've ever seen. I've been all these miles; I always try to keep myself happy. I'm a good-natured, fun-loving sort of guy, you know. But, man, it was like POW—like a big wave of fresh air. I didn't get to see him play. It had been raining that morning. I told the promoters not to worry. It was going to stop raining before I played. My guitar told me that. I also told him people would start showing up before I played. I just knew that. And I told them when Richie played "Here Comes the Sun," the sun would come out. And it did.

Hudson: I know we both visited the Van Gogh Museum in Amsterdam. Tell me about Van Gogh.

Van Zandt: The first time I visited a museum was the Metropolitan Museum of Modern Art in New York, and I was with Jeanene. I walked in and had to have a wheelchair because occasionally I get a touch of the gout. Terrible, terrible stuff. So I had to get a wheelchair. I also had a cane. I said, "Well, I'll just use this cane." Jeanene was looking around the corner, then she called to me, "Hey, Townes, come here. Here's that painting you love." It was "Starry Night." There it was, bigger than Dallas. I just stood there leaning on this cane. Jeanene kept looking at the many other wonders. I was kind of hooked on this one. I didn't move. I'd walk up closer just to see the paint. Made the guards nervous; they just sort of surrounded me. When Jeanene started looking for me, she asked one of the guards. He said, "Let me guess. He's in a brown coat and leaning on a cane. He's downstairs by the 'Starry Night' painting." That was three hours after we'd entered the museum. I also love the self-portrait. It's three-dimensional. I love stuff like that.

Townes and I continued talking on a regular basis until his death, January 1, 1997. He was a troubadour, a wandering bard. He was always filled with the stories he had to tell.

The Character Within

Blaze Foley

I just love it. There's nothing like it. Just to look out there and see your friends crying and laughing or whatever. It's the biggest thrill I've ever had. Just performing my songs for my friends.

Blaze Foley was a friend to many songwriters, and he chose a life of writing for himself. Often known as the character who would show up with electric tape holding his clothing together, Blaze became a regular in the Austin music scene. I met him at Townes's house. We went into the bedroom to sit on the edge of the bed, next to the big fishtank, and talked. From time to time Blaze would lean down and kiss Townes's dog. Upon Blaze's death, a tribute was held at South Meadows on Highway 35 south of Austin. I purchased a charcoal rubbing of his headstone. The crew paying tribute was motley, diverse, and interesting. Mainly a crew of people who really know what it is to love the music, the man, and the art. Blaze represents part of the spirit of Texas music, and that spirit is alive and well.

Hudson: Blaze and I are talking at the home of Townes Van Zandt. This is a fitting place to talk to Blaze because looking at your album here, *Blaze Foley*, I see Townes has written the comments on the back. So you guys have a friendship that goes back a ways?
Foley: Goes back a ways and it will last forever.
Hudson: Every song on here is written by you. How do you view your niche as a songwriter?

Foley: I'm just a songwriter.

Hudson: Do you write for yourself or for other people?

Foley: Whenever I get inspired, I write songs. I can't just sit down and write a song.

Hudson: How do you know when it's time to write one?

Foley: I just end up with a guitar in my hand.

Hudson: Is there a certain time that you write?

Foley: Usually when I'm going through a breakup of a love affair.

Hudson: So some kind of intense, emotional upheaval gets you going?

Foley: Yeah, or political stuff or funny. It's a mystery, and I want to keep it that way.

Hudson: Definitely something you're personally involved in though?

Foley: I figure it wouldn't matter if I described it. Whoever listens to it can describe it. It's up to them. I just do my part. I try to.

Hudson: Townes mentions a song on the back here. He met you in New York when you were making a record of "If I Could Only Fly." Tell us a little about what caused you to write this song and what has happened to the song since then.

Foley: I was living in Chicago and I was happily married to this girl, Cybil. She was an actress, still is. And I missed her. I was down here in Austin away from her, doing gigs. I felt like writing a homesick love song that would make me cry. But I started crying, I just broke down, and I had to finish it the next day. Willie Nelson recorded it recently and then Merle Haggard.

Hudson: How did they discover the song?

Foley: I played it at a friend's funeral, Clyde Buchanan, who is a great songwriter, rest his soul. Willie's daughter was there, Lana, and she liked it. And my friend Peggy Underwood was there, and they're best friends. It's been about four years now. It's finally like a dream come true.

Hudson: I'm sure. When's it going to come out?

Foley: He's got an album that's at number one now, so they'll wait till that goes down on the charts. Then it will come out in a few weeks. It was supposed to be out in April, but you know how those things work.

Hudson: Time schedules change. How does it feel to you to have someone else singing your song?

Foley: I'm flattered. Absolutely flabbergasted. And he didn't leave out any words. He changed two words from *but*s to *and*s. That's the only thing. I wish I had a tape of it. I'd play it for you. You have to hear it. I haven't even told my mom. I want to wait till she hears it on the radio, and it'll be a surprise. That's hard to do.

Hudson: Hard to keep something like that to yourself.

Foley: Yeah . . . I haven't told anybody.

Hudson: How long have you been involved in the Texas music scene?

Foley: Ten or twelve years or so. I don't stay here all the time. I used to hitchhike around a lot. I go to Georgia a few months a year.

Hudson: Where are you from?

Foley: Marfa. West Texas. Middle of nowhere.

Hudson: Do you think there are any particular places in Texas that have influenced you and your writing style?

Foley: San Antonio, mainly, or even the whole state of Texas. There's just something about it.

Hudson: What kind of influence could San Antonio have?

Foley: That's just where I spent my formative years. I think everything influenced me. Everything I've ever seen in my life, and that's the only way I can imagine it.

Hudson: Townes says, "Blaze is a lover of things and pleads their cause with every word."

Foley: I try to. I'm worried about that fish there. A fish with legs just doesn't makes sense.

Hudson: There is one with legs. Actually, there are two with legs.

Foley: Two?

Hudson: Maybe these are Townes's special pets.

Foley: That's a catfish there. That's a scavenger. It eats the acid algae-eater.

Hudson: Actually, the other little fellow has four legs.

Foley: I know. And an ugly head.

Hudson: Townes has a house full of live things here.

Foley: Yes, he does.

Hudson: Birds, cats, dogs, and fish. So you all share?

Foley: And people. There are always people here.

Hudson: How would you describe what is so important about Townes's music?

Foley: It's spiritual. It's scary at times, 'cause you just don't sit down and write songs like "Nothing," "Waiting Around to Die," or "Sad Cinderella" without really knowing something. He's the best I ever heard. He's a poet, he amazes me. But I was familiar with his music before I met him, and then we became good friends. We almost got thrown off a plane once at thirty thousand feet.

Hudson: Together?

Foley: Yes.

Hudson: Both of you?

Foley: Yeah, it was a group deal but they changed their minds.

Hudson: Have you spent time in Nashville? Have you tried that scene? Are you still a part of it?

Foley: Not really. I mean I go up there to visit Richard and Lacey and the people that recorded my album. They did have an office there. It was a tax write-off or something. I can't even get any of the albums anymore. They were sitting in the guy's house, three thousand of them. Last time I saw them, termites were eating the cardboard boxes they were in. It's kind of a bummer.

Hudson: Now that's a waste of time.

Foley: It is, but I'll get them. Just have to go through legal channels. I'm working on it.

Hudson: In the realm of Texas music, are there any writers or performers who have been a direct influence on you?

Foley: George Jones and Willie Nelson and Townes. There's a lot of good legendary country singers from this state. I grew up going to Panther Hall in Fort Worth when I was a kid and seeing Willie Nelson.

Hudson: Panther Hall—that was definitely a melting pot of a lot of talent. I talked to Ray Price when Willie was playing with him.

Foley: I used to see him there all the time.

Hudson: Ray mentioned the old Cherokee cowboys and their days at Panther Hall.

Foley: On Sunday afternoons they had a talent show. My sister used to go over there and sing. Every Sunday that was the family ritual. All pack up and go hear sister sing.

Hudson: How would you describe Texas music?

Foley: The essence of Texas. Texas is the only place I know I like. About everywhere you go in the world, you hear, "You're from Texas?" There's a mystique about the state. There's a lot of creativity because of the myth, if it is a myth. I'm sure it's exaggerated at times, but there's definitely something about Texas.

Hudson: You've mentioned the word *legend*, and you've mentioned the word *myth*. Both of these are very broad areas. The roots run deep and that does capture some of what goes on here. It becomes mythological in nature: bigger than life.

Foley: It's like it's a continent of its own. Every time I go away, when I come back in, I cross the state line, and there's this feeling. I'm sure people get that if they live in Connecticut or wherever, but I don't know if they get it like we do here.

Hudson: But we don't hear songs about heading back to New Jersey or heading back to Pennsylvania.

Foley: True.

Hudson: But all over the country you can turn on a station and hear a song about heading back to Texas.

Foley: Texas and Georgia are the two most mentioned states and songs that I know of. Chicago, maybe, or San Francisco. But mainly Texas, even cities in Texas, like "Does Fort Worth Ever Cross Your Mind?"

Hudson: You have an album out that is . . . ?

Foley: Hard to get.

Hudson: Hard to get right now. Some of the songs on it are "Loving You," "My Reasons Why," "Where Are You Now, My Love?" "Getting Over You" and "Picture Cards." Out of these songs, are there any that stay closer to you? Favorites?

Foley: "Darling" and "Oval Room." "Darling" is my favorite because you can skate backwards to it, if you wanted to. I figure if you can skate backwards to a song, then it's a good song. It makes people happy. I don't know why it makes people happy skating backwards, but I've seen them do it. It will be a hit in skating rinks one of these days, I hope.

Hudson: How do you feel about performing?

Foley: I just love it. There's nothing like it. Just to look out there and see your friends crying and laughing or whatever. It's the biggest thrill I've ever had.

Hudson: Do you have any favorite places to perform?

Foley: The Austin Outhouse is my favorite because they let dogs and kids in there and most places don't. That's kind of a rowdy place. That's where the hippies go. I'll be a hippie all my life. That's my favorite place. But I like to play anywhere.

Hudson: Do you ever go back to Marfa?

Foley: I haven't been there since I was five, but I'm going to.

Hudson: If you had your choice of any place that you could go play, where would it be? Either a town or a particular hall.

Foley: The Armadillo—but it's too late. Or Cain's Ballroom in Tulsa, Oklahoma. Or Liberty Hall in Houston, but that's gone too. The Summit. I want to play anywhere, Jerry Falwell's house.

I kept hearing stories of Blaze as he followed the Texas music spirit where she led. We never talked again, and he died an untimely death. It's these "characters" who make up the Texas music scene. We can't forget them.

For Love Not Money

Jubal Clark

I feel everything. I'm just like a big sponge; I feel everything at one time, but sometimes I'm not perceptive enough to know what I'm feeling. Maybe months later it comes out, and I say, "Oh wow," and I write something.

Jubal Clark moved to Marble Falls after years in Austin. He played the 1996 Willie Nelson Picnic at Luckenbach with two of his sons playing with him in the band. He had been battling cancer for a while, and this was his last picnic performance. He died in 1997. He represented the on-going beating heart of the Texas songwriter. He did not have a label, he had not sold a lot of songs, he was not heard on the radio, but he kept writing and playing. Even a serious bout with cancer did not stop him. He didn't know "why" he wrote; he just wrote. He was childlike in his joy in the process of writing. His eyes sparkled, July 4, 1996, as he reminisced with me. "Yeah, I remember when Willie asked me to open Farm Aid for him. I felt real special. Even if the hour was an early 7:00 A.M."

I first heard Jubal at a Rod Kennedy production at the Texas Arts and Crafts Fair in Kerrville. I was leaning on a bale of hay, just absorbing all the music, when suddenly this lanky cowboy took the stage and intently looked into my eyes when he started playing. Now, maybe he wasn't looking into "my" eyes, but that's what that intensity felt like. About three verses into "Gypsy Cowboy," I had tears rolling down my cheeks. I believe he saw them, and after his show he motioned me backstage. After asking me to sign his guitar (quite the role reversal), Jubal wanted to know what in the song moved me. "I knew you were telling the truth in a big way as you sang about this lone cowboy. I knew it was the truth for me and for many others," I replied. "Moving just for moving, that's all I understand," is one of my favorite lines. Yeah, the road is part of this scene, and Jubal Clark has documented that with his stories and songs.

Hudson: We talked first at the 1986 Farm Aid in Austin. I'd like to begin by talking to you about songwriting. Where do you come up with the ideas, and how do they get down on the piece of paper I saw?
Clark: Mmm, I see, right. Well, like this particular song I call it "America, America" by Jubal Jubal Clark Clark. Two names for song and writer.
Hudson: Where did you get the idea for that song?
Clark: When I heard that Willie was going to have this Fourth of July picnic, I started writing the song because I thought maybe Willie might ask me to pick, which he did—that was good—he's a friend. And I started writing. I wrote a whole bunch of verses, and I came back into town, and everybody said, "Jubal, Willie put you on Farm Aid Two," and I said "Great!" So I started writing some other verses, but it didn't work, and I thought well, I'll just do the song as I originally wrote it and repeat it. Then the other day I was ill, middle of the night, no place to go, no TV to watch, nothing, and I sat down and wrote two other verses and summed it up. Like it says in the Bible, you earn your bread by the sweat of your brow or something like that, and it's sweating with our toil, working hard in the soil, burning the midnight oil, nobody cares to know. Well, if the world, it don't need us—who the hell's gonna feed us? We need someone to lead us—stop reaping what we sow. So I'd summed up the first verse— "America, America, it's a politician's story, nobody takes the blame— America, America, now my Old Glory is flying with shame." And my mother, she was born in the old Indian territory before it became Oklahoma, and I'm proud of that Indian heritage. And the American Indians, they've been messed around forever, and for all the poor folks in the world, bless their hearts, and for the people that have heart, that have a heart whether they're rich or poor or nothing. I was raised on a farm.
Hudson: Where?
Clark: In Crosby County up close to Lubbock.
Hudson: What influence do you think environment has on you?
Clark: I feel everything. I'm just like a big sponge; I feel everything at all

times, but sometimes I'm not perceptive enough to know what I'm feeling. Maybe months later it comes out, and I say, "Oh wow," and I write something.

Hudson: Comes out in a song.

Clark: Yeah.

Hudson: What do you think the environment of Lubbock and West Texas might do? What's special about that kind of environment?

Clark: I am not that much influenced by it. My daddy died when I was about four years old, and he was born in Indian territory too—no big deal. And I lived in Bailey County about seven miles outside of Muleshoe. Everybody thinks of Bob Wills as being around Turkey, Texas, but Bob Wills came from there. They bought a farm about half a mile from this little two-room white shack I lived in, and I was always up there under Bob's feet every Sunday. We'd ride horses, and I knew Billy Jack Wills and Luke Wills and Johnny Lee Wills and Bob's daughter, and my mother used to baby-sit for them, and Uncle John Wills, he taught me my first cuss words, and me and Billy Jack we'd go track rabbits, and . . .

Hudson: In Bailey County?

Clark: Yeah, it's close to New Mexico—West Texas. So I grew up around music, but I didn't think about influences. Maybe just a little bit by hearing Leon McAuliffe and Jessie Ashlock and Bob Wills, but I think I'm more influenced by other things. I was living at my uncle's where he had a little shack, you know where the black people would come and pick cotton, and I'd go over there, and they use tissue paper and a comb, and they'd sing. I'd go in there when I was about five years old. I'd sit there and listen, and my mother would have to come get me—she was a widow woman by that time—"Come on, let's go home, back up to the house," but they were playing music. I didn't want to leave. I think my Aunt Lolo used to play at a Baptist church; I think all the girls played piano—even my mother. They played in an old empty church house on Saturdays. I'd just quit playing cowboys and Indians, and I'd sneak over there. I'd creep in the door, and I'd sit there and listen. I loved her! She knew I was alive. She tells me, "Hi—hey you're alive," and I didn't get too much of that. Aunt Lolo influenced me a lot—she played that piano. A lot of my songs got a lot of that kind of Baptist influence.

Hudson: More gospel stuff there.

Clark: Yeah, sort of, yeah.

Hudson: Okay, what about the song "Gypsy Cowboy"? I was sitting on the front row at the Kerrville Arts and Crafts Fair, and I heard you sing that song thirteen or fourteen years ago. It really moved me. Then you saw me crying and asked me to come backstage. Remember, I signed your guitar?

Clark: I wrote it in 1975. It was sort of the way I felt at the time—the way I feel—and it's sort of like—like being free, and you don't necessarily have to be an old Gypsy cowboy to feel the freedom within it—"living the dreams of other men," like one of the statements says. A lot of people they look outside their office windows, and they see a hippie or a longhaired person, and they say, "Huh?" But maybe they concentrate and say, "I've got to go home, I got to do a barbecue, I've got all these things I've got to do all week long." Maybe they look out the office window and say, "Maybe for one day I could just be like that strolling musician." So I say I'm living the dreams for other men. If they can't do it, I'm going to do it for them.

Hudson: How long have you been writing songs?

Clark: Since I was about five years old. Forever? There wasn't a period when I said, "I'm going to start writing." This is my thing. I don't know how to describe it, but you say something to me, and I'll put a rhyme to it. I might answer your question, but I'm always hearing rhymes. It started when I was a young child. I can't sleep at night sometimes.

Hudson: You can hear rhymes?

Clark: Yes.

Hudson: Do you have a collection of all your songs somewhere?

Clark: No.

Hudson: I mean I just saw a couple of pieces of paper up there covered with red marks. What's going to happen to those pieces of paper?

Clark: Do you want to take them and keep them?

Hudson: Somebody needs to.

Clark: I was at a friend's house one time. Somebody burglarized the place, and they took tapes I had of Willie playing at Willie's Pool Hall a long time ago. Different songs, and songs I can never ever recapture. They're gone, but I'm a writer, and I don't put that much stock in things I have. Some people say, "Hey Jubal, hey man do something," but I write.

Hudson: It's important to you just to get it out.

Clark: I write all the time, constantly. You want to hear what I wrote this morning?

Hudson: Yeah.

Clark: I'm going to the city—to see what I can find—yeah I'm going to the city—to see what I can find—gonna find a girl young and pretty—to blow my country mind. I woke up in the middle of the night—it's always on my mind.

Hudson: How do you figure that happens to you, and it doesn't happen to a lot of other folks?

Clark: I think it's a curse. Really.

Hudson: I thought you were going to tell me it was a blessing.

Clark: No, it's a curse because I hear it all the time. I hear things. I hear lines all the time when I'm awake. I do. I don't know how other songwriters do it. Now, sometimes I sit down, and I write poetry. I wrote some poetry the other day. A girl called me the other day, and she said, "Jubal, you remember you wrote in my logbook something like 'the wild piercing scream of the night now lies in quivering silence'?" or something like that. I don't know. I mean I've gone to parties and people say I talk in rhymes. I just talk Jubal. And they pick up pencil and paper and say, "Oh wow man, you said . . . ," and I'll say, "What did I say?" They said, "You said so and so and it takes two to make a song." And I said, "Yeah, one to sing and one to hear." "I'm writing that down, I'm going to write a song about that," and, in defense, I'd say, "I've already written that," but they still write it down. They say I talk in rhymes, but my children tell me, "Dad, I think perhaps you can answer any question with a line in one of your songs that you've written already." Like "Gypsy Cowboy."

Hudson: I use your lines when I answer questions sometimes. "Just rhyming words trying to stay free." I know it's real hard to focus on particular influences because everything around us is so important, especially when you are an observant, perceptive, feeling person. But are there specific songwriters that you know have had a direct influence on you?

Clark: I think, in honesty, I think that loneliness—being alone—has influenced me more than other performers. Yeah, I've heard Bob Wills. I grew up around him. I think Willie Nelson is one of the best songwriters in the world. Billy Joe Shaver is great, but that came along later. I was writing songs before that, and maybe I write a different style of song. I don't know. I'm not going to tell you the year, but I used to be in the navy, and I'd go out to the West Coast. I was playing an upright bass fiddle with a group called Jason Hillbillies, if you can believe that about a ten-piece band. But I wasn't influenced by that. I'd go listen to Stan Kenton. Louis

Prima playing trumpet and Benny Goodman when I was in New York. I would always seek out live music. I used to hang around the Berkeley campus. I'd go down to Point Richmond and hear Big Tiny Little banging on an old piano. Later on he's on the Lawrence Welk show. I'm glad the man made it. I used to hang out where there's live music. I'd be riding a bus down the street—I'd see some kid with a tissue paper and a comb, and I'd get off the bus and go listen—pat my foot and listen. Catch the next bus. I mean, I love music.

Hudson: Let's describe Texas music.

Clark: Texas music is a combination of interpretations. Gary P. Nunn's perception of Texas music—that's Texas music. Jerry Jeff, a friend, all the people—Mickey Newberry. Oh God, Lee Clayton, I love him, and all the different people. I've known so many people during the past, and they're always saying, "Hey Jubal, you do your own unique style." I think Texas music encourages us each to be unique. A lot of people don't understand me. Willie does because Willie said, "Jubal, will you come play the Farm Aid?" And I said, "You got it Willie." Bless his heart, he's a champion, and a lot of people perhaps don't understand that Willie doesn't place any restrictions. Willie says, "Hey, I like what you do—come pick," and I do. This year with a ten-piece band hopefully—twelve-piece. But that's Texas music.

Hudson: Texas music is the perceptions of that artist at that time.

Clark: I suppose so, but I'm not the stereotypical person to answer that question.

Hudson: Why not? You've been listening to it, you've been playing it, you've been here, you know all these folks.

Clark: I just play my music, and I love it, and I'll love it when I'm eighty-three years old, and I'll keep picking. I had my heroes you know. The ones that I'd admire when they'd do a catch line. People'd come to me and say, "Damn, Jubal, you wrote a good line there, wow that's good. It's a good hook line or something." And I said, "Well, I don't write hooks; I just write what I feel." It might not be Nashville, but I just write what I feel at the time, and I write all the time, constantly.

Hudson: Well I think that shows up in your work. It comes right through nice and clear. I know you have some demos and everything. Have you thought about going into the studio and getting all this stuff down?

Clark: Kathleen, I'm going to try to cut an album this year, but I need a thousand dollars. At one time some years back Willie told me, "Jubal, you want to go to Nashville I'll give you thirty thousand dollars. Go on down there and cut you an album. Do it the way you want to do it." And then things kind of changed a little bit, and times were changing, and then we both mutually talked about other things. I feel like if I ask Will, "Hey, can I come out to your studio and can I cut an album?" I feel that Willie would say come on. But I kind of want to do it on my own, and if I can get a thousand dollars from you, a thousand dollars from this friend, a thousand dollars from this friend, I'm gonna do an album. I want to go to Europe. That's my dream. I want to take one other person. I'm an authentic Texan. I want to go to Europe, but I need to take me an album. Lots of Texans go over there and do well. Look at Stevie Ray Vaughan.

Hudson: What's your favorite song?

Clark: I guess "Gypsy Cowboy" is my favorite. That's good, it says a lot of things. I mean I got friends but "peace of mind—that's my only friend."

Hemingway Lives
in Texas

Richard Dobson

It's like fishing. Maybe you're fishing in the unconscious, not the ocean. You just never know what you're going to pull out of there. Sometimes you have to wait. Sometimes you get lucky. Sometimes you wait days on end and never get anything.

I don't remember when I first met Richard. It seems he's always been around. I do remember one spectacular Sunday morning at my house. His band, State of the Heart, needed a place to crash after the Kerrville Folk Festival. My living room was perfect. In the early morning light, I fixed breakfast, and the three of them went outside to tune instruments. Standing in my rock garden, amidst cactus and animals, State of the Heart started playing beautiful music. I stopped the breakfast preparation long enough to sit out on the porch to watch and listen. I had been receiving Richard's newsletter, *Life and Times of Don Ricardo,* for years. I knew many of his stories. When I finally looked at his promo material, I also discovered that the poetry of his songs inspired covers by David Allen Coe, Carlene Carter and Dave Edmunds, Guy Clark, Lacy J. Dalton, Nanci Griffith, Phillip Donnelly, Pinto Bennett, Rick Densmore, and more. His albums come out in Europe first on Brambus Records in Switzerland. He tours Europe regularly, often finding the elusive audience. Richard is always working on daring creative projects. Just check out his tribute to Townes Van Zandt called *Amigos*. Imagine Townes à la bluegrass.

Known by an elite underground coterie of fans, Richard has been described as the Hemingway of the country music field. He divides his time between Nashville, Galveston, and Europe. Critics keep writing that "fame has eluded Richard Dobson," but he is a musical visionary whose songs are timeless vignettes, everyday tales of everyday folk.

He's often called a writer's writer. He has not crossed over that line that will bring his work to the masses, but he has crossed over the ocean many times. In England he has a serious, appreciative audience.

Listen to "Old Friends," a song he wrote with Guy and Susanna Clark. The love evident in that song is the love evident in the life of this Texas troubadour.

Hudson: Describe the way you see your career as distinct.

Dobson: I really have faith and confidence in what I'm doing. I see myself as someone who has tried to have a foot in each camp: to be a valid artist and try to write something that's commercially valuable. I've really worked pretty hard on that angle. I have to say, after all these years, I don't really have that much to show for it. At the moment I'm almost at the point of just chucking it. You can get your songs recorded by accident as easily as by beating your head against the door over there in Nashville. I see myself as being pretty lucky. On the whole, I've been able to pursue my career. Of course, I don't own anything. The best teachers tell us that's an impediment to real spiritual growth anyway. In this culture we're so bombarded by owning things.

Hudson: Is there any particular philosophy which has influenced you? I read in one of your newsletters a reference to the Tibetan Buddhists.

Dobson: I guess I'm a little guilty of just picking up what comes along. Things that I need. I get a lot out of Buddhism, but I don't think I'll ever be a Buddhist. There are certain guidelines you just pick up. The need to be positive is extremely critical. I run across these ideas in my readings which seem to help. I don't have much religion, as such, but a lot of spirituality. What else are you going to do? We're all on this journey, and we know where it's going to end. It behooves us to live our lives as best we can and help others. If a song can do that, that's the deal. Music sure does it.

Hudson: I've really enjoyed your live performances. Do you see yourself continuing to perform?

Dobson: As long as I can. It gives a lot to me. I think music is a communal thing. It gives to everyone involved in it. The people listening and the people playing. It's all a celebration.

Hudson: Let's talk about major influences.

Dobson: Leonard Cohen, Neil Young, and Bob Dylan. Those three guys. In addition to the heavyweight guys like Hank Williams and Merle Haggard. I kind of like those literary writers like Kris Kristofferson.

Hudson: What do you think Dylan's influence has been on Texas music?

Dobson: About the same as anywhere else. I don't think he was any bigger in Texas. He's a major influence everywhere. But from a commercial point of view, you couldn't pick anybody worse to have as an influence than Dylan or Cohen.

Hudson: They somehow managed to get commercial.

Dobson: I like Neil Young, too. He's pretty far out in left field. Some people just get away with it. I like songwriters nobody ever heard of, like Rex Bell. Crazy people. I always like the lunatic fringe. Butch Hancock, I've always liked his songwriting. Texas is full of craziness. Calvin Russell is a monster. Terry Allen, there's another one just kind of loopy.

Hudson: What's ahead for you?

Dobson: I hope to get a little interest in the book I'm working on. It's about stuff that happened twenty years ago, being on the road with Townes Van Zandt and a bunch of crazies. I've got an upcoming tour of Europe this fall and another in the spring. Our record is called *Love, Only Love*, which is coming out this fall in Switzerland. I hope I can write some more songs, just keep on doing it. It brings me a lot of joy and happiness. As long as I can keep living and keep doing it.

Hudson: I see in your newsletters you have a strong connection with nature.

Dobson: I would have been a pretty good game warden or naturalist if things had turned out that way. When I'm fishing, I get a really good feeling.

Hudson: Let me ask you some bizarre questions I don't ask anybody else. What animal are you?

Dobson: A bear.

Hudson: What direction are you?

Dobson: I never thought of that. Probably southwest.

Hudson: Are you earth, wind, fire, or water?

Dobson: Water.

Hudson: What color are you?

Dobson: I'm brown right now.

Hudson: What country are you?

Dobson: Wow, that's another hard one. Gee whiz. I'm Mexico.

Hudson: What city are you?

Dobson: Santa Fe.

Hudson: I know you don't usually answer these questions. You've got to make it up right now. Creative process at work. What room in your house are you?

Dobson: Kitchen.

Hudson: What item of clothing are you?

Dobson: Cut-off shorts.

Hudson: What vehicle?

Dobson: An old Ford truck.

Hudson: What body of water?

Dobson: Gulf of Mexico.

Hudson: What's the most beautiful thing in the world?

Dobson: Loving somebody, really.

Hudson: What's the ugliest thing in the world?

Dobson: Hatred.

Hudson: If you could change any one thing in the world, what would it be?

Dobson: Bad habits that come back. Stumbling blocks.

Hudson: Joseph Campbell said wherever you stumble, dig for gold. Tell me a story about some of our pals on the road. Townes, Roxy, Guy?

Dobson: I have a lot of stories about traveling around in a motor home with Townes Van Zandt and Mickey White. The Hemoridge Mountain Boys. We played in Denver and Boulder. It was a madcap cruise. The captain was crazy. Everyone was trying to keep up with the captain. I don't think it would play today. At the time we were drinking a lot. It was a nightly test of seeing how weird it can be. Twenty years later we said, "What was it all for?" We were partying. Just see how hard you can push the fun button and still have fun.

Hudson: Your songwriting is like . . .

Dobson: It's like fishing. Maybe you're fishing in the unconscious, not the ocean. You just never know what you're going to pull out of there. Sometimes you have to wait. Sometimes you get lucky. Sometimes you wait days on end and never get anything.

Hudson: That brings us back to Hemingway. Sometimes you drag that fish home, and there's nothing left of the fish.

Dobson: Townes said, "Where you go is good and gone. All you keep is the getting there."

Hudson: Townes is a good one to quote. Let's talk about *Love, Only Love*.

Dobson: It's about a long-distance love. There's a story in there. The love songs on the album tell the whole story. One woman inspired all this. There's a woman in Europe who inspired all this. It begins, "I'm so afraid of love."

Hudson: I was just listening to Kimmie Rhodes' new song which begins, "I'm trying hard to believe in forever."

Dobson: It's not easy. Sometimes you've just got to go for it. You can't look at your past mistakes and say it can't happen. You've got to try again.

Hudson: What kind of reading do you do?

Dobson: At the moment I've been reading South American things, *Love in the Time of Cholera*. It was synchronistic, my reading that at the same time as being in love with this woman. Before that I was reading *Paula* by Isabelle Allende. I was in Chile in the Peace Corps. I wrote her a letter, and she answered me and sent me a copy of another of her books. All the South American writers floor me. Right now I'm trying to read *Beautiful Losers* by Leonard Cohen. I like his songwriting better than this book. In spots, it doesn't work for me.

Hudson: I just read a collection of short stories by Gabriel Garcia Marquez. I wonder why these South American writers floor us.

Dobson: Magical realism.

Today's Jimmie Rodgers

Billy Joe Shaver

I was at the end of my rope, doing lots of things, just about to die and hadn't written a song in a long time. I went up on a mountain outside of town here and had a spiritual experience. I came down the hill singing that song. So I done all right on that, and I think it just come from God. As a matter of fact, I know it did. It went right through me. I was just a vehicle, and I appreciate that song.

Billy Joe Shaver signed a multi-album deal with Justice Records in Houston in June 1996. Billy Joe has long been recognized by his fellow artists as one of the most respected songwriters of our time. His songs have been covered by an impressive list of performers including Bob Dylan, Kris Kristofferson, Willie Nelson, Elvis Presley, the Highwaymen, Patty Loveless, and Marty Stuart. In the early '70s, Waylon recorded an entire album of Shaver songs, *Honky Tonk Heroes*. Billy Joe wrote ten of the eleven songs. That record brought Billy Joe's work into the limelight. It went on to become one of the most important recordings of the genre.

Billy Joe is a "honky-tonk hero," and "an old chunk of coal," and most certainly "a diamond." He climbed a real mountain of despair one day, wondering whether or not to jump, and returned with the song, which John Anderson recorded, "I'm Just an Old Chunk of Coal."

Listen to his songs and you'll hear his story. Beginning a classic love song that included the line, "There's no end to what I'd do, just because you asked me to," he said, "I've written these all about the same woman. Eddie's mother. I married her twice."

My favorite Billy Joe lines include "If I never felt the sunshine, I would not curse the rain," or "Just like the songs I leave behind me, I'm gonna live forever," or "I couldn't be me without you." This man has been in love. Eros has led him down some long and winding roads.

He admits to the influence of Jimmie Rodgers. His producer, Randall Jamail, said, "He's our generation's Jimmie Rodgers, and his music is Texas soul."

Billy Joe is a major voice in the story of Texas music. Not because of the number one songs he's written and not because of his rapport with audiences. He has an important story to tell, and he is willing to keep telling it in ways that are true to him. He knows, "Yesterday's Tomorrow Was Today."

We talked first in Nashville and then many times in Texas. In February 1997, he spent the day at Schreiner College telling his story to several English classes.

Hudson: Let's talk about the beginning.

Shaver: I was born in Corsicana, Texas. I got started when I was about five or six years old. My grandma raised me and my sister on her old-age pension. People down at this general store where we got credit from, sometimes we'd get behind on our credit and grandmother's check wouldn't come in and they all knew I sung. My grandmother would go down there wanting to extend her credit, and they'd say, we'll let you extend your credit if you'll get that boy to sing for us. They'd stand me up on a cracker barrel and I'd sing "Pins and Needles in My Heart" and just sing my heart out. I thought I was really doing something. Singing for a meal really. We didn't have a radio, and I would just listen to whatever I heard on whatever radio. They had one at the barbershop and I'd listen to that.

Hudson: Picked up a lot of music then?

Shaver: Picked up whatever I could. Whatever I couldn't pick up, I'd just make up. And that's how my songwriting got started.

Hudson: When did you pick up the guitar?

Shaver: I didn't start doing that until I lost these fingers on my right hand.

Hudson: Are there songs you remember as a kid?

Shaver: I can't remember how old I was. I know I was too little to be out at night. I was barefoot and I walked about ten miles down the railroad track up to the place where the Light Crust Doughboys were playing. Homer and Jethro were there in Corsicana, and they'd all come in for a big show. It was in the back of a bread building, I remember. And there was a lot of people in there. Corsicana has always been dry, and you'd see a man every once in a while with a pint of whiskey in his back pocket. I was just a kid, and I didn't have no shoes on, and my overalls were plumb up nearly to my knees because I was growing out of them. We was so poor—my God. We got our clothes from the Salvation Army. I mean we were real poor. But I got in there in time to see Hank Williams play. He looked at me all the time he was playing and singing. He didn't do but about three tunes, but he sang to me all the time. I was standing by a pole, and people were stepping on my feet, and I couldn't even feel it. I said, "Man, I want to do that—that's what I want to do." I didn't know who Hank Williams was at that time, but that's what they were calling him—Hank. I just knew he was good, and I got touched by him. And that ain't all that caused me to go in the direction I went. I felt like I was cut out to do this. My grandmother encouraged me. She used to rock me in a rocking chair and tell me how I was going to be on the Grand Ole Opry. I was only about five years old. She had no money or anything to send me to school or college. She just planted a seed in me, and that's the way it happened.

Hudson: And it's been growing ever since.

Shaver: Yeah, I'm doing all right—a pretty good crop.

Hudson: Are there any songs that have stayed with you over the years in your memory, songs that you heard?

Shaver: No, not too many. My own have been such a comfort to me. I've been so engrossed in my own stuff that I really haven't had time to learn anybody else's. I can remember a few old tunes, but most of them I can't even remember.

Hudson: Many major names in Texas music and in country music have recorded your songs.

Shaver: Yeah, I wrote *Honky Tonk Heroes*, the entire album, and Waylon Jennings recorded it.

Hudson: How does it feel to listen to other people do your music? Because the rendition is bound to change the meaning a little.

Shaver: Back then I was into my writing so much that I was really happy to hand the ball to Waylon. I couldn't sing as good as he could. As a matter of fact, he is just a damn good singer, Waylon is. He can take a song that somebody wrote and make it sound like he wrote it. That's a real art. Willie does the same thing. When Willie does "Old Five and Dimers," it sounds more like he wrote it than I did. That's good—it's real good.

Hudson: I think the person singing your song must feel the same honesty you felt when you wrote it.

Shaver: Yeah, and also, I've been pretty selective about who I pitch my songs to. I don't usually pitch my songs. It's caused me not to be as productive as other writers, but the ones that I give them to usually think the way I do. I'm pretty lucky there, that I've been able to survive and still be able to do that.

Hudson: Now you have some albums of your own. Billy Joe Shaver doing his own music.

Shaver: Yeah, top-secret albums.

Hudson: Those are my favorites.

Shaver: They're hard to find. I haven't even got all of them.

Hudson: How did you get involved in some of those projects?

Shaver: Kris Kristofferson produced my first album. He had to borrow money to do it. Nobody in town wanted to record me. We went in and did it. It was a very unselfish thing for him to do.

Hudson: He had a lot of faith in your writing and your performance.

Shaver: Yeah, and it didn't hurt my head none either. That first album had "Old Five and Dimers," "Willie the Wandering Gypsy" on it and "Georgia on a Fast Train."

Hudson: The Billy Joe classics today.

Shaver: Yeah, you're right. They are good. I did one for CBS called *Old Chunk of Coal*. I was just an old chunk of coal and I'm going to be a diamond someday. Then the next album was *Billy Joe Shaver*. It had a bunch of good tunes on it but they dropped me, fired me. Whatever you call it when the record labels say, get out, we don't need you no more.

Hudson: Mysterious reason?

Shaver: No, I think they just mysteriously didn't like me. It gets to be so personal and political sometimes; you just want to grab somebody and choke the hell out of them. But you don't want to do that unless you catch 'em where there ain't nobody else around.

Hudson: You're in Nashville instead of Texas for some reason.

Shaver: I'm wanting a deal with a record label. I'm expecting to do very well this next trip. I'm not going to take any prisoners. I mean, I'm going for the throat this time, so they better look out.

Hudson: You've done well before, according to your fans.

Shaver: Yeah, I did a lot of things I didn't particularly want to do because of the producers. They were all my own tunes, but there are a lot of things I want to do differently. This time I'm going to insist on doing them the way I want to.

Hudson: Keep hold of the reins.

Shaver: Absolutely. I'm either going to do it that way or go down trying, and I'm sure I'll get my way because I've been around longer than most of them have. The biggest mistake I ever made was thinking somebody was smarter than me. I swear it just knocks me plumb out—some guy sitting over here, can't even play the damn guitar, is telling me how to do my tunes. It's not that all of them are that way; they're not. Maybe the ones that produce my albums are not that way. We did hit some spots where I could have made things a whole lot better.

Hudson: And now you're going to.

Shaver: And now I'm going to, and I'm not going to take "no" for an answer either.

Hudson: Sam Phillips this morning at the address here for the Country Radio Broadcasters gave that advice. You can look back at his background and career and know when he stands up there and says go after what you believe in.

Shaver: Old Sam.

Hudson: He speaks out of experience, too.

Shaver: He's real active. He kicks ass.

Hudson: Do you have any favorites of the songs you've written?

Shaver: They're all like kids. Some with buckteeth. You don't say anything to them, either. It's hard to pick a favorite. The one that really moved me a lot and helped me at a time when I really needed it was "I'm just an old chunk of coal but I'm going to be a diamond someday." I was at the end of my rope, doing lots of things, just about to die. I hadn't written a song in a long time. I went up on a mountain outside of town here and had a spiritual experience. I came down the hill singing that song. So I done all right on that, and I think it just come from God. As a matter of fact, I know it did. It went right though me. I was just a vehicle and I appreciate that song. I don't know why I got chosen to write it. It was so simple and nice and good, and I'm such a big old sinner. But it came out of me and worked. It helped me out and it helped a lot of other people, too.

Hudson: And continues to.

Shaver: Yeah, it's going to be around forever I'm sure.

Hudson: What kind of things are you working on now?

Shaver: I don't really want to ruin anything by talking too much, but you'll be hearing about it.

Hudson: Your songwriting seems to come directly out of your life and your experience.

Shaver: Yes, I guess it's kind of good that I haven't been real successful. But it's good that I probably haven't been more popular because I'd probably be laid up in some bed watching TV instead of out on the streets where I belong, gathering all these experiences.

Hudson: Texas music has been labeled many different ways. What are some characteristics of it that perhaps keep it special?

Shaver: I call it Kick-Ass Country. Just flat ass kicks you in the head. Those people down there, by God, know how to say something; they get right straight to the point and it'll hit you in the head. I don't care if you're in New York soaking your feet, it'll kick you.

Hudson: That's a characteristic of good music wherever it comes.

Shaver: Everybody is direct and to the point down there. I've heard this all my life. It's everyone's job till we get the work done attitude.

Hudson: Community spirit.

Shaver: Not much complainin' or bullshittin'. Everybody get busy and do what they're supposed to do.

Hudson: Do you have a song that was really difficult for you to write?

Shaver: Not very many. I've had some challenges of things that I've thought, "Well, I'd like to write that." But it took me years. I never did put them down on paper. I just let it roll around in my head until it came out right.

Hudson: Do you know when it's ready to come out? Is there a time or a feeling?

Shaver: It just comes out. Sometimes I carry one around for a while, and it may not amount to nothing to anybody else, but it does to me.

Hudson: What place does writing have in your life?

Shaver: I always write. I think everybody ought to write. It's the cheapest psychiatry there is. I'm pretty happy when I'm writing. I'd say I'm successful if I'm writing, no matter what I'm writing on. If things are bothering me or I'm having to wait on this or that or I'm getting disappointed about something here or there, as long as I'm writing, I'm okay.

Hudson: So it's an outlet for you.

Shaver: Yes, it is.

Hudson: To get some things out of you, if they stayed inside they might . . .

Shaver: It would cost me a lot.

Hudson: I've often explained that horseback riding kept me out of the psychiatrist's office. That's one of my hobbies.

Shaver: There aren't many psychiatrists I've seen chasing horses [laughs].

Hudson: Writing is an outlet for you. Do you find times when you can't write?

Shaver: There are times, but I learned early on. I've been writing poetry since I was about twelve. I'd started doing that stuff I told you when I was five, so I was kind of putting everything together at a pretty early age. I found out there were going to be times when you'll have a period there where you don't write. I never have. I got past forcing things a long time ago.

Hudson: You let them happen?

Shaver: Yeah, they come out a whole lot easier.

Hudson: And the waiting doesn't frustrate you?

Shaver: No, just that one time when I had that problem. But it was because I was doing a lot of drugs and alcohol and not taking care of myself. Doing everything I wasn't supposed to do and feeling bad about it on top of that. Then an "Old Chunk of Coal" came along. Ever since then I've had no problems with that waiting stuff.

Hudson: What are some of the latest songs you've completed? We won't talk about what you are working on, but are there a couple you've completed in the last couple of years?

Shaver: I've got one called "Manual Labor." It's about two years old, but I wished I had it out. Sometimes I get so disappointed because I don't have anybody interested in 'em but me. They are so timely if they'd come out when I'd write 'em, it would be great, but they don't. So I have to wait around and listen to other people do some reasonable facsimile to it. I've written mine well enough to know if they come out, they're still going to be good. Regardless of whether it looks like I'm sucking hind tit or not; they are going to be good because I write them good.

Hudson: That is wonderful that you have a real core of positive energy about what you're doing. Have you always had that?

Shaver: Oh yeah. There has never been any doubt about the writing part. As a matter of fact, I think I can sing just as good as I write. This is what's been hard to convince people of. Their lack of enthusiasm has even caused me to doubt it. Then I came back and said, hey, when I first came to town these idiots tried to tell me to go home and find something else to do. I can't find those guys now. I don't know where they went to.

Hudson: Do you have any favorite places you like to play in Texas, any favorite honky-tonks?

Shaver: I like Gruene Hall pretty good. A lot of places I used to like are gone.

Hudson: Do you enjoy a crowd that's dancing or one that's listening?

Shaver: Either way.

Hudson: I know at some of the various Kerrville Music Festivals you've had an absolutely captive audience.

Shaver: Yeah [laughs]. We've been lucky on those. Those who come to Kerrville usually listen, but at the honky-tonks they like to hear loud stuff.

Hudson: What do you like to see happen when people are listening to your music?

Shaver: It doesn't matter to me. It's always a different chemistry every time you play because it's different people. They decide the way things come out. I just enjoy it all.

Hudson: Are you enjoying having your son Eddie as part of the show?

Shaver: He is real good.

Hudson: Music experience?

Shaver: He's on his way to being one of the best. He's been playing with me since he was fourteen. I took him out of school. Every time he'd go to school he'd vomit—so—what the hell?

Hudson: Let's go on the road . . .

Shaver: I took him out of school, nobody ever said nothing. I wasn't supposed to have taken him out that early, but I'll put him up against these guys who went through school any day. He's as smart as they are—

smarter. I'm going to give you a tape of some of my songs where Eddie is playing guitar on them.

Hudson: Do you have a set band you are working with now?

Shaver: As long as I've got Eddie is the main thing. But I just use four pieces. Actually just drums, bass, Eddie, and myself. A lot of times I don't even play.

Hudson: Did you pick up the guitar as a challenge?

Shaver: Yeah.

Hudson: What did you do with it?

Shaver: [laughs] With them fingers? [He holds his hand out.]

Hudson: What happened there?

Shaver: They got pulled off in a chain in a sawmill.

Hudson: Were you working there?

Shaver: Yeah, and I took the fingers—I picked them up out of the sawdust and took them over to the doctor's office with me. He said he couldn't sew them back on; they were ruined. But this colored lady over there, a nurse, she said "Mr. Shaver, can I have those fingers?" I said, "I guess so, what do you want with them?" She said, "I'm going to put them in a jar." I said, "What for?" and she said, "Well, we got religion a little bit different over here." So I said, "Well, I don't care." So, I guess my fingers are still pickled somewhere. I don't know, they might be dancing around right now [laughs].

Hudson: Where was this?

Shaver: In Waco. They got voodoo down there, too, by God [laughs].

After this first conversation, Billy Joe and I met on the road many times. Eddie was always there. Billy Joe is always serious about a performance, whether he's on the stage at a Willie Nelson picnic or at Farm Aid or at a roadside cafe. Billy Joe sings each song each time just like he means it. He signed with a label in Texas, Justice, which also produced a Waylon album, one on Kimmie Rhodes, and one on Willie Nelson. The label is committed to the sound of each artist rather than attempting to create new sounds. The label gave us an autobiographical album, *Shaver: Highway of Life*. Billy Joe tells his story through the twelve songs on this CD.

Time to Rock

Delbert McClinton

That's solitude. It's definitely the place where it is created. Sometimes the idea comes out of a crowd or in a crowd. But the writing usually comes from the solitude.

Born in Lubbock, Delbert grew up in Fort Worth. I heard Ray Sharpe sing "Linda Lu" at the Skyliner on the Jacksboro Highway in 1964. That same year Delbert and his band, the Straightjackets, shared the stage with Sonny Boy Williamson, Jimmy Reed, Big Joe Turner, and Howlin' Wolf during their stint as the house band at Jack's Palace. In 1962 McClinton played harmonica on the Bruce Channel hit "Hey! Baby!" It was while performing with Channel on a European tour that Delbert turned the Beatles (a then unknown group who opened some of the shows) on to the harp licks later heard on the well-known "Love Me Do."

His albums on various labels have been labeled blues, houserockin', southern rock, and soul. Many of his songs have been recorded by others. In 1978 Emmylou Harris scored a number one country hit with "Two More Bottles of Wine." In 1988 Alligator Records released *Live From Austin*, which earned Delbert a Best Contemporary Blues Album Grammy nomination in 1989.

He has always maintained a rigorous touring schedule, performing nearly 250 dates each year. I have heard him under a big sky at Luckenbach when Marcia Ball joined him for the last set. I have heard him in roadhouses and in concert halls. "I've never been rocked enough," says the tee shirt I bought at John T. Floore Country Store.

Each time I've seen him, we've talked. Once he told me about his latest reading: "Cormac McCarthy is my favorite right now. I've read most of his work. It's astonishing. I don't have the words to describe his writing. Once I was amazed to discover a critic mention both of us in the same paragraph. How is that? I wonder. He's so visual while he conveys the real emotions and situations." I told Delbert that I understood. It's about real emotions.

Back at the bus once he said about his life, "It hasn't all been great, but I can say that I do have a great life, and I really love where I am right now."

Once at Floore's he had nine musicians on stage with him, including another Fort Worth connection, Steve Bruton. On his Alligator album he said, "I just wanted to make a very eclectic record. I thought, why the hell not? Where is it written that you can't do this and you can't do that? I just did what I wanted to."

The following conversation took place one New Year's Eve afternoon, before a show in Austin.

Hudson: Let's talk about your musical beginnings in Texas.

McClinton: I have been playing Austin for a long time. Maybe twenty years. We started playing frat parties here back in the mid-sixties. I was living in Fort Worth at the time. Austin is a real good town for me, always has been.

Hudson: What about Fort Worth?

McClinton: I started playing there in junior high school. All the places have since burned down except the Blue Bird. We used to work the Red Devil Lounge out on 28th which has been gone a long time. They all burn down.

Hudson: How did you get started?

McClinton: Seems like I've always been playing music. I moved from Lubbock when I was eleven. I had musical influences from Lubbock before I moved to Fort Worth, but Fort Worth is where I really started. That's where I was old enough to really start getting out and get into it.

Hudson: What about writing?

McClinton: Songwriting started out as writing poetry.

Hudson: Any particular procedures when you write?

McClinton: Not really. It either comes to me, or I sit down and try to encourage it to come to me. Sometimes it does, sometimes it doesn't. Solitude is important in the process. I need to create time for myself, but it's something that is difficult to do. The writing usually comes from the solitude.

Hudson: Any favorites of the songs you write?

McClinton: They're all my babies. I don't write nearly as much as I'd like to. I used to write a lot more, but I was living a lot faster, and that seems to be something that brings about a lot more of those hard lines. I have been writing recently, and I'm really proud of what I write.

Hudson: What are your early musical influences?

McClinton: Lefty Frizzell, Hank Williams, and, of course, B. B. King. Bobby Blue Bland, Lightnin' Hopkins, Howlin' Wolf, Elvis. I've probably been influenced by everybody I've heard because I like a little bit of everything. The only conscious direction that I believe I've ever taken is that I'm not trying to copy anybody else.

Hudson: Are you influenced by locations? What's it like to be in "Cowtown"?

McClinton: It's got a lot of influence. I don't think of it as a railhead for cattle shipment, but the phrase does bring to mind Northside. I played down there before it was cool to play down there.

Hudson: What do you think about the direction of Texas music?

McClinton: Texas music is special and always has been. With Stevie Ray jumping out right now, he's really bringing a lot of us to light. Texas is in the mainstream. If you're going from coast to coast, you just might go through Texas. Dallas–Fort Worth is pretty heavily traveled by people from one end of the country to the other. So, it's got a lot of influence, it's got a lot of color. It's a wide path for various types of music, a midway point.

Hudson: What writers influence you?

McClinton: Billy Joe Shaver is probably one of the greatest writers that I've ever known personally. He's a real treasure. He's a longtime character. He is what he is, and his songs are just as real. Kris Kristofferson said something to me once. We were talking and somebody else said something, and he said, "Boy, that's as real as a Billy Joe Shaver song." Shaver is a real poet.

Hudson: What do you like to see happening when you're on stage?

McClinton: I like to see people enjoying themselves. I grew up playin' for people dancing. I relate to that better than any other aspect. We've always played for people dancing, and when we play, and they dance, I like it. People dance because they want to.

Hudson: Favorite honky-tonks?

McClinton: Yes, but it's not there anymore. The old Soap Creek in Austin was about as fun a place as I've been. It was one of those magic places off one of the bumpiest old dirt roads I've ever been on.

Hudson: Do you have any experiences in writing or performing when everything just crystallized and it all worked?

McClinton: A lot of times in songwriting when that happens you're standing off watching and saying, "Golly, look at this," and it's just coming out. It's sort of an out-of-body experience. That sounds a little heavy, but still, that's what it's like sometimes. And it's fun. It's a good feeling.

Ten years later we talked again at John T. Floore Country Store.

Hudson: Let's talk about your life right now.

McClinton: The most current thing in my life right now is the new record. It will be out in February of '97 on Rising Tide Records. I'm really excited about it. That's a new label in Nashville headed by a guy who understands Texas, Ken Levitan.

Hudson: Is that excitement any different than the way it has been over the years on all those different labels?

McClinton: Yes. I wrote most of the songs on this one. I've been writing for the last four years in anticipation of a new record, so when the time finally came, we went in and did it. I'm real happy with it. It's a good record.

Hudson: What makes you want to write?

McClinton: I don't think it's a matter of wanting to. I can't help it.

Hudson: What has stayed with you through the years?

McClinton: Fans. Fans have stayed and that's the best part. They really have, God bless them.

Hudson: You mentioned the need for solitude and that was important to you in your own writing process. How do you describe your process now?

McClinton: I've been co-writing in the last several years, so there has been a lot less solitude. But it's something I've come to enjoy. It's interesting and a lot of fun.

Hudson: Any slumps in the writing?

McClinton: One of the best turn-around songs I did that kind of brought me out of a writing slump was a song that I wrote for Wendy, my wife. The song is called, "I Want to Love You." Up until I wrote that, I had been in a slump for several years. That kind of opened it up, and the juices started flowing.

Hudson: You've been around so long. Why?

McClinton: Too broke to quit is the main thing that has kept me going.

Hudson: You love it.

McClinton: I do love it. I did write one song for this album, co-wrote it actually, that says it all. "If you can't lie no better than that, you might as well tell the truth." It's great fun to write those little stories.

Hudson: Did some of this come out of your life?

McClinton: It all comes out of life, my life or others.

Hudson: Is it hard to write songs?

McClinton: Sure it is. Sometimes we work all day and get nothing. Sometimes we work all day and get something real good. Sometimes we work for a short time and get something real good. The process of co-writing is just getting together, sitting down, starting to doodle around with a guitar to get a hook line, and then just build on it.

Hudson: Are there any misperceptions about you?

McClinton: I think a lot of people who watched me, the way I lived most of my life, probably think I'm still the same way. I'm not. I couldn't be and continue to live. I see a lot of people from my past, and they still want to act that way. I just don't do that.

Texas Energy on the Road

Joe Ely

There's not a formula. It's a little like roping a runaway motorcycle. You just have to hang on and ride it out till you pull it down. Some songs come like a flash of blinding light, and some take months to wrestle with until you get them. I think that the main thing is just to catch whatever comes in.

I first talked to Joe Ely at the Austin Opry House, December 28, 1985. Since then I've watched him rock the house in Cannes, France, in Frutigen, Switzerland, at roadhouses in Texas, in San Francisco, and many times, in Austin. On Saturday night, August 3, 1996, I was standing out under a huge Texas sky at John T. Floore Country Store. All was expected. All was predictable. No surprises here—only pure Joe Ely. And that's always "enough." I'd been listening to his new album, *Letter to Laredo*, over and over. The love of the road, the outlaw, the passion, the tenderness—they were all there, Ely style. In each listening.

I was ready to watch him now, remembering the night at Slim's in San Francisco when the crowd shoved against the stage in order to be close to his energy. Ready to participate when he leaned out over them with his mike aimed toward them. I remembered a similar night at Gruene Hall, a night that led to a roadhouse video.

In Helotes, at Floore's, he came out on stage, full of energy, picked up the guitar and began. He went through the album, song by song. He opened with the line, "I have stumbled on the plain, Staggered in the wind," and told of a man's search for a woman that takes him "from St. Paul to Wichita Falls across the desert sands and the Rio Grande—All just to get to you." The album is a travelogue through Texas and time, down to Mexico and across the ocean, to Spain and back again. Ely is a thousand miles from home but still next door. He becomes the mariachi, the fighter, the lover, the warrior, the rancher, the fugitive, the storyteller, each character driven by deep passion. Ely said, "Maybe I read too many Cormac McCarthy books the first couple of years, and it's rubbing off." Ely is a master storyteller like his longtime hero, Spanish poet Federico Garcia Lorca (one of Leonard Cohen's favorites, as well).

On stage with Ely that night in August was Teye, a Flamenco guitar player from Holland. His meeting with Teye led to the new album, which combines the textures of instruments in a way Ely appreciates. "When he played," Ely recalled, "it just added this weird thing I guess I'd always secretly loved, but I never thought that I could ever use on a record. When I got Lloyd Maines on steel and dobro with Teye, it was like some kind of long-lost sound that I was not sure if I'd ever heard before. If I had heard it, I didn't know where from, and I didn't know what to do with it." Listen to the album. He did a lot with it.

Back to Floore's. Ely went through the album, song by song. Jesse Taylor, longtime Lubbock compadre, joined Joe, as well as Teye. Glen Fuginaga held down the bass spot as usual, and Don Harvey beat drums. The evening not only showcased the songs, but also featured a truly Texas performance—high energy that hails back to Buddy Holly. This thread in the Texas music tapestry is of a rough and rowdy texture. The other side reveals the smooth tenderness of a man who would do "anything" just to get to you.

The crowd pushed up to the stage. All joined in on the encore, waving hands high above their heads to "I keep my fingernails long so I click when I play the piano." Joe's music crosses many borders. He played Midem in Cannes, France, one January after being held at the Italian border for eleven hours. He and his family showed up at the Frutigen Songwriters Festival in Switzerland. Currently on MCA, a label that has supported his music for years, Joe has created his own niche instead of continuing to search for one.

A true son of Texas energy, Joe Ely will rock you.

We had the following conversation in 1985.

Hudson: How would you describe your music?

Ely: I'd say it's got its roots in Texas. It's Texas rock 'n' roll that has country and blues roots.

Hudson: What influences are you aware of?

Ely: There are lots of them. So many that if I started naming them, I'd probably run your tape all the way out. One of my earlier influences was Jerry Lee Lewis. I remember seeing him when I was about seven years old. He was playing in a dust storm on a flatbed trailer out in front of a Pontiac dealership in Lubbock. The dust was blowing so hard the mikes were blowing over. It was almost surreal. It made a real big impression on me that a band could get out here in a dust storm on a flatbed trailer in the middle of West Texas and make something happen. I guess it was before Jerry Lee had any big songs on the radio because I remember the Pontiac guy would come out after he played a little and sell Pontiacs and then say, "Okay, let's get that piano player back up here." Everybody had scarves over their noses. It was an awful day. What impressed me was the fact that he pounded it out in a sixty mph wind.

Hudson: How have you heard your music described?

Ely: Every way imaginable, from cow punk to middle folk to rockabilly to rock 'n' roll. I just write the songs and work them out with the band the way I feel they should be worked. I have all instruments in the bands, everything from accordion to steel to saxophone. I like to use the textures of different instruments to do the song like I feel it should be.

Hudson: What problems do you run into being part of a group which defies a label?

Ely: I don't have problems with it. I think maybe radio has always said it's too rock for country and too country for rock. To me, that's not a problem; that's what Texas music is. It is widely diversified music. They called Bob Wills a jazz band because he took jazz chords and structures in a lot of his leads. People defined it as they went along. Now it's defined as western swing, which took the best of country and jazz and melted them together. Cultures combine and swap ideas, then music changes. That's what keeps it new and interesting.

I can't help but think back to Robert Johnson. He brought blues to Texas. He recorded in San Antonio. The only twenty-nine songs he recorded probably did more to shake the whole foundation of blues and rock 'n' roll. Just those few recordings, and Jimmie Rodgers. I know he had a home in Kerrville. I think he took a lot from the blues and added the country lyric—you know, trains and hard time. I think Buddy Holly influenced me a lot. We grew up in the same town. Texas has always been a good music state.

Hudson: Environment seems to affect music. Let's talk about yours.

Ely: I lived in Amarillo and heard Bob Wills there. I didn't know it at the time, but my parents told me. I developed an interest quite young. I started out playing violin when I was eight years old and a family guitar when I was about eleven. When I moved to Lubbock, I first started learning Buddy Holly songs from a guy down the street. We formed all these little bands. When I was fourteen, I opened for Jimmy Reed. Lots of goings on in people's houses, just getting together and playing and swapping songs and ideas. A lot of the Lubbock sound came not so much from the city but just from the fact that there wasn't a whole lot else to do except get into trouble. Waylon was out there. I started putting my songs together with Butch Hancock and Jimmie Gilmore—just looking at where we came from and laying down songs and seeing what happened. The Flatlanders album in the early '70s was the result of all that.

Hudson: I enjoyed the reunion of the Flatlanders at Jimmie's wedding.

Ely: That was the first time we'd gotten back together in about five years. It's a wonder we'd remember any of those songs, but it was a lot of fun to play.

Hudson: What are your influences as a songwriter?

Ely: I spent many years just kind of rambling back and forth across the country with just a guitar, jumping freight trains. I was looking for the source of where songs come from. After all that time, I realized that they come from down inside of yourself. When I sat down and started making records, I took from all my experiences. If something really touches you on the inside, then it usually ends up in a song.

Hudson: Who are some of your favorite songwriters?

Ely: That list can go on and on. How about Butch Hancock, Billy Joe Shaver, Jimmie Gilmore, Elvis Costello, Mick Jagger, and Bob Dylan? I think they were all influenced by Buddy Holly in some way.

Hudson: Do you have a particular procedure you follow when you write?

Ely: I wish I did. It would probably make it a damn sight easier. There is no formula. It's a little like roping a runaway motorcycle. You just have to hang on and ride it out till you pull it down. Some songs come like a flash of blinding light and some take months to wrestle with until you get them. The main thing is just to catch whatever comes in. I always keep real thick notebooks and scribble constantly. I've written a lot of songs on tabletops in restaurants when I didn't have anything to write on. I had to tell the waitress not to clean the table so I could run down the street and get some paper.

Hudson: Takeout with tablecloth!

Ely: Right. It's hard to take the linoleum though.

Hudson: What advice would you give someone writing?

Ely: Don't look for any magic—just write all the time. People ask me where I get a particular idea. I don't know the answer. All I can say is that I was just writing one day, and it came to me. If I had not been writing, the idea might not have come. Writing generates ideas. Don't just sit and wait for flashes of light. They might not come. Write anyway, about everyday ordinary things. Even though they might not seem significant, sooner or later, something will come that you'll wonder where it came from. Those are the things that make sense. I guess out of every hundred songs I write, I keep one and throw the rest away. I'm always working on something because it's something I like to do.

Hudson: What do you like to see happen when you perform?

Ely: I like to see the music and energy onstage transferred to the crowd to where they feel something we're doing. That doesn't always happen, but it's what I like. There's this kind of chemistry. When everybody in the band gets on fire, it's like a stack of dominoes.

Hudson: I know you're a reader. We both carry books. Any favorites?

Ely: I've always liked Henry Miller and Jack Kerouac. I've been reading a lot of Sam Shepard lately.

Hudson: *Cowboy Mouth* is one of my favorites.

Ely: I just read a little collection of stories he did while he was traveling around the South. It's called *Motel Chronicles*, and it contains pieces that didn't quite make it into his movie, *Fool for Love*. [Every time I talked to Joe we compared reading notes. Once in Switzerland, we were both reading *Weaveworld* by Clive Barker. We've also both read Cormac McCarthy.]

Hudson: How would you describe Texas music?

Ely: I'd say it's tough, rugged, hardy. It's not pretentious, it's straight to the point. I'd say it takes from its past and passes it along to the future. It's also about individuals celebrating their hardships with a Saturday night on the town. I think the songs that really jump out are by people who have been through some tough times and have made it through to the other side to tell the story. First you go out and do a lot of hard work. After the work is done, you go to the dance.

**Darrell Royal
with Randy Willis**

*All photos by the
author unless
otherwise noted.*

Willie Nelson

115

Willie Nelson

Floyd Tillman and
Roland Davis

Floyd Tillman

117

Sonny Throckmorton

James McMurtry

Steve Earle and Del McCoury

Steve Earle with the author

Guy Clark

**Richard
Dobson**

Billy Joe Shaver

**Townes
Van Zandt**

Ben Dorcey (a fan) and Delbert McClinton

Jubal Clark

Joe Ely
*(top portrait by
Merri Lou Park)*

Marcia Ball
*(top portrait by
Merri Lou Park)*

Kinky Friedman with Sweet Mary *(above)* **and Kinky with Gary P. Nunn**

Tish Hinojosa

**Katy Moffatt;
with her brother,
Hugh Moffatt**
(below)

Kimmie Rhodes

Carolyn Hester and a fan

Freddy Powers

Gary P. Nunn

Tanya Tucker *(courtesy photo)*; **Jimmie Dale Court with Anita Rodgers Court (Jimmie's mother) and the author**

Stevie Ray Vaughan portrayed in this sculpture in Austin; Stevie Ray in person *(below)*

Johnny Winter

Johnny Copeland

Ray Wylie Hubbard

Holly Dunn with the author and Sonny Curtis with Guy Clark

Johnny Rodriguez

Lyle Lovett and the author

Robert Earl Keen

139

Crawlin' Crawfish Circuit

Marcia Ball

A lot of times you just have to be a real workman about it. You just have to go in and sit down and write. Almost inevitably, if I sit down at the piano and focus on writing a song, I'll get something. It might not be the whole song though.

If you've seen Marcia Ball, you've seen a willowy Texas woman, sitting cross-legged at a piano, foot dangling over the edge of the stage, keeping time to the music. She'll be looking over her shoulder, hair flying, smiling while she belts out her tunes. Or she'll be crooning the blues. Or running up and down the ivories. It's blues, it's boogie woogie, it's soul. It's Texas music, for sure.

She played at the Frutigen Songwriters Festival in Switzerland under a huge white tent nestled in a valley surrounded by the original Hill Country. Over seven thousand folks gathered. She knocked them out, even with the language barrier.

Tish Hinojosa played the same night. The audience responded to these women, they responded to the music.

Marcia does the Crawlin' Crawfish Circuit with style. Whether it's New Orleans, the Gulf Coast, or the Hill Country, Marcia plays to the roadhouse crowd with the gusto of a Delbert McClinton (they both shared David Hickey as a manager). She joined with Lou Ann Barton and Angela Strehli on an Antone's album entitled *Ladies Sing the Blues*. In 1991 these three "divas" closed the Benson and Hedges Festival in Dallas to a large and appreciative audience.

She began in Austin as Freda of Freda and the Firedogs, yodeling Patsy Montana songs. She has been influenced by singers like Barbara Lynn, O. V. Wright, and Jean Stanbeck. John T. Davis once wrote, "And, ah, when she plays . . . Her arms pump like a weightlifter's; her body is transported; moving to the beat, all snakey sinew from the waist up. She plays with her wrists cocked high (like the piano teacher used to tell you to do), her long legs crossed, her right foot kicking hell out of one of the piano legs as she swings it to the beat." Yep, that's Marcia.

Marcia and I talked the first time right after the release of her album *Hot Tamale Baby* in 1986 at the Kerrville Folk Festival.

Hudson: Let's talk about the origins of this music.

Ball: It's a Louisiana-oriented album. Most of my music is. The title song is a Clifton Chenier song, and the album is dedicated to him.

Hudson: Are most of the songs on the album yours?

Ball: Not this time. I only wrote two out of the ten. There's a little bit of Memphis sound on it as well. If you had a collection of old 45s, and you picked out your favorite old labels, I've probably covered every one of them on this album.

Hudson: Did you have a particular theme in mind when you put it together?

Ball: No, just good music. Just a certain amount of balance.

Hudson: You mentioned onstage that you've been writing some this year, and you talked about the blues.

Ball: A lot of time I write songs that aren't suitable for my band to play. This has turned out to be more of a "blues" year, though.

Hudson: Do you enjoy a single piano set like this?

Ball: It scares me to death. I enjoy it to a certain point, but it's hard for me to do.

Hudson: It's a real direct communication between you and the audience. I loved it.

Ball: In Kerrville I can do songs I don't do anywhere else. These are not the songs that are my everyday repertoire.

Hudson: The crowd loved it.

Ball: It could have been a little more boogie woogie.

Hudson: How do you know when it's time to write?

Ball: Sometimes you really feel like saying, "Gosh, that's a good line," or "I feel like going in and writing something." But a lot of times you just have to be a real workman about it. You just have to go in, sit down, and write. It's inevitable. I will go in and sit down at the piano and focus on writing a song, and I'll get something. It might not be the whole song. Words and music come at the same time for me.

Hudson: Are the songs tied in with what's going on in your life?

Ball: Sometimes, and sometimes they're really off the wall. Sometimes I'll just decide that I'll make up a story. Sometimes somebody will cue me; sometimes it's a hook line that I'll work around. Sometimes I'll go in completely blank and start playing a rhythm, just mumbling words, whatever feels right with the rhythm, and pretty soon something will come.

Hudson: What's the easiest song you've written?

Ball: One of the easiest songs that I ever wrote was the one that's on my new album. It's called "That's Enough of That Stuff." I was in Fitzgerald's in Houston, the club I play, and they were trying to empty the bar. Pat, the bartender, said, "That's enough of that stuff" to the rowdy bar hangers. I said, "I believe I'll write that down." I did, and a song came as fast as I could write it down. A lot of times that happens, as fast as you can write it down. Sometimes I go back and edit, but sometimes it just comes out like that.

Hudson: What's the most difficult song you've written?

Ball: There have been songs I've kept around for years. One I did tonight, "Ozarks in the Snow," I started writing because of something that happened the first time I became aware it snowed in Arkansas. I was on the road. I had Luke with me, he was still an infant. We were trying to get from Oklahoma to Arkansas, and it was a mess. I started that song, the little nucleus of the song, right there. I got back from that trip in January. I finished the song on the hottest day in July. I remember the day that I dug it back out to finish. But I had really been working on it all along.

Hudson: Do you have favorites that you enjoy performing?

Ball: A lot of times it's just whatever is the newest thing I've got because it's fresh.

Hudson: You represent a Texas-Louisiana connection. Let's talk about your involvement in the Texas music scene.

Ball: I've lived in Austin for sixteen years, and I've played music here in Kerrville. I don't fit anywhere because to Louisiana people, I'm from

Texas, and to the Texas audience, I'm from Louisiana. It's hard to type-cast me. I've always been a little out of step. Once I was "Freda and the Firedogs." A booking agent in Austin once said to me, "Would you mind telling me, when country music is more popular than it's ever been in history, why you decided to quit playing country and start doing the blues?"

Hudson: Yeah, I've heard you introduced as the Queen of Country.

Ball: I had a hot little country band. We were kinda the first on the scene in Austin. Greasy Wheels was playing, and they had Mary on fiddle. There were not many female vocalists running around, especially playing country, and especially not hippies playing country. That's where our niche came in. We were bringing country music to the Hungry Horse and the Armadillo. This was months before Willie moved to town, during that whole period Steve Fromholz calls the Progressive Country Music Scare. We were quite popular, and we played straight country music, not to be confused with country rock. We really did not touch on the rock end of it very much at all. We didn't put out an album, but we did a reunion gig at Soap Creek and Bobby Earl and Joe Gracey put out an album of that. It's very rare. They only pressed about five hundred of them.

Hudson: Your other albums?

Ball: I did one Capitol album called *Circuit Queen*. I did two Rounder albums, *Soulful Dress* and *Hot Tamale Baby*. Rounder is a great label for what I do.

Hudson: You also spent time with the Texas Playboys?

Ball: Yeah, in fact, I recorded with them. We were both on Capitol eight years ago, and I sang a couple of songs with them on a live album. It was my greatest thrill to meet, know, and play with those guys. I sing and play piano with them every chance I get.

Hudson: What about other influences?

Ball: All piano players have influenced me. The obvious ones are New Orleans players like Fats Domino, Allen Toussaint, Tuts Washington, and Professor Longhair. The Gulf Coast is a hotbed of rhythm and blues and soul music. Everybody from Albert Collins to T-Bone Walker to Bobby Blue Bland on this side of the line.

Hudson: This Texas side?

Ball: Yeah, I was born on the border. I was born in Orange, Texas, and I grew up in Vinton, Louisiana. They're ten miles apart. Orange had the hospital and Vinton didn't, so I have always treaded that line.

Hudson: Are you heading off into the blues now?

Ball: That's kinda where I always was by nature. That's what I know best, that's what I like best. Being a piano player affects what I write. I don't use a guitar beat in my songs. If I were a guitarist or different instrumentalist, our sound would be different.

Hudson: Describe Texas music.

Ball: Do you have two or three hours? Let's see, I love Texas music. Texas has everything, and that's my description of Texas music. It's everything I love. It has spawned everybody from Flaco Jimenez to T-Bone Walker to Janis Joplin. It runs the gamut.

We talked again after she played the New Orleans Jazz and Heritage Festival in 1991.

Ball (from her mom's house in Vinton, Louisiana): I use whatever catches my attention. Sometimes I just sit down and write exercises, see what I can make up. I was an avid reader as a child. I've always loved language. But putting out an album that has seven of my own songs on it was a real feat of nerve for me. It took lots of support, lots of people encouraging me. Carlyn Majer, my former manager, was the most influential when it came to getting those songs out of me and onto a record. She said, "Good job."

Hudson: Now you have a third album on Rounder, *Gatorhythms*.

Ball: My record label is perfect for me. They allow total artist control while giving wonderful direction at the same time. This album took about three years, but they allowed me to do it on my sense of timing. I feel the product is better because it was not produced on demand.

Hudson: How do you balance your career with your family?

Ball: My family is important to me. I love to travel and perform, but I feel I can keep it all in perspective. My fifteen-year-old son, Luke, plays in the school band on trumpet. He looks forward to playing with me sometime. We have a household of teenagers. It's scary. Jeb, Gordon's seventeen-year-old, is playing drums, and Brandy, fifteen, is also offering support. It's even more demanding being a parent to a teenager. I can't just read them stories anymore. It's algebra now, and that's much harder. When I had the opportunity to play the New Orleans Jazz and Heritage Festival, my husband, Gordon, and I talked about the possibilities. His last words were, "Go for it." I wonder now if he really knew what would happen. I think so.

Hudson: What's it like playing to this crowd?

Ball: I'm still overwhelmed. People came up over and over to tell us they loved the music here, but that they especially came to hear us. We're open to what's happening, and, as Gordon said, we're ready to go for it.

Off the Wall

Kinky Friedman

Strange as it seems, the more inward I turn, and the more way out where the buses don't run the subject matter is, the more people identify with it. You would think the fewer. But it hits more people because there's so much crap out there anyway.

I moved to Kerrville in 1984. I met Kinky Friedman shortly thereafter. We had an uncomfortable conversation on the local radio show. I was an amateur trying to put together a series on Texas music. I'd never been in a radio station before. Since then we have talked many times in many places. Once, when he was running for Justice of the Peace, I received this phone call: "Hudson, get on your cowgirl clothes and come meet me at the post office. Drive your truck and pull your horse trailer. No need to bring the horse, though." It seems one of the New York talk shows was featuring Kinky, and he does like to create "atmosphere."

Other conversations have taken place at the Del Norte Cafe over bean jalapeño tacos, at the local laundromat, at the Hill Country Cafe over huevos rancheros, at my house in Kerrville South where his pig, Soppy, lived for several years, at Denny's on Easter, in my English classroom at Schreiner College where he surprised a few college students, at Farm Aid and Willie Nelson picnics, in Austin at South by Southwest Music Convention where he was a guest speaker, and the list goes on.

He's "home" in the Hill Country even though for Kinky, "home" is found in the wind. He lives in a green trailer on his parent's ranch in Medina. He brings in the camp laundry during the summer season for Echo

Valley Summer Camp housed on the ranch. He says, "Home is where the answering machine lives."

He first appeared in the national spotlight in the early 1970s as a rabble-rousing country singer, trying to carve out a niche in the scene with the Texas Jewboys. He was chased off campuses as a racist and sexist, only to be invited back twenty years later to give advice to young writers. One turn in his career came when he stepped in to rescue a woman in New York being mugged on the street. That event led to his first mystery novel, *Greenwich Killing Time*. Many more novels in the same genre have followed.

Always expect the unexpected from the Kinkster—the trickster. His counterpart in Greek mythology, Hermes, stole cattle from Apollo, then helped him invent the lyre. The Kinkster moves between the sublime and the ridiculous. He writes for "The People Who Read *People* Magazine" at the "Take-It-Easy Trailer Park." He convinces you to listen with his song "Sold American." Then he makes you wonder why you listened when he says, "Old Ben Lucas had a lot of mucus." He still reminds women to "Keep Your Biscuits in the Oven and Your Buns in Bed." Rumor has it that Joseph Heller's favorite Kinky line is "They're not making Jews like Jesus anymore."

Kinky says he wants a lifestyle that doesn't require his presence, but he has gone out on the road promoting books at music events and playing music at book signings. And he keeps pushing the music aside, even as he released *Old Testaments and New Revelations*, a compilation CD.

When you talk to someone who speaks of himself in third person, "The Kinkster is ready to go now," you quickly enter the story he has to tell about himself.

When we met at the Del Norte in Kerrville in 1989, he asked me, "Wait a minute. Is this an interview?" "No," I replied, "Just a conversation." Interspersed were references to his breakfast, "I've been a vegetarian for thirty-eight hours now; get that ham off my plate," references to his friends, "We need more people like Abbie Hoffman, people who are not content to just watch. People who see something unjust and do something about it," and references to his own artistic career, "There's a performance hype in music that doesn't come into play with fiction. Oh, sure, we have book signings, but hundreds don't mob the store. Rather a nice ebb and flow, a rhythm. You don't buy the hype in fiction like you do in music. Music is business."

The Kinkster is working, busy creating his own life in the story he tells about it. We may all do this, but the Kinkster is very aware of the character he's shaping.

The following conversation took place at the green trailer in 1989.

Hudson: You're a rare combination of performances, Kinky. Your singing and the comedy that goes with it. Then I see you sitting onstage after the show signing stacks of your novels. Where did the idea come from?

Friedman: This is part of a thirty-city solo tour that I'm doing in thirty-four days. We kind of Frisbeed the idea out there, and Waldenbooks brings the novels to every nightclub as we play. The club owners were a little gun-shy about it at first, but they got a very good response. We'll be driving with my friend and agent around the country with nothing but a guitar and a suitcase in hand. I thought it could get rather tedious, but in fact, it's fun—a nice, old-fashioned tour not sponsored by any record company or beer company. People come, I think, mostly because of the books now, not the music—maybe fifty-fifty.

Hudson: The show the other night, which I thoroughly enjoyed and thought brilliant, had all these high spots and then it had moments when you just quieted the crowd and they listened. Have you always been aware of your ability to do that with an audience?

Friedman: I think playing at the Lone Star Cafe every Sunday for several years in New York helped. Of course it made me feel like Lenny Bruce in the last month of his life, but if you can play for that audience consistently and successfully, you can do just about anything.

Hudson: What was the newest song you did last night?

Friedman: Probably two of them. "Dear Abbie," about Abbie Hoffman, is not a new song, but I never did it much before. The newest one is "Saying Goodbye" from the Broadway show that Don Imus, the disc jockey, and I worked on for about four years. It's now just about brain dead, I think—it's crawling in Broadway. We had hoped to have some homosexuals tap-dancing by this time, but that hasn't transpired.

Hudson: Abbie Hoffman came to Kerrville to speak at Schreiner College a few years ago, and the way you performed that song was extremely moving to me, especially after I met and talked with Abbie.

Friedman: Looking around now at the Exxon Oil spill and the pro-democracy protest in China, there is definitely a place for Abbie today in the world. In fact, he was a troublemaker in the great tradition of Jesus.

Frankly, I think looking at all those college students is what killed him. I think it got him very depressed. His brother Jack told me that before he died, Abbie confessed that he just couldn't deliver the message anymore. But I think the legend is going to grow. He's the one out of the Chicago Seven who never sold out. He had a light message to begin with—he was always good, a person who cared about people, not someone out to destroy anything. As the '60s and '70s begin to come back, I think Abbie's going to become very, very big. It's like Mick Jagger says, "Nobody wants to hear any new stuff anymore." When he says, "Here's a new song we wrote," the crowd all goes "Oh, God." If they want to hear the old stuff, Abbie's among the best of the old stuff that we have.

Hudson: Your fourth novel is out, you're working on a fifth one, doing screenplays, Off-Broadway productions, movies.

Friedman: As Joseph Heller says "Nothing succeeds as planned." My guess is that I've always wanted to be a country singer, which is why I'm sure that I will be a best-selling novelist. Things are looking very good with *Frequent Flyer,* the new book. A paperback of *When the Cat's Away* is coming out next week. What has happened to the first book, *Greenwich Killing Time,* is that Ron Howard's company has bought it. The screenplay has been written and they're going to give me a screen test in a month or two. Of course Hollywood made fun of my not being right for the part of Kinky, but I have to take it as it comes. My guess is that the soundtrack from the movie will be a big hit—maybe I'll be a hero with millions of Americans clamoring for me to return to the States. All I know is that for a long time now I've been looking for a lifestyle that does not require my presence, and by God, I think I've found it as an author.

Hudson: So where did you get the title "Surrounded by Indians Tour" for these shows?

Friedman: That was my agent, Cleve, who belongs in a mental hospital. His new one is "The Charming the Pants off of America Tour."

Hudson: That's certainly a different focus.

Friedman: I think the key issue is: Will the Americans come to a nightclub drawn by books? Young people aren't going to be drawn by my music, since they haven't heard it in fifteen years. My first album, *Sold American,* from 1973, is being reissued on CD and cassette by Lawrence Welk. He bought the company, so this will be the first time my records have been out there for anybody to buy. It's an irony not lost on me. It's still called

Vanguard Records, but it's now owned by the Lawrence Welk Group. I understand the distribution system is great and the CD and cassette will be easy to get.

Hudson: Are we ever going to have some more songs from the Kinkster?

Friedman: If I'm going to do any more music, it will probably be around a conceptual deal like a Broadway show or a movie. I do think that songs like "Get Your Biscuits in the Oven and Your Buns in the Bed," "They Aren't Making Jews Like Jesus Anymore," "The Ballad of Charles Whitman," "Old Ben Lucas Had a Lot of Mucus," "We Reserve the Right To Refuse Service to You," "Ride 'em Jew Boy"—they seem to be very popular. In many places, everybody in the audience is singing every word to these songs. Charles Whitman climbed the Texas Tower and killed those people twenty years ago—that's yesterday's fish wrappers now. Nonetheless, there's a little bit of him in us all. He was just an all-American boy, nothing weird about him. The point is as true today as it was then and it's a good song. Most of my stuff was never really commercially received the first time around.

Hudson: What kind of highlight are you anticipating in this thirty-day blitz of shows?

Friedman: I feel like Dashiell Hammett with a guitar. The music is not the main thrust, though if it wasn't for the books, I probably wouldn't be doing the tour. The media's interest level is extremely high. For instance, in Philadelphia, we're playing a small club but we're getting the same press that The Who got when they played the City of Brotherly Love—huge newspaper and television and radio exposure. We sold a hundred hardcover books in a nightclub in Dallas last year. I don't think that's ever been done before. Reading is a very personal thing and a book's success is made largely on word of mouth. Especially for mystery writers who'll be spitting these little boogers out like sunflower seeds, one every year. When they finally get hot, the whole shelf gets hot. It's an interesting thing, and it gives me more control than I've had in the past. I have editors and agents, but it's not like when you're with a record company and you've got producers, managers, booking agents, and club owners to deal with. I feel more autonomous, much more my own man doing things my own way.

Hudson: Fill in the blanks: Writing is like . . .

Friedman: I'll go with what F. Scott Fitzgerald used to say, "Writing is a lot like swimming underwater and holding your breath." Good writing is very much like that. Writing prose is easier for me than writing songs. I use a Smith-Corona electric, and I try to get out four or five pages a day. Much more than that and I start going downhill pretty quick. You've got to listen to that voice inside your head. I don't really write much fiction, although it's sold as fiction.

Hudson: Is there ever a time when you just have this feeling of being full and overflowing, and there's just something you have to write down?

Friedman: I wish there was. I mean, not often. Usually I don't know what to write, and I can't get started with an idea. So I use substitutional therapy—I type with my toes and take a very light attitude toward a heavy subject. That's one reason I like mysteries a lot. Mysteries offer resolution and life doesn't, so rather than write some ponderous tome, I prefer to write to amuse Americans on their aircraft. That's the way I approach a typewriter.

Hudson: You've obviously got some discipline in your process, but do you have any sort of trick that you use to get beyond that block or that stale time?

Friedman: If you're working it's more difficult. It helps to be unemployed. I can spend more time with it whenever the mood catches me. I find if you approach it not as a great genius, poet, and novelist, but as someone who's got to produce so many pages, then you may find that some of the work is pretty good. It'll start right from the first sentence. If it's good. If it rings wrong you've got a serious problem. Especially in the mystery field—it's got to ring right. I hope my books are funny but they're also real. Part of the reason they're real is because I'm writing to a very small group of living people and a larger group of dead people that I know. That's my audience.

Hudson: Steinbeck said he wrote for one person that he knew.

Friedman: I stole that notion from Steinbeck.

Hudson: Do you see yourself moving into other genres of writing?

Friedman: Writing screenplays is like putting together lawn furniture. I'm not too excited about that unless somebody pays me a lot of money to do it, and still I'm not spiritually excited about it. I think I'm rather trapped in the mystery genre. People want what they start to like. On the other hand, I must say that it's very rare for a guy like me who's known as an outrageous kind of musician to get another chance and be received now as a novelist. It's unusual because in this world we don't often take a guy that may be a star athlete at one time and then later accept him as a rocket scientist. Usually we get one chance. This is like another reincarnation for me, and I intend to make the most of it.

Hudson: When are you having the most fun with writing?

Friedman: Truman Capote said that he hates writing and he loves having written. Like Agatha Christie said, "When people actually come up to you and say, 'My spirits were very low and I read your book and it really picked me up' or 'It made me laugh'"—that's very gratifying. It makes writing one of the most important things in the world to do when you're getting that kind of reaction to it.

Hudson: What is absolutely the most difficult aspect of the whole writing business?

Friedman: It's probably when you reach a certain point, at least in mysteries, when you wonder if it's working. You got nobody to really check on whether it's working or not except flying by Jewish radar. You don't know until you're through with it whether what you've written is gibberish or a diabolically clever plotted novel. It's a risk you take when you don't diagram or outline things. I don't really know what's going to happen until it happens. I'm not saying I'm the vessel for God like John Denver. I don't know who the murderer is or how the thing is going to resolve when I start the book. But I do find out eventually.

Hudson: Some final advice?

Friedman: What I always like to say is what my friend Doug Kennedy said before he fell off his perch in Hawaii some years ago, "You've got to learn to roll with the bullets." And the poet Kenneth Patchen said, "Never eat at a place called Mom's, never play cards with a guy called Doc, and whatever you do, don't ever sleep with anyone who falls in love more easily than you." My own personal advice is "If you're driving, folks, don't forget your car."

One morning in October 1995, Kinky and I met at the Hill Country Cafe in Kerrville for breakfast. He was in a hurry to return for the O. J. Simpson trial. I was surprised he was keeping up with it.

Hudson: Let's talk about your books now.

Friedman: This whole bit with the Kinky books has been unexpected. For some reason, it's not a path that's often followed. It's one thing you're known for, and that's it. If you happen to have several facets to your personality, which some of us have, like say, Dr. Jeckyl and Mr. Hyde, you only get known for one of them.

Hudson: You write in the mystery genre.

Friedman: I think the flavor of the atmosphere is the most important thing in the kind of writing I do. You won't find a mystery writer who writes mysteries. They all write something else, and I guess I'm with them as well. I'm really writing novels with a kind of atmosphere. They'll make your apartment smell like someone's smoking a cigar in there, hopefully. That's really what I'm doing, with a few asides about life, liberty, and the pursuit of whatever. We're all pursuing, and I hope we all find it.

Hudson: Do you listen to criticism?

Friedman: I briskly look it over once. People think I'm the next Mark Twain. You don't want to dwell on that, you know. That'll fuck you up. The main thing I want to do is entertain myself in the middle of the night when I'm typing. If I can keep doing that, sometimes I slay myself at two in the morning. If I can do that, that's what I want to do. Because I do believe Tom Joad was right in *Grapes of Wrath*, that we're all just part of one big soup. Strange as it seems, the more inward I turn, and the more way out where the buses don't run the subject matter is, the more people identify with it. You would think the fewer. But it hits more people because there's so much crap out there anyway.

Hudson: How do you stay in touch with what you really have to say?

Friedman: By staying out of touch with most sources of input. I've almost totally tuned out music now. I listen to some Hawaiian schlocky music. I don't have an extensive CD collection.

Hudson: What's the connection with Hawaii?

Friedman: I've been there a whole lot of times. I'm being drawn spiritually more and more to Hawaii. But I don't want to get into a clinical recall about it. The islands have a certain melancholy about them and a certain joy that you don't find anywhere else. In the spirit, anyway, I'm drifting out there. Also, I'm very taken with a lot of the stories. The same way James Michener was in *Tales of the South Pacific*. That's why I'm angry with the frogs for doing their nuclear test out there but, getting back to the topic of writing and songwriting. I don't know why a man like Kris Kristofferson couldn't write an autobiography. I'm talking about a book that makes it on its prose. Why those people haven't tried that, I don't know. The only guy who's tried is Jimmy Buffett, and me. I might point out I was doing it about eight years before Jimmy Buffett was, and I will be eight years after Jimmy Buffett. That is a little surprising. There are some really great poets that are in songwriting, and we know a lot of them. I'd like to see a Guy Clark novel.

Hudson: I have a copy of a screenplay Billy Joe Shaver wrote. What would you imagine for yourself as a writer in ten years?

Friedman: I will probably be the next Mark Twain. That's my guess.

Hudson: Now you're heading out on a tour of South Africa.

Friedman: Yes, to explore my roots. I've never been to Africa, but it's one of those places I love because the books have preceded me, and the music has not. It's like Australia.

Hudson: You won't be asked to sing a few little ditties?

Friedman: Oh yes, I'm doing concerts there, but the people coming to the concerts—only a handful will be cult Kinky fans. The vast majority will be book readers to see what this is all about.

Hudson: What do you think about the cult Kinky fans? You love us, don't you?

Friedman: Yeah, but I think you know I do. For some time I've been aware that I'm in danger of losing my cherished cult status. Some of the cult people who are referred to as insects trapped in amber are not healthy. I do prize these people to some degree. I've always thought cults are important. I mean Robin Hood was a cult, Jesus was a cult, and Jim Jones was a cult. There've been important cults before, and this Kinky cult might be another one.

Hudson: What happens when you get popular with mainstream culture?

Friedman: There's a distinction between someone like Danielle Steele, who has a large audience, and Kinky Friedman, who has readers. Stephen King has a huge audience. I have readers. The best books are not on the best-seller list, that's for sure. I'm not going to say too many bad things about the best-seller list because I may soon be on it myself. I never made the money that Johnny Rodriguez or Charlie Pride did, and I had as much to offer. Good material, probably better material that was never heard by the public because I shot myself in the foot or in the head or wherever. But I shot a few other people around me at the same time. The result was that with this body of song, I established a cult following. People aren't sitting around waiting for me to sing "American Pie," you know.

Hudson: But maybe they do wait for "Sold American"?

Friedman: Yeah, but it's a healthier thing for me. It would be a drag to just have that one big hit. Nobody cares what you're working on now. That's the way it is with the Rolling Stones and with Bob Dylan. Abbie Hoffman once observed, "Nostalgia is a sign of illness in a society or an individual." So I've never believed in nostalgia—I don't deal in the past. I'll tell you who has gotten fucked a lot worse than me is Willie Nelson. He's lost more money than I ever lost in country music. I just never got a chance. I mean, I had more of a chance than many people, but I didn't really have a chance to be taken seriously. I'm a serious soul, as Billy Joe Shaver says, but I've come to take myself very lightly. To the point where, when I meet people, they say, "Oh, you hocking your boots these days, Kinky." You write the stuff and let the chips fall where they may.

Hudson: I like what you said, bottom line, you're entertaining yourself in the middle of the night.

Friedman: Do that and possibly writing for a silent witness somewhere along the line. It's a little hard to distinguish because there's many. I've also said that I write mostly for dead people. I conjure up dead people when I write. I'm not writing to think what would a living person think.

Hudson: So you're off to catch up on the trial now?

Friedman: I don't like reality to intercede on fiction or on this interview, but I would like to put a positive spin on this whole thing. It's been an absolute privilege to do what I'm doing and to be able to do it. And it's a joy to work on these books. I'm writing a book on Willie Nelson now. *God Bless John Wayne* is out. *Love Song to J. Edgar Hoover* is now finished. The Willie book is number ten. It's a murder mystery involving Willie, tentatively titled *Roadkill and Willie*. With all his ex-wives and all his colorful past, we don't know who's trying to kill. I seem to blither in on the scene somehow, and then it starts happening. This will be a nice behind-the-scene look at country music the way it used to be and the way it still is in some circles, in some forms like Willie. Willie's a very funny guy and a very insightful guy, so it should be a very philosophical book. Witty with a lot of one-liners.

Hudson: Does your philosophy blend with his? The two of you are bound to have had some serious conversations.

Friedman: He's more faithful, more fated. I'm a lot more cynical. One very valuable thing I've learned from him is that there's one prick in every organization who will say you can't do it that way. There's always someone like that. What keeps him in the game is to defeat that person, show him it can be done this way. He said he's fought that in everything he's done successfully. *Stardust* is probably his best example. He said nobody would let him release that record. *Red Headed Stranger* is another example. I know what he's talking about. You have to pick your battles carefully in life and decide what you want to do.

On Dreaming
Tish Hinojosa

It's like walking through a museum. Something catches my mind. There's never enough time. Things just flash by. I end up desiring things—time to dream, for example, and the things I desire lead me. I write from this desire.

I first met Tish when she played a Mexican restaurant in Kerrville in the late 1980s. She invited James McMurtry to sit in. She sang one of his songs, "Flashing Yellow Lights." At that time her performance did not compel me. Rather, I was interested in her talent as a songwriter. Now her performances grab me by the throat. Her depth is apparent in her choice of material. Her dedication to her culture, her interest in various causes, her willingness to stay authentic in a world and a business asking for conformity are just some of her strong attributes.

I had last seen Tish at the 1996 Kerrville Folk Festival. Her presence onstage is pensive at times, altogether charming and clearly focused. She is a spiritual force to be reckoned with when she is singing from her heart.

Just a few blocks from the 170-year-old former convent chapel where she recorded *Dreaming from the Labyrinth,* Hinojosa grew up as the youngest of thirteen children in a family held together by her Spanish-speaking parents' faith, pride, and resilience. As a teen she played folk and pop tunes in San Antonio clubs, covering Dylan, Baez, and Ronstadt. In 1979 she moved to New Mexico and embraced the progressive country music of that period. She did the stint in Nashville and the stint in Austin (her current home). After several successful albums on independent labels, she signed with Warner Bros. *Destiny's Gate,* in 1994, was her first release. In 1996 *Dreaming from the Labyrinth* followed. In this album, with lyrics that traverse the commonly shared territory of the soul, she transcends all categories.

She knows she has many stories to tell, and like many of the other Texas artists in this series, she is willing to tell them in many ways. We spoke on September 19, 1996.

Hudson: Let's play a game of word association. What comes to mind when I say "labyrinth"?

Hinojosa: Lost . . . church . . . maze . . . confused . . . discovery.

Hudson: How did your recent work evolve?

Hinojosa: It made itself backwards. Some start with a theme and create the songs. I have been reading Octavio Paz for several years. I actually carried it [Paz's *The Labyrinth of Solitude*] for two or three years, both the English and Spanish versions. The songs came, then I saw how the project could come together. The fun part was volleying between the languages and letting them weave together. They're not really all that similar, so to paint similar images in the two tongues was a very different way of looking at the languages.

Hudson: Let's talk about one of the songs on the album.

Hinojosa: "God's Own Open Road" is a Bob Dylanesque thing that isn't like what you usually hear in Spanish. I wrote it in English, but I also did a version in Spanish. Hopefully, we'll release an all-Spanish version of the whole record one of these days. When I wrote the translation, I said to myself, "I never thought I could say this in Spanish." It was really a unique experience, and it made me see a lot of possibilities. Spanish tends to be the language of poetry—it's such a rolling, romantic language—so this album forced me to find equally romantic language in English. It sometimes took a little time to find it, but I did. Generally, I'm not much of a puzzle-doer, but I realized that I was really challenged by putting this together.

Hudson: You seem to be on the road most of the time. How do you create time and space for dreaming?

Hinojosa: It's like walking through a museum. Something catches my mind. There's never enough time. Things just flash by. I end up desiring things—time to dream, for example, and the things I desire lead me. I write from this desire.

Hudson: Describe a time when you felt "inspired" to write.

Hinojosa: After the spring 1995 Border Tour with Santiago Jimenez, Butch Hancock, and Don Walser, I returned to Austin and the tunes just poured out of me. I don't usually do this, but I let the tape recorder run. For about an hour I let the songs pour themselves out, with whatever lyrics came—some starting in English, some in Spanish. I'd never really written that way, and it was an interesting journey into the mind.

Hudson: Just the word *labyrinth* brings up a journey motif to me. What's significant to you now?

Hinojosa: I'm at a crossroads now. I see where I've come from and how I got here. There are divisions to the various dimensions. Looking ahead, I have three projects in mind. All my work is chronological. It all reflects where I am right now, in time and space. My challenge now concerns the elements of storytelling. I have many stories to tell. For example, a song like "Something in the Rain" puts a personal face on an idea. It strikes closer to home with that personal face. I also enjoy the introspective stuff.

Hudson: How do you spend your time now?

Hinojosa: I am naturally involved with my kids as they grow up. They are interested in creative things—music, writing, sports. Sometimes I take them on the road with me. I don't want them to walk down every road I take, but I do want them to enjoy the interesting ones with me.

Hudson: How do you see your career now? I first met you playing in Kerrville. You have worked with several independent labels, and now you have two albums on Warner Bros.

Hinojosa: I love where I am right now. Jim Ed Norman is head of the label and head of A&R [Artists and Repertoire] at Warner Bros. He understands what I'm doing, and he can represent me that way to the label. In turn, I know they need to make money and sell records. I'm committed to having my songs heard by the widest audience possible. I'm able to work with the label without that sense of compromise that can be so damaging to an artist. Yet I don't operate alone, either. We take each other into account. It's a tough compromise, being on the fringe and also being heard. Texas musicians have dealt with that a long time.

Hudson: What are some high points in your life? Moments of extreme joy?

Hinojosa: I've noticed cycles of seven around me. Every seven years I get worn out, something happens, and a shift occurs. A new discovery, a new form of art. In 1979 I moved to New Mexico. The album *Taos to Tennessee* resulted from that period. Then I moved back to Austin and struggled with my career as a songwriter and/or singer. I took a deal with A&M [*Homeland*] as a singer-songwriter. Then bigger labels came after me as a singer. As I look back, I know I made the right choice at the time. I did spend two years in Nashville trying to become a country singer even before I started writing songs. When I moved back to New Mexico, I decided to get my tools out and work on a project. *Taos to Tennessee* was released as an independent cassette in 1987. It was a collection of songs which represented something to me. I titled it and wrote the title song. That, to me, was the start of something that made me realize what it takes to do that kind of thing. I have since done two albums for Rounder Records, including an all-Spanish border music project and a bilingual children's album.

Hudson: Tell me about your writing process? Is there an incubation period for the ideas? Do you spend a long time on a song? How do the ideas come?

Hinojosa: First, just pay attention. I don't create a certain time or space in which to write. I have a pool in my head and from time to time I stop and put the line in. It's a constant motion process. It's like fishing.

Vulnerable

Katy Moffatt

When I step on a stage, I'm in the middle of my insecurity. I really want to be there. There's no other place I'd rather be. I care very much how the audience is feeling. I want to know.

Katy had just finished her set at the Kerrville Folk Festival on June 10, 1989. Her last song, composed by Cindy Walker, gave her voice an opportunity to exercise its full range. "You give your hand to me. And then you say hello. . . . But you don't know me." She sings traditional numbers as well as her own compositions. Touring Europe regularly, Katy is a favorite with audiences around the world. Her phenomenal success overseas is linked to a warm and open way of being with people, both onstage and off.

A Fort Worth girl, Katy Moffatt has played the folk club circuit with a duo named Moffatt and Flower. I first heard her at the Rubaiyat Folk Club in Dallas. She has tried the music scene in Nashville and Los Angeles. Rounder Records, in Massachusetts, has given her a good home for a while. Her brother and songwriter par excellence, Hugh Moffatt, is also on Rounder. This label preserves the integrity of each artist by supporting the individual person as they are rather than insisting on changes to meet a particular market.

A Katy Moffatt performance is infectious with her laughter, exuberant with her *joie de vivre,* and permeated with a sense of the real. Whether she is yodeling through a Jimmie Rodgers tune or softly singing a song that she has recently written, Katy Moffatt cuts no corners.

Hudson: Let's begin by talking about your last song, one penned by Cindy Walker from Mexia, Texas. Your voice has new ranges in that song. Your interpretation was brilliant.

Moffatt: That song is, without a doubt, my very favorite song in the world. It has been for a long time now. It's called "You Don't Know Me." I think it was first recorded by Eddie Arnold. I think he claimed on the record a part of the writing credit. Big artists used to do that. I know Elvis did as well. But it was Cindy's song. To my knowledge, I've never heard a woman do that song. I heard it and I had to do it. I had to change a couple of lyric perspectives to do it. I would like to know more about Cindy Walker. I was talking to Dee Moeller about trying to find Cindy and just go and get an interview with her. Meet her and talk to her about her life. She must have an extraordinary story to have been the only woman writing in that era and being taken so seriously. As well she should have been.

Hudson: I was interviewing Merle Haggard at the San Antonio Rodeo, and we got to talking about writers. He said, "You've got the greatest right there in Texas. Cindy Walker, in Mexia. She has sent me some songs recently that are great." Now let's talk about your writing. You mentioned a lot of songs tonight that you had co-written with Tom Russell.

Moffatt: This is a subject that is very fresh to me. I've been writing for a billion years [laughter], but I feel like I'm just now starting to learn how to be a writer. Which is different than just every now and then having an inspired song come through me. I have had that occur occasionally. The process I'm going through now makes the songs that I'm writing by myself a little scary to me. A very recent one is a song about a woman being mistreated by a man who is a drinker. It's called, "She's Driving Home Tonight." There's a brand-new one, unfinished, called "The Blue Hotel." This, too, is a frightening song.

Hudson: Where did it come from?

Moffatt: Tom Russell and I were in Switzerland a month ago touring together. We were both sick, and we were touring on the road with these separate illnesses. We mentioned that we each spent time hanging around our hotel a lot, feeling poorly. In this kind of depressing place this story came to me. We are always walking, and at every moment we have a choice. At any one moment we are choosing between safety and danger. You know what I mean? At any moment it's your choice whether to go absolutely stark raving mad or change the course of your life in an instant. The song's not finished yet. I think someone's died in this hotel, and I've got to fix that. The songs that I'm writing on my own are songs that I've got to deal with a little bit before I put them on the stage.

Hudson: Do they come to you as an idea or theme? Or do you hear a line of language? Cindy Walker reported that she writes from a title. Eddy Arnold gave her a title at a party. Three weeks later she gave him the finished song. Three weeks later he recorded it. Let's talk about your awareness of the beginning of a song, of the writing process.

Moffatt: There are many different ways that songs begin for me. I would have to say the most coherent way is with a title and then, of course, there has to be an idea that is expressible. With a title and an idea, that's where a song usually begins.

Hudson: Do you do much rewriting?

Moffatt: No, I really don't. I probably should [laughter]. There are also exceptions. "She's Driving Home Tonight" has been rewritten quite a bit. Only specific parts though. The majority of the song was not rewritten. Other songs have begun through melodies. I often write with a guitar in my hand, but I also begin composing in the car, in the shower, without an instrument anywhere nearby. One real trick which every writer knows, you've got to write everything down, no matter what kind of fragment it is, you've got to write it down. I don't know why it took me so long to figure it out.

Hudson: Do you write a lot?

Moffatt: I'm beginning to. I honestly feel like I'm just beginning.

Hudson: Do you have any definite structure to your writing process?

Moffatt: It's notebooks for me. I run through those spiral notebooks. I like to get a nice, new bright color when I start up a new project. I keep them; they have all kinds of stuff in them. I'm not organized enough yet to have a "songwriting" notebook. It's really good to go back and pick up shards of things that are very old but never used by me.

Hudson: Let's talk about something that has been difficult for you in the writing process.

Moffatt: Right now, the most difficult is co-writing. I don't know if it's truly a difficulty or just a fear that I'm going to learn how to overcome. I don't know what this is going to mean to me, but I've done a little bit of co-writing with some Nashville writers. It just scared the hell out of me to be in the room with Don Schlitz, who's fast, like greased lightning. What I brought in was truly difficult for me. I had a song started that was two years old. I had an entire first verse, a chorus, and an entire melody . . . everything. The idea was very clear. Because of the subject matter, I could not progress beyond the first verse. I didn't know what happened beyond that first verse. It was about something I've never experienced. It's called "The Honeymoon Is Over," and the idea is that you get to a point in a relationship when the honeymoon is all over, but the loving has just begun. This is where it really starts. Now I've come to that place before, but I've never really gone beyond [laughter].

Hudson: Me too.

Moffatt: I really felt like I didn't know what happened next. I thought Don Schlitz would know. He's quite the family man; he's lived that. We got together to finish this song. I felt way out of my league. He was so facile, so fast. And I'm so slow. I was glad that I brought in so much of the song all ready. A principal difficulty I was having with the song was not feeling free to project myself into an experience that I had not had. I'd like to learn how to do that.

Hudson: My friend, Joe Heffington, who used to own Raven's Club in Austin, says he is mesmerized by your performance. So am I. After all these years and all this experience—I do remember the Rubaiyat in Dallas—your performance is as fresh and natural as if you were on the stage for the first time. How does that happen?

Moffatt: [laughter] I don't know, but it is fun to me [more laughter]. It truly, truly is fun. It's the most fun for me. Every time I get on a stage it seems so different.

Hudson: What gives you all that energy?

Moffatt: Having fun is a real goal in my life from moment to moment. As far as the performance situation. Maybe it's because I feel insecure every time I step onstage. I honestly do. I've seen so many wonderful performers, like John Prine, Steve Goodman, and on and on who are just so special. They seem so spontaneously marvelous and funny. I don't feel like "one of those" at all. When I step on a stage, I'm in the middle of my insecurity. I really want to be there. There's no other place I'd rather be. I care very much how the audience is feeling. I want to know. It affects me very much.

Hudson: You are one of those artists you described. Let's talk about some favorite songs.

Moffatt: "You Don't Know Me" is definitely a favorite. There are several of my brother's songs that I feel that way about. Two are on my new album—*I Know The Difference Now.* The song I did tonight, "Papacita," is like that for me. "Wild Turkey" is a favorite, too. That allows me to connect with a certain kind of energy that I love. I had a conversation with Hugh, my brother, a year ago. We were talking about stage fright and how one manifestation of it is the thought that you might forget lyrics. It can be so frightening. It can really be one of those chilling kind of fears. One thing I have really learned through performing my brother's songs is there are songs that I know I can trust. When I start them I know I can finish them. I don't have to worry about that. I know what songs they are. I know how they feel. That makes me relax when I start. Just having faith in the songs is the key to me.

Hudson: A song that rings true for you?

Moffatt: There is a moment of truth, but there is something else, too. The song is so well written that each line comes after the one before, so naturally. How could you forget the lyrics to one of those songs?

Hudson: A quick talk about record labels. You're from Texas. You've spent time in Nashville and L.A. You're playing festivals across Europe. All those connections. Tell me about how you see the business of music.

Moffatt: That's a big question. I'll try to make my history brief. I was on a small folk label out of Denver with Mary Flower. Actually, before that I was in a movie called *Billy Jack*. I did the sound track for that with Warner Bros. That was the first real record I ever made—just two tracks on an album. Then Mary and I did a compendium album for Biscuit City, a label in Denver. We were one of four acts. Then I signed with Columbia Records, and I did an album with Billy Sherrill in Nashville. Then I did another one in Macon, Georgia, with Johnny Sandlin. That album was rejected. Then I took several of those songs with a producer to Los Angeles and made an album called *Kissing in the California Sun*. They wanted me to do a pop kind of thing. One thing I've discovered about record labels, unless you really pin them down, they won't tell you what they want. They won't tell you anything. I was struggling at that time to find out why they wanted me. That was a long, hard trail. I was with them for four years. We released two albums. Then I signed with a label in Texas called Permian Records. It was distributed by MCA Records. We released three singles. We did an album that Jerry Crutchfield produced, but the album was never released. At that point I learned a lot about independent labels. I learned that if you're going to enter the game, be in the game, you've got to be on a major label. You really do. I've never felt that artists are in competition with each other. But records are. Singles truly are. So, if you're going to be in that game, you've got to have the juice. You've got to be with a major label that is used to that kind of competition. A year ago I made this album in Switzerland which was a big surprise for me. Just myself and Andrew Hardin, who is Tom Russell's guitar player. Andy and I produced it, and he played on it. It's mostly two acoustic guitars and one voice. We created the label. A gentleman acting as my Swiss German agent currently said, "I want to build something for you in central Europe, but we need product." I thought, "Well, I'm leaving the country in three days. How could I make a record?" Suddenly I realized that Andy was in Switzerland with a couple of days off. So we just got together and made a record. We called the label, which belongs to my agent Jurg Shapper, Red Moon Records. My brother is recording for Philo/Rounder. He had a copy of this record. He played it for Ken Irwin, who got interested. So, Ken and I made a licensing deal for this album with Steve Berlin and Mark Linnett producing, a more rock-oriented sort of album. We made an album for Wrestler Records, and they are currently being distributed by Rounder. So, I'll have two albums on Rounder. The Steve Berlin album is a country rock. Actually, it's more like a blues, rock, country sort of thing. Kind of hard to describe. It has a harder edge. None of my songs are on it. It is a heartfelt kind of effort because a lot of my friends in L.A. played on this, contributed songs. The latest thing I've done is to start a project in Nashville. The intention is to find the right major label.

Hudson: So is the focus aimed at radio play?

Moffatt: This album has a specific focus. We'll see if it's something that Nashville thinks is radio oriented. I do. It feels like an older kind of country blues. I did a Floyd Tillman song, which I love. He's one of my favorites. The song "Gotta Have My Baby Back" has been part of my show for quite a few years. We had such a fabulous band. It was a treat to sing with these guys. We did a Judy Smith song—real honky-tonk—called "Stand in Line." Then we did a song Tom and I wrote called "Walking on the Moon." I find the four-song package very focused.

Hudson: I heard you sing a Jimmie Rodgers tune at the Kerrville Folk Festival. Rodgers is the epitome of country blues. What provoked a dashing young lady to include old, traditional music in her repertoire?

Moffatt: When you're talking about "Waitin' for a Train," I live in that place. I always have. I can't really say I know how he felt when he sang that or wrote it. But I know how I feel when I sing it. And it makes me feel good. Like I'm not alone. Yeah, that's the stuff.

Hudson: Henry Young, who started this tribute to Jimmie Rodgers in Kerrville, said he always heard "hope" when he heard the songs of Rodgers in 1929, after the crash. There were always better things around the bend. Even singing the blues provided relief. Songwriting is like . . . ?

Moffatt: A big blank. No real comparison comes to mind. I don't have experience writing books or articles, but I would imagine songwriting is a mercifully briefer version of that same process.

Hudson: Except you are compressing so much in a song. Isn't that harder? I can ramble around in a newspaper article so much more.

Moffatt: You also have that much more space to fill, and every sentence must follow the other. I've always heard that writing a novel is very difficult and painful. So, I enjoy the short form of the song.

Grace and Spirit

Kimmie Rhodes

Artists record the human experience, just how it feels to be a human being in your time. It's a way other people can see the world through your eyes. I think human beings feel compelled to put that experience down. They may not even know why, but the end result is that people come along later. They're able to learn from it and relate to it. It also ends up being the only record of what went on a lot of times.

Kimmie Rhodes has shown up around the world, and she's a regular at Willie Nelson events. He heard her and appreciated her talent long before the world sat up in recognition. She was born in Lubbock, the town that gave us music from Buddy Holly, Waylon Jennings, Joe Ely, Jimmie Dale Gilmore, and Roy Orbison. Her spirituality seems based in the wide open spaces of Texas, even as her vision is worldwide, and her audience shows up more in Europe than in her own home state. Our conversation for this book took place at Central Market in Austin. Sitting out on the back porch, eating pizza cooked over an open fire, we had a heart-to-heart talk about her life and about Texas music.

Her ability to focus and be present in the moment created a space for genuine talk. No "canned" responses for this Texas lady, no rehearsed dialogue. She is "real" and that's part of the Texas mystique. The ongoing urge to explain and create, the willingness to stay in touch with one's own driving force, are all characteristics of Texas songwriters.

Her CD on Justice Records features twelve of her original songs and includes duets with Waylon Jennings, Townes Van Zandt, and Willie Nelson. This Houston-based label is committed to documenting Texas music, and the Texas voices on this label are all distinct. Kimmie is one of those voices.

Hudson: It makes sense that I would naturally start off talking to you about Europe because, in my adventures in Europe, your name comes up more often than a lot of other singer-songwriters.

Rhodes: Almost my whole career has taken place in Europe. That's the place where my records have always been out. Up until recently there hasn't really been a market in America that could accommodate my artistry the way it is. Fortunately, in Europe there is a market that can accommodate the singer-songwriter the way they are.

Hudson: Why do you think that's so?

Rhodes: My music has not been considered to be a viable product here in America until recently. When I first started singing, I went to Nashville looking for a record deal. That was when Barbara Mandrell, Dolly Parton, and Kenny Rodgers were doing all their duets. Country music was real pop then. I was a real kind of an Austin honky-tonk singer, and that wasn't what they were doing in Nashville. I was too country for L.A. and not pop enough for Nashville.

Hudson: That's almost exactly what Katy Moffatt said.

Rhodes: That's how it was.

Hudson: Why would people in Europe pay attention?

Rhodes: Because people in Europe pay attention.

Hudson: They know more about heritage than we do.

Rhodes: Yeah, but that's not to blanket everyone in Europe. There are a lot of people there who are still kind of trapped in another story. They are still running around with guns and holsters, but there's a large section of the population there that appreciates singer-songwriters, the songs they write, and the way they sing 'em. That's why people like Townes Van Zandt, Nanci Griffith, Katy Moffatt, Rosie Flores, Butch Hancock, and Jimmie Dale Gilmore have been able to have a career there. We're in the record business, and those are people who will buy your record and come to your show. Here it has been a little harder to find, but it's not so much that way anymore. This record that's out on Justice is my first American record release since the Jackalope record which we put out ourselves.

Hudson: Which I have.

Rhodes: Which was my first album. You should probably hang on to it. We only pressed five hundred or a thousand copies of that record. People all over the world have that record. It's really weird; it was like the bread and the fish. Artists record the human experience, how it feels to be a human being in your time. It's a way other people can see the world through your eyes. Human beings feel compelled to put that experience down. They may not even know why, but the end result is that people come along later—they're able to learn from it and relate to it. It also ends up being the only record we have of what went on a lot of times. Like with the pyramids, sometimes there's a mystery hidden in it that we can't unravel. But for the most part it really shows us the common thread that runs through human experience no matter what age you were then. I think that's why most songs tend to be love songs.

Hudson: I listened to a taped conversation on the creative process. The first thing I heard was Isabel Allende saying the story I have to tell and share is part of my soul—it's something I need to say. When people read this they relate to it out of who they are and a community is created. Then she went on to say we're all particles of the same spirit. I knew that you and I had already alluded to that sort of oneness of everything as well. What is your background in reading?

Rhodes: My songs are like my journal. I don't read a lot. My ideas come from my experiences. I think musically I'm influenced by a wide range of sounds, from the Beatles to Hank Williams through the years. My songs are really what I want to say. I was writing a song with Waylon that's on his new album and we were talking about it. The song is called "Lines," and it says, "I want to be free from the noise of the grind so I live on the outskirts of the back of my mind with a strong hand, a song man and God on my side. I'm writing my freedom a line at a time." We wrote that together, so we spent a lot of time that day in order to write that song to get to the heart of it. I was revealing to myself why I write. We were sort of exploring that—what are we doing, why are we doing this, because that's what the song's about. I told him my songs are like my journal. They're how I understand what's going on in my life. It's a thing that is real natural for me.

It's not so much of an intellectual thing. It's more impulsive for me. Ideas come to me when I'm not looking for them. I end up with all these little lines that I write down—scraps and bits and pieces and given time and if I'm patient . . .

Hudson: Do you keep all the pieces?

Rhodes: I got mizillions. I don't always keep all the little scraps of paper once I've got 'em kind of wrestled down to something. Sooner or later they all kind of fall together. In fact, there was one little bit that found its way into that song that I wrote with Waylon. When my little girl was two or three years old, she was lying on the couch and she said, "Momma," and I said, "What?" She said, "You know, in my mind I'm having a beautiful life." I just thought that was the most wonderful thing, and I just kept that in my heart. I knew someday that would find its way into a song. It happened to find its way into this song that I wrote with Waylon that day. You just sort of keep all these little bits and scraps and thoughts and stuff in your mind and in your heart and then sooner or later, right when you need it, it's there.

Hudson: Why do you suppose some people notice those things and other people go through life with similar experiences happening to them, but they don't notice?

Rhodes: That's the gift. To some people that wouldn't be a gift, and so it's not their gift. They're good at fixing your car and so different people have different gifts. I think some people are meant to be recorders. Like the little person in mythology who sat there. I'm not the gods, I just write it down, just follow them around and write it down.

Hudson: Now even more so that's the way I perceived myself. I mean you're up onstage singing your songs—I'm really walking around recording this stuff.

Rhodes: That's your gift. You can't see yourself like other people do. One of the biggest jokes in life is that everyone in the world gets to see your face, but you never see your face. You only see the reflection of it. I figure that's one of the things we'll get when we get to heaven; we'll actually get to see our face. Sometimes it takes an outsider—someone outside of yourself, that can actually see you differently because it's so noisy on the inside. Outside it's a little quieter and you can just get a look. It's like the horses in the merry-go-round. You can see the merry-go-round a lot better if you get off it. But if you're on it, you just see this bit or that bit. It's your gift to see. It's my gift as well.

Hudson: Is there one thread which ties together your entire life, one theme, perhaps?

Rhodes: Singing is that thread for me because there's this part of you that's the same age. It's always been, and that age is weird because it's a timeless age. It can be either really young or really old based on the little moment that was frozen in time when you felt that you knew. For me, I started singing when I was about five years old. I had a gospel trio with my brother and my dad. I think I was meant to be a singer the same way I was meant to be a person who writes it down. The first song I learned was "The Old Rugged Cross." I have this realization when I sing that song. It dawned on me that this was occurring in me when I was at Electric Graceland in '79. I was recording that song, and I realized that when I sing that song, I'm the same age I was that first time. There's this part of me that hadn't changed since then. It hadn't gotten any older. It's as wise as it's ever gonna be. It's just this frozen moment of being that I still had. I think there are a lot of those with a song. You associate it through a singer, and especially if you're a writer. But those become little souvenirs of your life where you can go back and feel like that again.

Hudson: For me it was "How Great Thou Art." It's so interesting how many musicians and songwriters in Texas do have that gospel experience. I mean Billy Joe, Willie, Bobbie Nelson.

Rhodes: It really colors our music. I was playing a gospel record for my friend in France, and he said, "This is country music." I was playing Willie and Bobbie—the gospel record that they made.

Hudson: I interviewed Bobbie one time. I asked her to describe her favorite musical experience. She replied, "Singing gospel music with my brother."

Rhodes: It's unbelievable. I don't know if it's out or anything, but it's great music. There're times when it's especially good to have it around. For this friend of mine it was country music, and I realize how much it really has colored our music. To someone with an ear, that's just listening to the music fresh, you can't tell the difference from Willie singing "How Great Thou Art" to Willie singing "Night Life." You know, it's there musically. And you know that was their background.

Hudson: I was raised in a Southern Baptist church [**Rhodes:** Me too.] with the most brilliant music department led by Paul Paschal in Richland Hills. I had a hard time not worshipping our song director. It was the most amazing experience and then going to a church camp in the summer with neon lights over the choir stand that said How Great Thou Art. So every night over a Texas plain I worshipped with that tune blowing in the breeze. What comes to your mind when I say "exciting moments" in your life?

Rhodes: There have been millions of them, but I think a real turning point for me was the day I met Joe Gracey. I was living in the country and I'd been writing. I was living in Sunset, up in North Texas on a family farm. I'd been pretty much alone artistically and I was about twenty-five. I was still trying to figure out what it was that was making me different from all of the people around me in this little town. I was pretty lonely artistically and I didn't even realize it. I can see now that I was doing things that were lonely. I would sit on the porch, I had these birds that would come listen to me sing, and I would sing to these birds, and they would listen to me. They were like my audience. Then I came to town, and Joe Gracey had his studio in the basement of KOKE FM. It was after he had lost his voice, and he moved from radio and singing into recording and producing records. He had been working with Stevie Ray Vaughan on his first album, which was never released. He had a studio called Electric Graceyland. That day was a huge turning point in my life because suddenly I met all these people who saw me and knew me. It really changed my life because that was the day I started making records. That was the day I actually found my real niche in life, the place where I belong.

Hudson: How did you meet him?

Rhodes: Through Randy and Kim Banks, who were married at the time. I knew them from Lubbock. I was at a party and I was singing. They introduced me to T. J. McFarland, and then T. J. said we should go and record some demos. They introduced me to Joe Gracey. From that day on we started working together. We started playing music together. I think that was the biggest turning point for me artistically because it was the point at which I found my place in life. You can just drift around in life forever and not know where you belong. It was like an answered prayer to me.

Hudson: I know Willie Nelson really supports you. How did that happen?

Rhodes: A few years went by doing demos, recording, kicking around town and writing songs. I formed a band with Bobbie Earl Smith and Joe

Gracey called Kimmie Rhodes and the Jackalope Brothers. We played the Alamo Hotel, Emma Joe's, and some of the acoustic places around town. We started doing this album. We had this dream that we wanted to make an album, and we went out to Willie's to look at his studio one day. It was still privately owned by him at the time, and Bobbie Earl and Gracey introduced me to his daughter Lana. She's been a dear friend ever since that day, and I met Willie that day. The first thing he said to me was, "Do you write?" and I said, "Yes." He asked me how long had I been singing, and I said since I was six years old. He said, "Why don't you come out here and make a record?" Within two weeks we were back out there recording the album. He just opened the door and let me on in. It kind of pulled the plug that was keeping me from getting that first album done. After that it got a lot easier to make albums. I didn't really know Willie then, but since then we've become really good friends and work together a lot. We put out the album ourselves. Wes McGee took it back to England and distributed it on his small label, Terrapin. From there it ended up in Japan and all kinds of places. It's weird how that record made it around. Later I signed with a label called Heartland Records in London. I did two albums for them—one called *The Man in the Moon*, which I also recorded at Willie's studio. Then the next one, *Angels Get the Blues*, I went to Memphis and recorded that at Sun studios when they reopened. They had just done that movie with U2. We were visiting our friend Jack Clement up in Nashville, and he'd just been working on it as a sort of creative director. He'd been an engineer there in the old days, and we just thought we'd just stop in at Sun studio. This tour was beginning, so we wandered along with the tour. We already knew everything they were telling us in the tour, so we were going around the room clapping our hands and checking acoustics. At the time I was really feeling like music was getting so technical. I was starting to feel like it was really closing in on me with head phones and isolation booths and now plug this in and now turn that on and now we got this effect and that effect. I was feeling claustrophobic in the whole thing, so I got this idea at the end of the tour when they said, "Does anybody have any questions?" I said, "Yeah, what are your rates?" Within a month I was back there recording with a Texas band that I put together. We recorded the album for Heartland there.

Hudson: Did you meet Sam Phillips while you were there? He really has some stories to tell.

Rhodes: No, I didn't meet Sam Phillips. Gracey got to hang out with him one day. Joe Ely came and joined us for that session, and we did one of my favorite records I've ever done—my version of "Just One Love" that I recorded with him there. That was a day I'll always remember. Not just because I think I'm supposed to always remember it, but because it really was neat. Through those three albums that were released in Europe, we toured a lot over there, and I've made a lot of really great friends. If I had it to do over again, I'd just do it the same way. Although, at the time, I was probably whining and thinking why can't I get a record out in America, and why are things so screwed up here? Why won't radio play our music, and why can't things be more organic? But really sometimes God just has a better plan for you than you have for yourself. In the end my life turned out to be a lot more successful than what I would have done on my own. I have redefined my thinking about what success is. When I was sitting by a swimming pool in France, I was watching all these people I'd met walking around, and I had my British band that I'd had there for a long time. I was just thinking, "My life is so successful because I know these people."

Hudson: Yeah, I've had those moments too.

Rhodes: It's then you realize it's not what you thought it was gonna be, it's what it is that matters. That's what's rich about the whole thing. It's what you get. And I'll take it.

Hudson: It's really about the relationships.

Rhodes: Yeah, and I just have all these incredible friendships. I've gotten to play with gypsies in Switzerland. I know the guy who is in the *Guinness Book of World Records* for peeling asparagus faster than anyone in the world. He owns a hotel in Switzerland where we can go hang out anytime. I have friends there, and we play music in the cafe at night. I know people who will close their restaurants in Paris and have dinner for just us, people who own vineyards and people who write songs, and I mean just incredible people.

Hudson: Have you always operated out of a pretty strong sense of trust and faith with that kind of openness?

Rhodes: Yeah, it was amazing for me because it isn't something I had to learn. Maybe when I was a teenager, I kind of turned my back on it and sort of decided I'd taste the fruit of different things. Some guy once asked me if I was born again, and I told him, "No, I just got born." I was just born. I didn't forget anything so I didn't have to remember anything. I feel lucky that whatever that illusion may be, it works for me in my life. It's as real as a lot of the things you can't see. It's as real as love, it's as real as electricity. It's amazing because the things that you can't hold in your hand are the sneaky things that are the strongest, be they positive or negative, they're strongest. One thing I have found is that you can either keep running into the doors that are closed, or you can go and take the doors that open. There's an element of faith in that. How much faith does it take to keep running into a closed door? None. But if you take the door that's open, then it kind of comes—it's what you get with experience. I thinks that's why the older people get the smarter they get. You learn to trust. I'm not saying just take any opportunity that comes along, but I'm saying don't turn your nose up at something really sweet because you thought something different was supposed to happen. Because sometimes those little bitty roads lead to some great big highways. I try everyday to start the day with a little reality check. I don't mean a success check. Every morning you can wake up and find you've got a lot to be thankful for. If you start like that, then it puts you at the center of yourself. If you get in touch with what it is you want, what it is that really matters, what it is you're really thankful for, then it's a lot easier to go through the day at the center of yourself instead of running around and grabbing at things.

Hudson: What do you do in the face of disappointment?

Rhodes: I can't remember just being crushed. There have been times when it looked like things weren't going to work out, but they always ended up working out, so I really can't look at them like disappointments. It's more like I was saved from my own devices. I'm trying to remember being disappointed. Life hasn't handed me many disappointments.

Hudson: How do you handle the integration of a personal life and a career?

Rhodes: Willie's really good at that. You sort of look around you and see what's there and use it. It's sort of like life is your sculpture. You look at what you have to work with and work with it. It's like junk art. I was married real young. We both got older and became more who we were. We became two people who didn't belong together any more. The friendship was still there, but the thing that made it make sense wasn't still there, so I had to get out of that relationship. It's better to have a calling and a place where you belong in life than it is to stay someplace where you don't belong just out of fear. So it's all in how you look at it really, but basically, like

I said, the heavens just looked out for me. The thing that's been in my life has usually been the thing that I needed. When I met Joe Gracey we weren't lovers or anything for years after that. I mean, I was married and had two kids. But as time went by our friendship grew really strong and our love for each other grew really strong. It just became obvious to both of us that we belonged together.

Hudson: It's not a struggle to maintain it?

Rhodes: Almost everything you need is just right there, somewhere, no matter what you're doing. Whether you're building a house, building a career, building a life, or building anything. It's either right there or it's right around the bend if you just keep your eyes open. Maybe it isn't exactly what you had in mind, but it will get you to where you're going. You might have wanted a Mercedes, and you might get a Volkswagen, but it will still get you to where you're going.

Hudson: Do you have a favorite song?

Rhodes: That's always a real dangerous question to ask me because I know so many different songs. I love the song "Row, Row, Row Your Boat." I think it's all in there somewhere. It's short, it's easy to remember—people can sing along. It's a round so it's not boring even if you know it's short. It's like the script to *The Wizard of Oz;* it's all in there somewhere.

Hudson: Do you have a distinct reaction to some of the other songwriters in the business? What about Townes Van Zandt?

Rhodes: I love Townes.

Hudson: Give me an image that comes to mind.

Rhodes: What I see is a personal experience of when we recorded "I'm Gonna Fly." I have that song as my image because Townes is a very fragile and special person. There are people in this world, sort of birds of a feather. Blaze Foley was one of those people in this world that was so fragile and special that life was hard. Townes is fragile and strong at the same time. There's a lot of strength in that vulnerability.

Hudson: He's got that line, "She's as soft as glass."

Rhodes: I guess sensitivity's the first thing that comes to mind when I think of Townes. There's a thing that I love in Townes's writing. He tends to trust you as a listener just to get it. He doesn't go in to this whole big long complicated whatever to make sure you get it. He just says it. I like that. It's beautiful when someone sings that vulnerable to the world.

Hudson: What about Guy Clark?

Rhodes: I love his stories and the imagery that he chooses to make his point. I love the song about the pocket knife. A little boy looking at that knife. I love anybody who writes like that.

Hudson: What about Billy Joe?

Rhodes: Billy Joe just kills me. There's nothing I love more than a Texas man with a real voice with a sweet heart. I love a tender-hearted man. I really do. I love all those guys the same for the same reasons. There have always been a lot of great Texas writers. A lot of the best country music has come from Texas.

Hudson: What about this new label, Justice, based in Houston?

Rhodes: One thing I've learned from my career and from my climb is that the people who I think are making the best music right now are the people who have set themselves free from any concept of what you should do commercially. I don't mean that in a trite sense; I mean that in the biggest way you can imagine. I think that you know the stretch I'm trying to make artistically right now is one where I'm free creatively to do whatever, in the way I sing and the way I write. I don't want to do anything based on what I've done before, and nothing based on anything anybody else has been doing, just freedom. I'm starting to see that a little bit in the commercial world as well, because there seems to be a trend toward a commercial appreciation of those who are free. Justice Records gives me that freedom. I think there are some really good alternative acts right now that are doing really great because they are real free in their writing and thinking and singing. Music seems less categorized than I've ever seen it be. I think there's a trend toward that change. Americana Radio is affording a nice opportunity for people who haven't had the opportunity to prove themselves commercially. The ones who've proven themselves artistically beyond any reasonable doubt. Like Townes Van Zandt. What Top Forty country radio is going to play Townes Van Zandt? Americana Radio will. You have to cultivate the public's taste in music. I think that's why music was so much better in the '60s and the early '70s. I think that's why there was this nice growth period in music when the Beatles came along. Music was in a really creative period because the public taste was open to new things. They were ready to be cultivated—they were ready to expand their pallet. In the last fifteen years it's just gotten smaller and smaller and smaller until finally it's like cooking for a three year old. You can't get 'em to eat anything because radio hasn't cultivated their taste. The creative music world needs to breathe, and I think I feel a little bit of air coming in. I don't feel as claustrophobic.

Hudson: I know KFAN Radio in the Hill Country is the number one Americana station. They play the widest range of music I've ever heard on radio. "Texas Rebel Radio." Let's talk a little bit about Texas music as a distinction even though it's not a clear distinction. I, personally, think one of the characteristics is the sense of freedom, of getting in touch with who you are and what you have to say and being willing to say it the way you need to say it.

Rhodes: Texas music is distinct. Many of our influences are from Mexico and Louisiana. It's definitely an art form based on the people in the region.

Hudson: And for you personally the creative process is what?

Rhodes: It's a way to understand. It's an answer to a question. It's how I answer myself.

Hudson: Kris Kristofferson said, "Life is the question. Life is the answer. God is the reason and love is the way."

Rhodes: It's true.

Hudson: Let's end up with one last story about my newest favorite song of yours, "Hard Promises To Keep."

Rhodes: It came from a pretty personal experience. Basically the thought behind that song is that you know your walk in this world is alone with God. We love each other, and we make promises to each other, and we want to keep them, but sometimes life has something else in mind for you. You can't feel something that you don't. Things change. Sometimes you've kept promises for someone that you feel it's time to give those back. I think people blame themselves too much for relationships that don't work out. Take one day at a time, and if it stays good forever then it stays good forever.

Hudson: And forever really happens one day at a time.

Rhodes: Yeah, it does, so you just "try to believe in forever." That's what I'm saying. "I'm trying to believe in forever, and I'm trying to believe in this little jewel-box life." I was married to my first husband for thirteen years. That's a lot of laundry, a lot of dishes, a lot of babies, and that's a lot of love. If you give that long to someone, and you don't feel that way anymore, then why should you kick yourself in the ass because you can't keep doing that? That's all I'm trying to say except I'm saying it from the point of view of the person giving the promises back in an understanding way.

Hudson: That's the truth. My favorite Greek philosopher is Heraclitus. He says you can't step in the same stream twice, or there's nothing permanent except change. Something has opened to me as I've gotten older. I have really become aware of the way things open and close, the rhythm of the process. It's all process.

Rhodes: A lot of times change can be like a torture rack in that it hurts while it's happening, but have you ever had bad change?

A Texas Heart

Carolyn Hester

I developed great admiration for anybody who would take the time to sit down and tell what they thought and believed and wanted to share with people. I felt I could do it.

I met Carolyn Hester at the Kerrville Folk Festival in the early 1980s. She radiated joy when she was both on- and offstage. We immediately shared stories about powerful women, about love and understanding, about sharing and giving. When the folk music "movement" moved on, she also continued to evolve and grow. And she still represents all that is real in folk music, the music of the people. Texas music has these elements of folk. Robert Earl Keen has been living with the label "folk" musician. Anyone who doesn't get airplay on country or rock music often falls into a "folk" mixed bag.

Carolyn has been onstage with all the major American folk artists; she continues to write and create her own music. Based in California now, her roots still run deep in Texas. Just ask her.

Hudson: Since you're in Kerrville for the Kerrville Folk Festival, let's talk about your association with that organization.

Hester: I've known Rod Kennedy since I was on Columbia Records in about 1962. He often acts as if we've known each other even longer. He had a radio station in Austin, and my mother called him to say, "I have a daughter who is a folksinger. I know you play primarily jazz, but could I get you her record?" Rod received the record, played it, and got interested in folk music. She called him back in six months, saying, "My daughter is coming to town. Would you be interested in putting on a folk concert?" I don't know where she got this idea. It was sent from heaven because this is what Rod says did it. He produced a concert for me in Austin, and in the front row was Allen Damron. Right there he got some of his first ringleaders of this Kerrville Festival. Now there are fifteen of us who are his board of directors. We don't do anything much. All I did this year was give him John Stewart's phone number.

Hudson: How are you still dealing with the label "folksinger" here in the '80s?

Hester: I do a few of the traditional folk songs, but my true label might be singer-songwriter today. That would be accurate. As Rod's festival turned into a songwriter's festival, I changed along with it. Several years I judged the songwriters' contest, and I developed a great admiration for anybody who would take the time to sit down and tell what they thought and believed and wanted to share with people. I felt I could do it. I had written some songs on some of my folk albums in the past. In 1982 I brought out a tape called *Music Medicine*, which was all written by me. My next tape was *Warriors of the Rainbow*, and that's all by me except for maybe one song about Martin Luther King. My husband, David Blume, wrote that one.

Hudson: Those are wonderful titles. You obviously have an interest in the Native American. When did that begin and how has that evolved throughout your career?

Hester: It began with my having a series of dreams, and one was to do with an Indian woman who I saw in my dream. I dreamed the song, and it took me about a year to finish it. When I sang it for the very first time in 1980 here at the Kerrville Folk Festival, there was a storm with heavy winds and the lightning was going in swirls and streaks around the sky. I'd never seen this before or since. People don't believe me when I tell them. Gail Ross was doing the sign language version of the song. It was a sign of some kind; it was really thrilling for me. Bobby Bridger, my first guru into that world, told me to read *Black Elk Speaks*. Page four of that book talks about an Indian woman in a dream, on a horse, and that was like my dream. I asked others about this, and I was told that, in actual fact, many tribes have an Ascending Woman, so that's what I named the song. All I knew was that this Indian woman had come; she'd gotten off the horse, she walked off and started going up a staircase, and I felt the need to follow her. So I did in my own mind. I had a dream about Geronimo that's in the *Warriors* album.

Hudson: How else do you interpret the dream?

Hester: What I know is that male and female powers are going to come into balance, and this is probably why Ascending Woman is being sent. I loved all the women onstage with me last night. Merri Lu Parks always joins me, and she's a real healer as well as a great photographer. I get healed in Kerrville.

Hudson: What about your education?

Hester: I didn't go to college. I was offered a music scholarship at the University of Colorado in Boulder, but I wanted to hit the road. Some were family reasons. A lot of time people want to do music, and their family doesn't like the idea of the gypsy life for their youngster. But my mother felt that I needed to sing very badly, so she backed me up on that, and I went to New York. She asked me to enroll in a school so she'd know where I was part of the time. I was eighteen and looking for Pete Seeger. I found a folk movement, and all my dreams came true. It took awhile. I had to find out where Washington Square was, who the folks were who wanted to be friends, but in a couple of years Tom Paxton showed up.

Hudson: Were you billed as a Texas girl?

Hester: I was. That caused me some problems. When Lyndon Johnson was president, it caused him some trouble that he was this big old Texan. I'd grown up a little girl knowing LBJ all my life, and he was quite a character, a great fellow, someone I really got a kick out of, and then on TV, they were trying to package him. I, too, was really noticed as different in New York. Dave Van Ronk was in the scene. Eventually Eric Anderson came, Joni Mitchell, Buffy St. Marie, and more. We all got contracts with big-time agents like William Morris. I was mostly with APA, Agency for Performing Arts. There were a group of people who broke off from one of the other big agencies. Their big act was Harry Belafonte. It was a very good time, and we were building our own audiences, so the big record companies wanted to get in on that. Some of us really did break into the pop field, but I wasn't that commercially oriented. I was very interested in social-conscience type songs. I knew Peter Yarrow then. We did some shows in England and a couple of political fund-raiser type shows. I knew Al Grossman, and of course, Bob Dylan was discovered on my album for Columbia, and that's how he got signed by Grossman. Then he wrote "Blowin' in the Wind," and Peter, Paul, and Mary made it a smash hit. I'm from that era. Dylan taught me one of the songs, "Come Back Baby," on my first Columbia album. That album sells for fifty dollars today. Isn't that horrendous?

Hudson: And you really seem to enjoy performing?

Hester: I love it. John Hammond had signed Pete Seeger, thinking he would attract other folks. So he signed me. I was his first lady folksinger, and through me, he got Bob Dylan. I've done all this kind of stuff, and I'm still feeling great and still coming to Kerrville.

Hudson: How does it feel to be talked about as a major influence? You were in the tradition, and now you're introduced as the reigning queen of folk?

Hester: That's very nice, and it does help people want to hear you because they may remember one of the old songs you did.

Hudson: But you've also evolved.

Hester: That's really thanks to Texas. My original musical influences were like the English ballads. A lot of American folksingers were influenced by the English. I was friends with Buddy Holly, and he helped me get my first recording contract with Coral Records. Buddy and his manager, Norman Petty, got me my first contract.

Hudson: Let's talk about the Buddy influence. I've been writing for *Buddy Magazine* in Dallas.

Hester: The odd thing is that because of my being friends with Buddy, Dylan wanted to pal around with me. Isn't that interesting? He plays harp on my album with "I'll Fly Away" on it. I'd never sung the blues, and Dylan taught me "Come Back Baby." I don't think I was that good at it, but with Dylan playing harp, you couldn't resist. Knowing Buddy influenced my friendship with Dylan.

Hudson: I talked to Sonny Curtis two hours yesterday. Do you know him?

Hester: I sure do. In 1986 when Rod took us on the road, we made a stop in Nashville. We did a concert there, and ASCAP was at the concert giving Rod a plaque for all he'd done for songwriters. BMI gave a party too, and I heard Red Sovine saying, "Where is Carolyn Hester?" He said Sonny Curtis was at the gathering and wanted to say hello. When I found him, he thanked me for recording one of his songs, "You Made My Life a Song." At that time Sonny was making a stack of money from that Mary Tyler Moore show song. I re-met him then, having first met him at Clovis in the Buddy Holly days.

Hudson: What experience has been a thrill for you?

Hester: You know, all of them! I did get to know Buddy pretty well, and I was backstage at the Brooklyn Paramount with Chuck Berry, the Everly Brothers, and Fats Domino. What a thrill.

Hudson: Did Buddy have a lot of charisma?

Hester: Both on- and offstage. He was a magnet. He still is. His records sell in the tons every year. I met Maria Elena, his wife, and I'll say that Norman didn't want Buddy to marry anybody, which was probably the basis of the dispute that broke them up. But Buddy didn't have much longer. He was going to be on that fatal airplane that crashed. I was real sad about it because Buddy himself was so delighted with Maria Elena, and they were going to have a good marriage, while it lasted.

Hudson: I look forward to seeing you every year. You always perform with such heart.

Hester: You know I love what I'm doing. That's the secret, isn't it? We both love what we're doing. That's obvious.

Back to Texas

Gary P. Nunn

Texans never have conformed to the norms, so to speak, and they never have toed the line. They always have been a little rebellious and a little rambunctious, and it's hard to get them all dressed up and make them sit in any one place for any length of time.

The name Gary P. Nunn is synonymous with Texas music. He's been an ambassador for the state with songs like "That's What I Like about Texas." "London Homesick Blues," his signature song, is heard on the widely syndicated TV show, *Austin City Limits*. And at one time he was designated by the governor as the Lone Star State's "official" spokesman. In spite of all the apparent success, Gary still has stories of struggle, growth, goals, and regrets. He has a spirit as wide and expansive as Texas, and he conveys this spirit on CD, from a concert stage, or from a corner spot in a Texas honky-tonk while crowds scoot their boots across wooden floors.

Gary P. Nunn began his musical career as a seventh grader in a garage band in Brownfield, where he was an honor student and all-around athlete. After a couple of stints in college, he ended up in Austin and was part of the progressive country music scene, the "Texas Outlaw" scene, or, as Steve Fromholz often says, the "Progressive Country Music Scare." He led the Lost Gonzo Band, first appeared on *Viva Terlingua*, the million-selling LP by Jerry Jeff Walker, and served as some of the glue holding the entire scene together. Often an unsung hero, Nunn has been recorded by Willie Nelson, Jerry Jeff Walker, Michael Martin Murphy, to name a few.

He has earned several gold and platinum records for writing, publishing, and performing.

Since then Gary has assumed responsibility for his own career and, without the aid of an agent and a manager, has built a substantial music business organization that handles his bookings, houses his music publishing companies, and publishes a newsletter that is distributed to over ten thousand fans. He has entered an agreement with an independent Texas label, Campfire Records, which has produced *Totally Guacamole* in 1993, *Roadtrip* in 1994, and *Under My Hat* in 1996, as well as licensing four previously released CD's.

I attended Midem, a worldwide music conference in Cannes, France, with Gary one year. Watching this humble, honest, talented, and self-effacing man move among the European fans, I became even more aware of how well he represents this state. My favorite Gary P. Nunn experience occurs when he's sitting alone at the piano, singing "The last thing I needed the first thing this morning was to have you walk out on me." The following conversation took place over a ten-year period. The first, in 1988, was on his front porch, in Austin, with his son Julian nearby.

Hudson: Gary P. Nunn is the author of "London Homesick Blues." Let's talk about the story of that song?

Nunn: It was in March of 1973, and I was in London traveling with Michael Murphy, whom I had been working with a couple of years at that time. He had the trip lined up. He was going over to England. His wife is English, and he was going to visit the in-laws, plus he had some business. He asked me to go along with him. During the course of the trip, I was more or less stranded for days at a time. For lack of anything better to do, I had this guitar in my hands, wandering around the room . . . just looking out the window, making up a song.

Hudson: As a songwriter, is there any theme that runs through all of the songs you write?

Nunn: I try to be there in the song myself as far as where I am, who's with me, and what's going on. Generally, I'm either headed to Texas or out of Texas, so Texas comes in there from time to time.

Hudson: You traveled quite a bit. What are some comments you get about Texas from outsiders?

Nunn: There's a fascination about Texas. It's a love-hate situation. They have a sense of the freedoms and the frontier. The cowboy is a classic example of the independent frontiersman. People admire that. The wide open spaces we enjoy, they're envious of that because most people don't have so much space to operate in as we do. But also because Texans are so proud and walk around justifiably braggadocios.

Hudson: Do you have any specific ways you approach writing?

Nunn: When it comes to writing, the critical factor is having the time and the quiet space. When you get an idea, have the pen and the paper in your hands and have the time to follow that train of thought to its conclusion. It's very hard to say, "I'm going to write a song," unless you've got something in mind already beyond that stream of consciousness. You can write a song in one sitting without blinking an eye if you're not distracted from the moment you have the thought until the time you complete the thought.

Hudson: What is the easiest song you have ever written?

Nunn: The easiest one was probably the one called "Loose and on My Way." I did it back with the Gonzo band. It's a piano piece that said, "I never thought I could get over not having you looking over my shoulder." I sat down at the piano, and it just came. All the good lines came when I needed them. I just pulled them out of the air.

Hudson: Must have been ready.

Nunn: I was ready, coming down, and had the record button on.

Hudson: Do you ever have that feeling that you are an antenna, receiver, or transmitter?

Nunn: Definitely. Every day. I was having a lot of good thoughts and good lines today just out raking up the leaves in my yard. Usually that's it. You have some time and you're doing some kind of busywork with your hands. It's mindless work where you sit there doing something, but your mind is free to wander.

Hudson: Is there a particular high point in your career that stands out in your mind? Some point where everything fell together to make a real magical moment for you in Texas music?

Nunn: There was a real high point for me when I finished doing "London Homesick Blues" down there in Luckenbach. It was the first time we had ever done the song. It was the first time the audience had ever heard the song, and they went nuts. That roar, that overwhelming approval, was definitely the high point. That was down in the dance hall. We were doing a live show and had been there a week recording an album that became *Viva Terlingua* for Jerry Jeff Walker. We did a Saturday night show and charged a dollar at the door. The place was packed.

Hudson: Do you have any favorite dance halls in Texas?

Nunn: Gruene Hall is definitely one and also Broken Spoke, here in Austin. They are the ones who keep the traditions of Texas alive. They don't try to modernize themselves to a point to where they are competing with the latest modern thing. They're just staying the way they were. That's what I like.

Hudson: What are some of those Texas traditions in music?

Nunn: You have your western music. I call it western music because country and western music started with the singing cowboy movies out on the range with the bunkhouse boys. That's why I named my band the Sons of the Bunkhouse because it's kind of a continuation of that spirit of the Sons of the Pioneers. Then your dances come, your waltzes, your polkas, and your cotton-eyed joe. To me that's all part of the culture. We have our folk dances and we have our folk songs. Here in America, with such a young country, we don't have many real traditions that are truly American. That's why I like Texas music; it's truly American folk music.

Hudson: We're still pretty close to our roots, aren't we?

Nunn: We created our own tradition. We didn't bring over the traditions from the Old World. We're not preserving a German or Irish or English tradition. That's unique in the United States—this part of the country has developed a culture and a tradition over a relatively short period of time. I identify with it, and it makes me feel good that there is a culture, my culture, out there I feel I'm a part of. That's why I go with the western music and country dances.

Hudson: How would you summarize what makes Texas music unique?

Nunn: Texans never have conformed to the norms, so to speak, they never have toed the line. They have always been a little rebellious and a little rambunctious, and it's hard to get them all dressed up and make them sit in any one place for any length of time. It sorta breaks the ice a little bit. It can be a little rowdy and tempestuous. It's a little yahoo, letting it out a little bit, which makes it unique. I was talking to a friend of mine today about what makes a real good country Nashville type band. They need to be straight and clear and not jump around because their audiences are orderly and basically Christian oriented.

Hudson: Texas audiences aren't quite so orderly?

Nunn: They're Christian, but they aren't afraid to hoop and holler, too. After they hoop and holler, they do a good ol' gospel tune, and everybody goes home singing "Will the Circle Be Unbroken."

Gary and I talked many times over the years. He performed at the first two Willie Nelson Picnics at Luckenbach. He performs over forty weekends each year. The man is on the road. The following conversation took place October 2, 1996. I had a chance to call him, catch him at home at the AO Ranch in Oklahoma, and I did.

Hudson: First, let's talk about the stories you have about times in your songwriting career when things were really fun for you or when they seemed to be mostly struggle.

Nunn: It would be easier to talk about the difficult times [laughter].

Hudson: But you always have fun, right?

Nunn: Yeah, I always seem to have fun myself. I'm always kind of disappointed in the way the music ends up sounding. I always seem to be upset with the way the band's performing. I don't know if that's me or what. I've had a lot of problems getting the guys in the band to pay attention to what I'm doing.

Hudson: Maybe it's just a matter of getting the right group around you.

Nunn: Yeah, well, it's been twenty years or so.

Hudson: You've had awards, recognition, fame, and success.

Nunn: It may look like that from the outside, but they've had very little impact. The only thing that really has impact is promotion and the trappings of success. Like you roll in to the gig on a bus, or you've got a big sound system, or you've got a record company behind you. Those things seem to make a difference. It doesn't matter what you do as an individual if you don't display those trappings of success. On the other hand, I feel like I've been pretty successful as far as my business, the money I can generate, the lifestyle I'm living. It's a pretty comfortable life.

Hudson: It does look pretty good for you. You get to play, have fun, have your family, produce music, enjoy life.

Nunn: I've put together over eight hundred acres of ranch land. My wife has built a pretty nice house, we drive two vehicles, we go skiing twice a year.

Hudson: What's missing? What's not happening that you want to happen?

Nunn: I feel if I could really get a crackerjack band backing me up enthusiastically, singing harmony, not making mistakes, taking pride in a group type of thing, then things would jump up rather quickly. Everything else is in place. I have a tremendous following of loyal people. I've got a full calendar of bookings for decent money. You just can't step up to that next level if you don't have a real tight band with you. If I were in my own audience, I would say, "You know, Gary P. has been around a long time, and he still doesn't have his band bullshit together." But, I work so much it makes it difficult to just take off and switch bands. I do have some time blocked out at the end of the year to work on things.

Hudson: Let's talk about your writing. What shift has occurred in that area?

Nunn: I'm so busy with the work. Like Roger Miller said one time, "I tried too hard to get my shit together, then I realized when I got it together, I couldn't carry it." It's pretty much all business. Your brain can only concentrate on one thing at a time. To be creative you need some real quiet space and uninterrupted time so what's inside of you can come out. About the only time I have is when I'm driving up and down the road by myself. I rarely sit down and finish a song nowadays. Frankly, I'm more impassioned now by the publishing aspect of it. I'm really focused on finding a tune that works. I like the idea of getting another person involved in helping me promote this thing. He goes out and promotes it as well; then there are two guys working on it. That way, I don't go around saying, "Me, me, me."

Hudson: I know you have quite a group of songwriters who supply you—Larry Joe Taylor for one.

Nunn: Yes, it feels good to help others get started.

Hudson: What do you see ahead in the next ten years?

Nunn: I want to slow down, really. At least the road stuff. I want a music business, a company where I get into the management, the production, the promotion of young talent. That's really what I'm hanging around for. I'm hoping I can somehow get a "hit" (for lack of a better word) to generate some mailbox money so I don't have to work by the hour. Or get some financial backing to start a company. I really believe I could start a record and publishing company to promote three or four artists. I have several in mind right now. That's what I look for. I'm fifty now, and hopefully, by the time I'm sixty, I can get off this road deal. I enjoy the travel, but it's not always that much fun.

Hudson: I'd love to see you do a solo concert—you and the piano. Do you ever do that?

Nunn: I wouldn't mind at all, but the calendar is booked with band dates. The band thing is a blessing and a curse. They're sensitive artists as well, and they have their own needs.

Hudson: Give me a story about a time when it was all raucous and glorious.

Nunn: That was back during the Jerry Jeff days. I was happy and creative. I wanted to write songs. I enjoyed playing. The relationship with the Gonzo band was exciting. We were unselfish players, and we would always surrender to the song instead of saying, "Watch me, watch me." Ever since that's been over, I've been looking to recapture that magical feeling, and it just hasn't been there. Guys now don't do this naturally, and they don't understand what it is when you tell them about it. They wouldn't recognize it if it did happen. It seems, since then, I've been kind of walking around alone.

Hudson: What's a song you really like doing?

Nunn: I still get a kick out of "What I Like About Texas." I always kind of get a little tingle—patriotic.

Hudson: You really are central to the Texas music scene. You represent some major stories for some people, and you have always been there. What's another way you'd like the world to see you?

Nunn: I would like for people to know I've had a silent hand in the careers of a lot of people. I feel I've been a bridge between being "out" and being "in." The business, that is. I've been disappointed a lot by what appears to be an "obvious omission." I was the one who got Joe Ely his record deal with MCA. As soon as he got the deal, they cut me out, pretended I wasn't involved. Same thing happened with Shake Russell and MCA. They didn't want me anywhere around. I feel like I could have helped both of those guys from the beginning. Joey's demos were better than the record he made. I wanted to be on the team, but they went to the big producers and that was it. It's obvious the contributions I've made. I told Michael Murphy to move to Austin, move into my house, and I found him a band. That was the beginning of the country music progressive scare. We built a stage for Willie Nelson to walk out on, and he generated all the glory. And that's fine. I just wish more people knew about it. You can't go around bragging about yourself. My whole career has been a series of insignificant events that add up to something a lot bigger.

A Walking Conversation

Freddy Powers

It's like telling the world your story. It's talking to a lot of people at one time and telling them your story.

I met Freddy at Top of the Marc, a nightclub above Katz's Deli on Sixth Street in Austin. Randy Willis, a music promoter who had worked with Johnny Rodriguez, thought we should meet. Our next visit was at Bill McDavid's house, located on the Pedernales Golf Course, home of Willie Nelson. Catherine, Freddy's wife and most serious fan, helped orchestrate the meeting. It was September 6, 1996, two days before Jimmie Rodgers's birthday, and two days before Merle Haggard was playing in Kerrville. I knew Freddy had written a lot of songs and toured with Merle a long time.

Later I learned Freddy's major influences included Willie Nelson, Paul Buskirk, Merle Haggard, and Django Reinhardt. Listen to his guitar licks and you hear Django. I also found out that he had five BMI awards for number one songs, including "I Always Get Lucky with You," "Let's Chase Each Other Around the Room Tonight," "Looking for a Place To Fall Apart," "Natural High," and "Friend in California." When I heard Freddy and Sonny Throckmorton play at the Saxon Pub in Austin, I watched Darrell Royal listening intently. "Silver Eagle," another Powers tune, says it all. Life on the road. Life playing gigs. He captures something with that song. Freddy became known for his "country jazz" sound. No three-chord unit for him. He caught the attention of Willie Nelson, and they collaborated on "Somewhere Over the Rainbow," Freddy playing guitar and co-producing. He's working on a new album, *It's the Hottest Thing in Town*, featuring a gypsy jazz style—another example of the broad way Texas music gets interpreted. Talking to Freddy is like talking to the guy next door; he's willing to just pull up a chair and talk and listen. He really enters a conversation.

Hudson: Let's talk about writing songs. You've had so many hits.

Powers: I never thought about writing songs as a way to make a living or to make money. I started writing songs because I had something to say. I was a performer long before I was a writer. The first big excitement came when someone told me I had a number one song. I couldn't believe it. I had been writing for years. George Jones cut "I Always Get Lucky with You." That was my first number one song. Merle also had it on a number one album. That was exciting. I remember when we would get a number one when I was writing with Merle Haggard. They didn't even celebrate; they'd just say congratulations and go on. I was champing at the bit to throw a big party. A number one song has always been exciting to me.

Hudson: How do you feel about someone else taking your song to the top?

Powers: It's an honor to have someone else go out and make my song sound good. I would have always rather had the number one myself, of course, but when somebody else does it, it's damn sure the next best thing. I had a song I wasn't crazy about until I heard it on a record. My sister and I wrote a Christmas song, "Silent Night, Lonely Night," and I wasn't real fond of it. Merle recorded it with the London Orchestra, and I was flabbergasted when I heard it.

Hudson: What do you feel about the writing?

Powers: It's a habit, I'm addicted. I didn't realize it until I got started. Once you write a song and you're singing it, then you have a letdown. You need another one. You need another one right then. After every song, I always feel like I'm never going to be capable of writing another one. It seems like an ending. That's what keeps songwriters going. They get addicted to the tension of a new song. It takes up all your mind. You're singing it all the time and you're showing it to people. Once the song is in the market, it's like a child. It's there when you need it. You want to pull up your guitar and enjoy yourself, sit around and sing some of your songs, reminisce about whatever the song is about.

Hudson: Does it sound different to you in ten years?

Powers: Nope. Once it has sunk in, the idea that you wrote it for, that's what it is. Singing the song brings that moment back.

Hudson: What do you share with other songwriters?

Powers: Ideas. I've been with one of my heroes, Sonny Throckmorton, all day. He's a true country hit songwriter. He has written fifteen to twenty number one songs and is very prolific. His songs are stories. We also share feelings. For me the time for writing is early in the morning. That's when you're awake. You wake up in the morning and fire up a cup of coffee. That's when your mind is fresh, while everybody is sleeping. When the world is moving real slow—that's the time when I get my ideas.

Hudson: What's the creative process like for you?

Powers: It's like telling the world your story. It's talking to a lot of people at one time and telling them your story.

Hudson: Are you aware of that when you write?

Powers: Yes, it is part of the process for me. I write songs for myself. For years, when I was writing with Merle Haggard, writing for his company, most of my stuff leaned toward him. I wasn't as pleased with the writing or thinking as I am when I'm writing about something that I personally can sing and perform. You know, Bill McDavid and I are partners now in Rogers and Hammerhead Publishing. I'll tell you what you'll hear tonight at the Saxon Pub. I'll probably throw in a few new ones with the classic tunes I have. Then I love those old 1920s and '30s kind of pop-top songs. I'll do a bunch of those. And I'll pay a little tribute to some other great guys, like Cole Porter. My primary influence on songwriting would have to be Floyd Tillman. Floyd dated my sister and used to come through my hometown every now and then. My sister, Mary Lou, wrote a couple of songs for Hank Thompson, and she wrote a song for Eddie Arnold, so it started kind of blooming in my family early on. I always wrote songs as a kid. I didn't have the nerve to go out and show people my songs until the '70s. I'd run across Merle, and we were running around together playing guitars. He was a real guitar enthusiast like myself. Deanybird, my bass player, and I used to get together and play for hours. Bill and I do that now. Deenie kept hearing, "I always get lucky with you" and saying, "Man, this is a hit." After Merle recorded it, I got a royalty check in the mail. It was three thousand dollars. Then I had three or four songs going, and I was getting thirty-thousand-dollar checks. I'd almost faint each time I got one. And I started getting really serious.

Hudson: Did you ever think you needed to stop and start a business?

Powers: No, I never thought of that. I gave a lot of my songs away to some loyal employees in my band. Merle and I used to swap songs around a lot. If he thought it was going to go, we'd get an idea and brush it around a little bit. A lot of the songs with Merle and my name on them were really mostly written by only one of us. We never sat down and said, "We're going to write a song." We would have an idea, and he'd jump in the car and say, "Let's go." We'd drive around; usually I had the guitar. No one could interfere with us that way. There's very few people I can really write with. Merle was easy for me to write a song with; he's a masterful songwriter to start with. Bill McDavid is another. He's a great lyricist. He's only written a few songs so far, but he's got some real good potential. He wanted to start a publishing company so we started Rogers and Hammerhead—a country version. That will take care of my songs from now on. There's a lot more money in the business when you publish yourself. You got more control of what you want to do.

Hudson: Where do your songs come from?

Powers: The life I've lived and the places I've been. That's all it is. Some aren't about anyone in particular; some are about feelings in general. At my age you don't look too far ahead. I've got to where I buy bread a half a loaf at a time. There's a bunch of us who have had three or more number one songs in a year, about fifty of us. I would love to have another big hit song, songs I'm proud of and a lot of people hear. I've found out one thing. I can't write on demand. I have to just get up in the morning and get my guitar and start humming. Then I get in a melancholy type mood and maybe come up with an idea, then write it out. I don't mind telling anybody that I get up in the mornings, drink a cup of coffee, and smoke a joint. I'm sorry to have to say that, but it puts you in a dreamy state. People who don't smoke probably don't understand. It opens up my mind a little bit. I don't say I use it as a crutch. I'm just saying that is usually when I can really get to burning in here.

Hudson: Any disappointments?

Powers: All my life I've been playing the circuit out in Nevada and Texas. I've been opening the show for Merle all these years. I was always known as a singer and performer. The very minute I got a number one song I was considered a songwriter. In almost every article on me they don't emphasize the fact that I've been a performer all my life. All the emphasis seems to shift to the writing. Performing has been the largest part of my income. Willie Nelson got his career going real good. Guys like Willie and Merle are also considered singers. For some reason, I became a songwriter.

Hudson: What advice would you give?

Powers: I used to write a song and then ask everybody what they thought about it. Sometimes you ask the wrong person. They'd say no good, and I'd dump the song. Now I've learned to decide for myself. You have to learn to critique your own material. If you absolutely think it's good, buster, it's good. Know what I mean? That's the way you have to look at it. Trust yourself.

Family and Friends

Tanya Tucker

My friends keep me sound. I have lots of really good, close friends. That's hard to find in the business that I'm in. You're here today and gone tomorrow.

At Aqua Fest in Austin on August 10, 1988, I stood in line for the interview. Everyone wanted to talk to Tanya Tucker. My turn finally came. I entered the backstage trailer and there she sat, in a white short outfit, calm and ready to talk. I was amazed after the display of energy and fire onstage that evening. Our conversation showed me a woman with something to say. Until that time I only had a stage image of a rowdy female performer. This conversation reminded me to be careful of quick assessments or hasty judgments.

Tanya Tucker at age thirteen debuted in 1972 with "Delta Dawn," a song written by Alex Harvey. Now she's the youngest woman in pop or country in history to have a boxed set of her music available to the public. Liberty Records, *Tanya Tucker Collection* contains fifty-eight recordings, including eight that were previously unreleased. Her career of over twenty-five years has been full of peaks and valleys. She has weathered many storms, and now she says, "I want to be better at what I do, who I am, and what I am. I think it's time to do that now, because we are representing the best music in the world: country music."

Hudson: Let's talk briefly about the beginning.
Tucker: I was born in Seminole, Texas, in 1958. In fact, Larry Gatlin and I

and my sister were all born in the same hospital. I lived in Texas for about nine months, then my family moved to Arizona. I stayed there through the sixth grade. In the seventh grade I went to St. George, Utah. By the time we had moved, my dad discovered I could sing. By about eleven, we had moved again and never stopped moving until we finally got that big break. That was in Las Vegas. It's such an incredible story, and it's kind of time-consuming how I got started, but I'm hitting the main parts of it. We met a guy named Billy Sherrill in Las Vegas. He'd come to town on a vacation, and he'd heard some of my demo tapes. He said he wanted to see me, so we met. Of course, Billy is one of the greatest producers in country music. He produced George and Tammy and all sorts of great country artists. I didn't know what was going on because I didn't really know who he was. I just wanted to get started any way I could. We signed a record contract with Columbia Records in 1971. I flew to Nashville in March of '72 and recorded "Delta Dawn." That hits the high points, but it was quite incredible how we got started because my dad never gave up. He kept trying and trying. He was real persistent, and he believed in my talent so much. It was really difficult for a man to say his daughter could sing. It was tough, but I finally got that one magical record, and it was the first one. That's absolutely incredible. "Delta Dawn" came at the right time in my life. I'd like to have about ten more just like her. We've had some good songs on Capitol Records, and it's really great to be back on the radio with new material. For a while there (three years) I didn't have a record label. I think I got kind of frustrated with it all.

Hudson: You put on a tough show out there in the Texas heat. You talked onstage about your Texas roots and how you felt. You ran around like Mick Jagger or Rod Stewart. Now you're sitting here with all this energy getting ready to go to Oregon tomorrow. Many would expect you to be burned out after having a first hit as a major hit. What accounts for the energy?

Tucker: I get to those points where I get real frustrated, and I think things are absolutely going nowhere. I'm in the back of the bus going, "where is the bus going?" I do have those bad times. But I have a lot of support. What keeps me really stable is a lot of good friends and a great family. I have a great foundation and a lot of wonderful roots. I had a great childhood. A lot of people think I missed my childhood. I don't think I missed anything. I've gotten to do so many more things than I normally would have because of my career. I got to travel, go to different countries and perform. That was quite exciting, going over to Europe. The people over there just love our music. It's absolutely incredible the way they love country music over there. Mainly my friends keep me sound. I have lots of really good close friends. That's hard to find in the business that I'm in. You're here today and gone tomorrow. It's hard to make good friends quickly, and I think that's what really keeps me going. Friends and the fans, of course. The fans are the bottom line. It's the most incredible feeling to walk onstage like tonight and have them just roar. They were singing so loud at one point I had to shut my ears so I could hear myself. I think that is probably the biggest rush that anyone could ever have. I feel very, very lucky and fortunate to be able to go out there over and over and get that kind of response from people.

Hudson: Yeah, that's love.

Tucker: It's really love, and that's what keeps me going. I mean, how can you burn out on that? I burn out on a lot of other things in the business as far as some of the sound and lights and things like that—band members changing. We're going through a lot of changes with my band right now. It's really difficult, but when you can go out there and overcome all that, and they're still roaring, it's quite an incredible feeling.

Hudson: Let me ask one more question before your fans break down the door. They didn't like my walking up with a tape recorder, bypassing the line.

Tucker: The press can be good or bad, but it's important because people out there don't know you. There's only one way they can really get a feel for you and that's through the press. What they read about and what they hear about you. So, that's real important in this business to have good press. Even bad press is good.

Hudson: I've been doing this series for a couple of years. My whole focus is to feature artists and give readers the chance to know how they feel and what they think.

Tucker: Exactly. It's important to get their feeling for things, too—what they feel about different entertainers. I know you've spoken with a lot of them, and speaking with you I get a feeling of where they're coming from and what they want to hear from me. I can't talk to every one of them on a one-to-one basis. You're the only way I can connect with them.

Hudson: I just looked at a video and album which seem to emphasize family quite a bit. Let's talk about that.

Tucker: I'm really excited about the new album. We recorded it down in the Bahamas because I thought it would be neat. First of all, I thought it was a great studio. But we wanted to get out of town so we could really concentrate on our music. It turned out really well. I enjoyed recording down there, and the songs were good. I feel like we're getting back to the basic roots, the acoustic sound. You know, sitting around a tree, a family reunion, acoustic guitars and mandolins. Everybody's coming out and having a family reunion. I used the same guy I used in "Love Me Like You Used To" video, and we were fighting in that video. So I wanted to use him. His name is Billy Long. He's a very dear friend of mine. I wanted to follow through and say look what happens; we stick together, we stuck together, and we're strong enough to bend, and we're going to stay together through it all. That's why I wanted to continue that same look of me and him. We created this scene at my ranch around this wonderful tree that I've just adored for years. I hope someday to build a cabin by that tree because it's a big strong tree, and it has a lot of big strong roots. I feel that way about my music and my family. It represents that to me. That's sort of what we built the whole video around—that tree with all my friends and loved ones around it and underneath it, sharing in the love underneath its limbs. It was a wonderful feeling.

Hudson: Let's talk about writing.

Tucker: Gary Stewart and I are real good buddies, and we were writing a little bit together down in Florida. I'd been writing this song about this guy I've been seeing that went to L.A. from Oklahoma to become an actor, and Gary helped me finish it. The guy's an Okie. He was driving out there, and I wrote this song about him driving out there. It's called "A Song for Ben." I think it will be on my next album. I'm excited about writing because it's a creative force inside. When it happens, it's the most incredible feeling. Absolutely fulfilling. When you finish that last line in a song, you sing it and record it and then it's a hit. That's just the icing on the cake. I mean when it's approved of by all your fans, and they love it too, that's great. I call it guts on vinyl, you know, my guts on vinyl.

Hudson: That's beautiful.

Heritage Matters

Jimmie Dale Court

I'm trying to go as deep as I can with my music. It's basically blues and country with a little flavor of rock. . . . I'm trying to get my own style because I think people with their own style are going to make it in the world.

After we put together the Fourteenth Annual Tribute to Jimmie Rodgers in Kerrville, after we celebrated Rodgers's birthday on September 8 with an intimate gathering to hear Merle Haggard and his band, the Strangers, playing in Kerrville, home of Blue Yodeler's Paradise, Jimmie Dale Court unexpectedly died on October 9, 1996. We had been talking about music and about songwriting for years. He had plans. He wanted to put out a tape of himself interpreting his grandfather's music, and a tape that included his own original songs. At our September tribute, he always sang an original, "I'm the son of the daughter of the father of country music."

He took me to San Antonio one Sunday afternoon to visit his mother, Anita. What a rare and special day that was, hearing Anita reminisce about her own life, her mother, Carrie, and her father, "America's Singing Brakeman," Jimmie Rodgers. Jimmie Dale (also named after Ernest Tubb, a true Rodgers fan) just wanted to play music. His best gig was perhaps the 1996 tribute to Rodgers held at the Broken Spoke. His band agrees with his Aunt Mildred Pollard, Carrie's sister, "This was the best night ever." Perhaps Jimmie knew it was time to do his best. We turned on the recorder one night in 1987 and captured the following conversation:

Hudson: You're playing with the Original Rolling Stones tonight. How did that happen?

Court: I've known Leon Carter for several years, and he needed a drummer. When he said the original Texas Playboys were going to be here, I just had to make it there. I think the Original Stones started in the early '50s. Leon said, "If you're going to dig a well, you might as well dig a little deeper to get to the sweeter water." He does that with his music.

Hudson: What are you doing with your music?

Court: I'm trying to go as deep as I can. It's basically blues and country with a little flavor of rock. I grew up with the music of the Beatles and Jimmie Rodgers. I try to mix what I've gotten accustomed to doing myself. I'm generating my own style because I think people with their own style are going to make it in the world.

Hudson: But you know where your roots are?

Court: My roots are in Jimmie Rodgers. Some people say he started it all as far as popularizing this kind of music. He was a great guitar player, and I don't think the world knows that. Dicky Betz, guitar player with the Allman Brothers, once told me that Jimmie really started a lot of different riffs on the guitar that people follow today. He was the Bing Crosby of country, back when they called it hillbilly. His voice was unique.

Hudson: Are there any problems living with the Jimmie Rodgers connection? Do people expect you to sound like him?

Court: Some do, but I've got to go my own way. There's lots I don't know about Jimmie. He died before I was born. But I lived with my mother and grandmother until I was about nineteen. They embedded me with a certain soulful feeling.

Hudson: Let's talk about the blues.

Court: Jimmie just got put into the Memphis Blues Hall of Fame last year. I think he really started the white blues along with the white country back in the '20s. To me, he was more blues than country in a lot of ways. Louis Armstrong recorded with him a couple of times. Listen to "Blue Yodel Number 9," and you'll understand where the blues in Jimmie Rodgers came from. He combined blues and pop music to actually create country music.

Hudson: He's the only artist in the blues, country, and rock and roll halls of fame. All three!

Court: Except maybe Elvis. I went to the ceremony in New York. It was a magical moment for me. He was also the first to be inducted into the Country Music Hall of Fame.

Hudson: That speaks for the diversity you find in Texas music.

Court: Yes, Texas music is where it's at. Jimmie loved Texas, and I'm a Texan. Went to high school in San Antonio. Jimmie had a duplex there after he left Kerrville. Come visit with my mother someday. She'll really tell you some stories.

Hudson: Texas music crosses a lot of boundaries.

Court: There's two kinds of music, really: good and bad.

Hudson: Any favorite Rodgers tunes?

Court: Ernest Tubb and I were talking about that. We agreed it was a hard question. I love them all. I always include a tribute to Jimmie Rodgers in whatever performance I'm doing. I'm a writer, and I've got a lot of material I'd like to get out there. I've been working with the same band for a long time, a very loyal bunch of guys. Sometimes it's hard for me to be a bandleader and play drums at the same time. It's best when I'm not playing drums. John Van Vleck has been with me a long time; he plays guitar. Appa plays bass. I'm really into rhythm. I've been a percussionist since I was ten years old.

Hudson: What comes to mind when I say "Texas music"?

Court: Bob Wills and the Texas Playboys, Willie Nelson, Waylon Jennings. There are so many great Austin musicians. I hate to even start that list. Texas music goes to the soul, it goes to the heart. You can get up, you can move whatever way you want to. There's that feeling you get when you're dancing and you're feeling good.

Jimmie's Texas Blues, the final band for Court, consisted of John Van Vleck, Steve Edwards, Rick Hassen, and Jay Hitt, with others sitting in from time to time. There were plans to tour Europe, plans for a movie on Rodgers, plans for a CD of Court's original music. All plans were cut short by Jimmie's early demise at age forty-five in 1996. He was buried in San Antonio, close to the home of his two sons, Austin and Cody.

Generous with Life

Stevie Ray Vaughan

The song was called "Life Without You." It was written when a friend of ours died. What I was trying to talk about was what drugs do to people. It kills people in their heart, and sometimes it's bad enough to kill them physically. You know when I say heart, I mean soul.

The first time I talked to Stevie Ray he had just come out of a rehabilitation program. Our phone interview focused on his new attitude rather than his music. When I got off the phone, I said, "Well, I missed that opportunity." Then I suddenly realized that allowing him to talk about whatever was on his mind was the opportunity. We met several more times, backstage and briefly, once at the Majestic Theatre in San Antonio where he followed Chris Holzhaus. Chris was thrilled to be playing on the same stage with Stevie Ray. Stevie Ray was thrilled to be giving Chris the chance at a larger audience.

The last time we talked was November 26, 1989, before his Austin show with Jeff Beck. I was always impressed at the sincerity and generosity of Stevie Ray Vaughan. He was a superstar in his career and in his talent; he was a humble man interested in his family, his friends, and the world.

First our talk at the Majestic:

Hudson: I'm overwhelmed by your performance, and the stories you told about each song. I'm not sure we can add much by talking about the music, since the performance speaks for itself.

Vaughan: That's the best I could do today. That's how I do it everyday now.

Hudson: I heard you first at Aqua Fest several years ago. You blazed under a full moon that night. Something real special was happening.

Vaughan: We were having fun.

Hudson: Let's talk about that song you played toward the end of the set tonight. You talked a little about your own feelings as an introduction.

Vaughan: The song was called "Life Without You." It was written when a friend of ours died. I was trying to talk about what drugs do to people. It kills people in their heart, and sometimes it's bad enough to kill them physically. You know when I say heart, I mean soul.

Hudson: The song portrayed pain in some places and then suddenly I felt this burst of celebration that came into it. There was so much intensity; it's hard to differentiate between the intense pain and the intense happiness that sometimes overlap or go hand in hand.

Vaughan: Sometimes no pain, no gain.

Hudson: Are there any special circumstances that drive you to put pen to paper?

Vaughan: Sometimes it's easy to write about something, sometimes it's not. I just hope it continues. It's all a gift. I'm trying to do the best that I can with the gifts I've got. And not try to stand there and say it's all me, 'cause it's not.

Hudson: Is there one performer that has influenced your style?

Vaughan: I can't nail down one. If I hadn't heard Hendrix and Clapton or others, I wouldn't be able to do what I'm doing now. What we all do is try to pay attention to what we've heard and give it back our own way.

Hudson: Is there any particular song you like to play more than another?

Vaughan: Which night are you talking about?

Hudson: I like that.

Vaughan: I like "the next one." What is it going to be? I keep doing the best I can to keep going with it.

Hudson: You're well respected and loved by many other performers.

Vaughan: I'm just glad to be alive and be playing and know about these people as well. I played a set with Otis Rush the other night. Just being there playing along with him and being able to stand right next to him, feel what he was doing; it was like coming home. He invited me to come home and hold on to a note and see where it goes. Thank God for people like Otis Rush.

Hudson: Chris Holzhaus said a turning point in his career was "tonight, playing on the same stage with Stevie Ray Vaughan."

Vaughan: Well, I thank him. We've got to hold hands and keep walking.

Hudson: I loved the ending of your show where the band lined up, throwing arms around each other, saying, "Hey, we're a family."

Vaughan: We are.

Our last conversation took place in Austin during the Jeff Beck–Stevie Ray Vaughan show on November 26, 1989.

Hudson: You're in the middle of a tour with Jeff Beck that's gaining a lot of national attention. I'd like to give you a chance to describe briefly where you see your career right now. Of course we're sitting right here in Austin, Texas, and that's bound to create some feelings, too.

Vaughan: The way I see it, it's like a new beginning. A lot of things are really working real well. We were able to do an album that represents the band a lot more so than some of the previous ones. A lot of it has to do with being sober, being more aware of what's going on, and, to some degree, being less intimidated by the whole thing. The tour's going real well. It's something that we like doing with Jeff. There's all kinds of good things going on, career-wise. I'm not on my way to death and destruction anymore. That's where I was headed and that's not the case now. Although life can be a little bit difficult without crutches, it's still a lot better than it ever was before.

Hudson: Could you describe how, on a grueling tour, you continually allow the art to take over?

Vaughan: I have to work at it. We're real fortunate. The band is like a family. Our crew is like a family. There is business involved—there has to be, but it's still more like a family on the road doing what we really enjoy doing. The music is the most important thing—what we're saying with the music and how we're presenting ourselves. Most bands don't have that opportunity. It's more business than anything. You go out and do exactly the same notes every night. I wouldn't be able to do it that way. It's got to be something that's alive and growing and that's what we keep trying to do. That's what keeps it going: caring about each other and trying to continue letting the music grow.

Hudson: What's been a real magical moment for you when things just crystallized and came together?

Vaughan: There've been several of them. God, it's hard for me, because there's so many shows closely following each other. I'm not sure how long a year is anymore. My favorite night was last night. Sitting around with Jeff and just jamming has been a lot of fun. We listened to tapes that somebody gave him of steel guitar players, so we're trading ideas. We have a blast when we play together. It's always fun because you never can tell what the guy's gonna do. I watch his band every night, their whole show, and I look up when we're playing and there they are standing, watching, enjoying us. There's a lot of respect going on here, and we're just trying to have fun every night. There are some nights that seem stronger than others or seem more to click, but that's just the way life is, too. If this sounds awful bland, it's not the case.

Hudson: It doesn't sound bland at all. It sounds like you're in the middle of something that's positive and growing and changing. It's going to have all the ups and downs and you're riding it out. At the same time you're in control and I think that's really exciting.

Vaughan: I don't know about "in control." I used to think I was in control of a lot of things that I never was in the first place.

Hudson: You're doing everything right now that every young guitar player would look and say, "Man, he has it made." Are you looking ahead to other things that you still want to do?

Vaughan: There's records with various people. The first one is to be with my brother, Jimmie. We're starting work on pre-production the first of January. I've always wanted to do a project with him. There's also the finishing of the worldwide tour of this album and then the next album with this band. There's talk of all kinds of different things—some of 'em are nearer than others, so we'll see. The main thing is this tour going through the end of December and then getting a little time off.

Hudson: Roy Buchanan told me that a steel guitar player, a little old lady who lived on his block, was his hero. There seems to be something with guitar players and steel players.

Vaughan: Steel guitar players have the best tone. Somehow that instrument's just got it all covered. I've always been a fan of them. I have no clue how to play 'em.

Hudson: But Jimmie's doing some of that. Is he still playing with that?

Vaughan: Yeah, and that's part of this deal we're doing. Anything Jimmie picks up, as far as I'm concerned, he plays it right. It's always been that way and I'm jealous.

Hudson: What about Dallas, your roots? Is there a place there you can come back and play?

Vaughan: I've been finding lots of places to play lately. Hanging out when B. B. was in town, and I got to sit in with him. Omar and the Howlers—I got to sit in with them at Poor David's Pub in Dallas.

Hudson: I'll bet that thrilled them.

Vaughan: Yes, the fast and cool.

We had another conversation planned, one in which we could talk even more about the writing. That day never came, but his music lives on. Monte Montgomery, a guitar wizard based in the Hill Country, played his version of Stevie Ray Vaughan at Schreiner College in Kerrville in November 1996. An original interpretation of a Stevie Ray classic is, indeed, a tribute to the life and career of this man who gave so much to the body of Texas music. He died in a helicopter accident in Alpine Valley, Wisconsin, August 27, 1990, and the world mourned. Claude Nobs still plays Stevie Ray in his chateaux in Montreux. Jimmie wrote, "Another blues player called home." Eric Clapton came to Austin to pay tribute along with Robert Cray and Bonnie Raitt. The world does not forget.

Blues on the Edge

Johnny Winter

You're not going to make it if you play other people's stuff. Then as soon as you do make it, they want to plane off the rough edges and turn you into the same thing they didn't want you to be before. I can't do that. It just makes me ill, and it really isn't the direction I want to go. Music makes me feel so good and it's such an important part of my life that it doesn't work for me to try to do something that I don't really love to do.

It was a winter weekend in July 1987 when I went to the Arkansas Blues Festival for the sole purpose of hearing Texan Johnny Winter. I have been listening to his records ever since. I was a bit late on the scene; Johnny burst into national attention with a much-publicized, lucrative record deal with Columbia Records in 1968. But 1988 was the first time for me to be in his presence. All the stories about Johnny didn't quite prepare me for the onslaught of guitar and passion I experienced that evening. There have been guitar slingers before Johnny, and guitar slingers to come, but he stands alone in his ongoing commitment to burning shuffles, scream-ing-on slow blues, rocking with raw abandon and singing with emotion-ally charged passion.

He's so original in his interpretation that classic tunes take on a new life, like when Johnny plays "Highway 61." One of his own songs, "Johnny Guitar," co-written with Johnny Watson, is autobiographical, a characteristic inherent in all genres of music. "When I was young I wanted to play the guitar, Now I'm a playin' son of a gun," is one line in "Johnny Guitar." Johnny says, "I'll have a ball as long as it lasts." Twenty-six albums later, four as producer of Muddy Waters' last albums, Winter is still having a ball. Johnny represents the roots of a tree with many branches.

Johnny was born in Beaumont in 1944. He was playing clarinet at age five and formed his first band at age fourteen with his brother Edgar on piano. In 1968, playing with bassist Tommy Shannon (now Double Trouble) and drummer Uncle John Turner, he attracted the attention of *Rolling Stone*. He returned from England and signed a lucrative contract with Columbia Records. For many young listeners back then, Winter became a bridge to the wilder, crazier side of the blues. The music of guys like Howlin' Wolf and Muddy Waters was a combination of acoustic country and electric urban, previously unheard in white, mainstream America. A highlight in Johnny's career was the opportunity to produce Muddy Waters for Blue Sky Music.

But Johnny's sound has always been his own. Bruce Iglauer, owner of Alligator Records, gave him the freedom he wanted in his music. The three Alligator albums are high points in his career. After an album on MCA, which disappointed his fans, *Let Me In*, his debut album on Point Blank, returned him to the rootsy form this Texas guitar slinger doses up in such good form.

Johnny makes no apologies for the sheer speed of his single-note lines or the cutting intensity of his slide work, he just rears back and wails. I saw him perform in Austin at Aqua Fest following our conversation at his hotel. And I listened to the music with a new ear, one that had heard many of his stories. Knowing the stories adds another level of appreciation. As I listened I remembered the tray of vegetables in his room as we talked about his health and the trip to see Rollo at China Sea to get tattoos. He got the bird of paradise on his thigh; I got my first tattoo—Pegasus on my left shoulder. As I listened to "Illustrated Man," I recalled all those tattoos, all those stories. I followed him to Houston the next night. I've been at Sneaker's when he played to a packed house in San Antonio. And I've always remembered the stories I heard.

Hudson: I bet you get asked all the time about roots music.

Winter: People want to know how the music relates from, say, Blind Willie Johnson to now—and whoa, I don't know.

Hudson: They are asking you to be a historian, right?

Winter: I guess from listening to all the records over the years I know a little bit about it, but there's still a whole lot I don't know. Some of those European guys just seem to be able to tell you everything that happened and when all the sessions were done and who was drinking what. It's amazing to me. I'm just real interested in the whole thing. I usually don't think of myself as someone who analyzes it. But over the years I think some things have just seeped in.

Hudson: Texas-style blues strikes me as something unique and different from anything that's out there. It's not Delta and it's not Chicago. Who would you interview on the subject?

Winter: I know you've already spoken with Johnny Copeland and, of course, Albert Collins. Curtie Ferguson is a good person to talk to, and it's too bad T-Bone Walker isn't still alive. He had been around for so long and done so much, he would have been a great guy to get on tape. I wonder if Blind Willie Johnson still has any relatives left. He died in Beaumont around the late '40s. I don't know if anybody's still left that knew him, but they could tell you stories about the lives of the musicians. They're also important.

Hudson: Who was the first musician you heard who made you want to play?

Winter: I don't know how much he knows about the technical parts of the music, but the first guy, the first white blues guy that I ever saw, was Joey Long. He's still playing around in Houston. When I was thirteen or fourteen, he was playing straight blues, opening for people like B. B. King and Fats Domino. Playing all the little clubs around the city. I think he influenced just about all the younger guitar players in Houston. Joe still hasn't really made the kind of record he ought to make. I was talking to the people at Alligator Records, trying to get somebody to become interested in Joey.

Hudson: Johnny Copeland mentioned a fellow, Joe Hughes. He said that Joe had sort of taught him to play the guitar.

Winter: Joe Hughes. I had forgotten about him. He's real good people.

Hudson: There's a fellow in Austin that Tary Owens has worked with, someone called the "Gray Ghost," who's eighty-three years old.

Winter: I've heard that name.

Hudson: Do you know Robert Ealey?

Winter: I'm familiar with him.

Hudson: I spent Saturday night at the Bluebird in Fort Worth, and Robert was a wonderful club host, working behind the bar, talking to everyone at the tables. Then he took the stage about eleven o'clock. The crowd loved him and I really enjoyed being there. That old, falling down, one-room building contains a lot of music. I think some legendary places like that still exist around the state, but they seem to be dying out. Let's talk about where you grew up. I've never been impressed with Beaumont—in fact, it's always depressed me.

Winter: It always did me, too. I was just talking to all the guys in the band about that last night. When I was growing up, I always knew that I had to get out of Texas. But it seems like all the things that made me want to leave it back then are the same things that I love it for now. That's crazy but it's true. What I mean is that it was a great place to grow up musically. I guess because there wasn't a hell of a lot else to do. It really did get boring. A lot of time, playing music was the only thing going on and there were so many great people. I didn't realize that at the time, either. I just figured those kind of great musicians were everywhere and that things would probably be a hell of a lot better in Chicago or New York or California. After I got to all those places I realized I was all wrong. The music was really better where I came from.

Hudson: When did you first discover this?

Winter: When I was in Chicago. That was always where I wanted to go—all the records that I was buying and learning to play had Chicago, Illinois, on the label. So as soon as I got out of high school, Chicago was where I went. None of the white musicians knew where to find Jimmy Reed or Muddy Waters or Bo Diddley. People would look at me like, "What? No, not here." It took me so long to even find out where anybody was playing. Nobody even knew what was going on there, and finally I met Mike Bloomfield. He had a little coffeehouse called Fickle Tickle, and he knew everybody. He was saying, "Why did you want to come to Chicago when there are all these great people in Texas, T-Bone Walker and Lightnin' Hopkins and Albert Collins?" I started thinking there *are* a lot of people down there. I was making more money in Chicago than I'd ever made in my whole life, but I was playing music that was so much worse with people who were so much worse. After about eight months I was real ready to go back home and take less money for doing what I really liked to do.

Hudson: What kind of music were you playing there?

Winter: There was this one club where we had to play all twist music for six hours, nothing but twist. The deal was that the waitresses had to dance with the customers, but they weren't allowed to touch them, so you couldn't dance slow. Because of that we had to play fast songs for six or seven hours a night. Even if you were making good money, that still got to be a drag. The more music I was seeing in other places made me realize how good things were at home. I figured, since I was hearing Chicago music, they were hearing our stuff too, but in a lot of cases that wasn't true. A lot of the local artists just remained local. I didn't have any idea of the difference between the local scene and the national scene—it was all just music to me, and I figured everybody heard everybody.

Hudson: You think there's wisdom in that old phrase from the Bible "A prophet is not without honor except in his own country."

Winter: So true. It's nuts. I feel like Texas musicians have never been appreciated down here. It's the whole business thing. I think it used to be a kind of set rule that musicians didn't get paid. Maybe they figured, "There are too many musicians around and why would we have to pay these guys? If one gets tired of us we can always find another." There were so many managers that I made records for ten years and never made a dime off of any of them. That was what was so bad; there just weren't any real good music lawyers or managers or people who could help you out. The few that there were made sure that if there was any money to be made, they were going to take it. It made it impossible to stay down here. At least a few people have done it now—ZZ Top, Stevie Ray and Jimmy Vaughan still manage to live down here—but it used to be really impossible. There was an article in the *Village Voice* maybe ten years ago about how many Texas people had made it in New York. They spoke with me and a lot of other Texas people. One of the guys said something that's really true; that some of us played a lot better in New York than we ever did in Texas.

Hudson: Kinky Friedman talks about that. He enjoyed his days at the

Lone Star Cafe and he's back, too, living at his family ranch outside of Kerrville.

Winter: That's great. Seems like I saw him on some kind of talk show where he was talking about his book.

Hudson: He ran for Justice of the Peace in Kerrville, and national television came down to film him walking the streets shaking hands.

Winter: He didn't make it, huh?

Hudson: Kerrville was too conservative. But to get back to that article in the *Voice*—you talked about guitar players and their influence, and I would like to ask you how you feel about your own music reflecting Texas.

Winter: I've wondered about that a whole lot. I used to think that it really didn't matter very much because the people that I was really interested in were either from Chicago or from Mississippi or both, people like Howlin' Wolf and Muddy. People who had harp players making a sound that was a little bit dirtier than the Texas thing was, always a little bit cleaner and more musical than Mississippi or Chicago. I guess T-Bone Walker was my biggest influence out of the Texas people. T-Bone and Bobby Blue Bland had a group of guitar players that were really excellent. Most of them were from around Texas. I really didn't feel my music was strictly Texas, but when you go from Blind Lemon Jefferson to Albert Collins or T-Bone Walker, none of those guys have a whole lot in common. And that *is* Texas music. It has so much variety: country and western, jazz and western swing, and all that stuff that you hear even if you don't like it. I didn't grow up liking country music at all, but there's so much that got in there anyway, that just seeped in. The variety of music that you have to play if you're going to play bars in Texas, you have to be able to play everything or you are going to get killed and not have a job. That was a big influence on me, listening to so many different people. There isn't one kind of music that you can point to and say "This is what Texas music is." Blues was something that was, but now people think of Texas and they think of black blues players. That just wasn't the case when I was growing up.

Hudson: Rather a new phenomenon here. Of course, you've been a part of making that happen.

Winter: Yeah, I'll have to take credit for that.

Hudson: I'm sure it's hard to be aware of that while you're doing it. Maybe it's even hard to look back and realize it as people write about Texas blues. They can't do that without talking about Johnny Winter.

Winter: I'm really proud of that.

Hudson: And your commitment to it. The fact that there were points when you said it doesn't matter about playing Top Forty, I don't care if I starve, this is what I love.

Winter: It is strange though, because you're not going to make it if you play other people's work. Then as soon as you do make it, they want to plane off the rough edges and turn you into the same thing they didn't want you to be before. I can't do that. It just makes me ill, and it really isn't the direction I want to go. Music makes me feel so good and it's such an important part of my life that it doesn't work for me to try to do something that I don't really love to do. It leaves a big void in my life if I'm not playing music that personally makes me feel good. Something I still don't understand is why I can put on a Muddy or Howlin' Wolf record and love it and other people can put on the same record and it drives them up the wall. They don't like it at all. I don't understand how something that makes me feel so good can do exactly the opposite to other people. I guess it's just emotional music and real overpowering.

Hudson: I happen to have eclectic tastes. Blues is my favorite. But I have sat and watched old fellows play the fiddle, old guys playing dobros, watched some of the country music that springs up in all of these small towns. You can go find some old guy sitting on the front porch somewhere and be equally as moved because of its sincerity.

Winter: That's what I think of the whole thing. It's a lot more real, you just see more of that in Texas. Most of the people that I knew who grew up to play did it because they liked to play. I didn't know anybody who just decided "I'm going to be a star" and then learned how to play a guitar as an afterthought. But I see those people all the time now. They grow up and think "I want to be Ozzie Osborne or whoever—Johnny Winter, even." They first get the idea of being a star and then decide to learn how to play music because that's something they have to do to be a star. That's going at it completely wrong. Most of those people wouldn't be too good even if they do learn how to play. Music has got to be the main thing.

Hudson: How do you explain your own longevity? I think you may have just answered it.

Winter: It just won't stop. I have to do it. As long as there's someone out there who wants to listen—whether it's three or four hundred people or three or four thousand people—as long as there's somebody that wants to hear me, I'm going to keep trying to get to them and play.

Hudson: That's my attitude about the Jimmie Rodgers Festival we do every year, to show as much of the public who cares the connection between blues and country music and the important role that Jimmie Rodgers had in integrating those two sounds.

Winter: Before I'd heard Jimmie Rodgers, I didn't realize what a huge connection there is. Bluegrass really is the same notes as blues, and it gives me the same feeling to hear a good bluegrass record as it does to hear good blues.

Hudson: When Jimmie Rodgers yodels on "Waitin' for a Train" . . .

Winter: It's just blues.

Hudson: When I was at the Blues Awards in Memphis, more Texas artists won national blues awards than anyone else—Johnny Copeland, Albert Collins, Stevie Ray, Clarence "Gatemouth" Brown, Sippy Wallace—and they were all talking about that connection.

Winter: Something that has bothered me a lot is this idea that you've got to be a certain color to do a certain kind of music. It never did make any sense.

Hudson: There's a black club in Kerrville and the folks there have really taken to this band of four white guys I manage. No one else in town seems to want to hear the blues, but this older crowd really enjoys them, and believe it or not, sings along with them.

Winter: That's exactly what I did when there wasn't anybody white that wanted to hear blues. We just played whatever kind of music white people wanted to hear and got paid for that. Then we would sit in and play for nothing, play blues at the black clubs.

Hudson: So how did you end up working for Muddy Waters?

Winter: Just loving him over the years. I didn't meet Muddy until we opened for him here in Austin at that old hippie place called the Vulcan Gas Company. We opened two different nights, four sets. I talked to him there and did a TV show out of Chicago called *Sound Stage* with him. I think it was his sixtieth birthday, and everybody—all of the people he influenced—sat in on the show: Dr. John, Buddy Miles and Junior Wells, Koko Taylor, Mike Bloomfield, Nick Gravenites, just like a father and his sons and daughters. Everybody came to do one or two songs. Seems like it wasn't too long after that, his manager called my manager and asked,

"Would Johnny be interested in playing on and producing an album for Muddy?" I said, "Definitely." We hadn't talked about it until then, it just kind of fell together real easy.

Hudson: Had you produced an album before?

Winter: Not on anybody but myself. I was worried about making sure the sound came across, because Muddy just played. He didn't know anything about the studio, and he was expecting me to make it all sound right. I was hating the way his records had been sounding at that point. They weren't near as good as the early Chess stuff. Rather than try to modernize things, we got an engineer to listen to the old records and listen to the new records. Then I talked to him and explained how I wanted to get the old. I had a good friend I had been working with, Dave Stillen, and he didn't know anything about those old records. We figured out that miking everything real close and getting a lot of separation was not going to work. So we got everybody in one big room, and even though we miked everything individually, we had one big room mike. It was a nice, echoey room so what came out the mike that we used most was that big room. Of course that makes it impossible to do over-dubs. If anybody does anything wrong, it's on that mike, so you just had to be able to play it right without doing a lot of technical changes. That turned out not to be a problem; in fact, it worked real well. I was real happy with the way those records were recorded. They were strange sounding.

Hudson: To be able to capture the essence of the music in the studio has got to be real art.

Winter: It's hard to do, and in those days the technical things were ahead of people knowing what to do with them. They had all this good equipment and they were making hard blues and rock 'n' roll sound too nice. Instead of a big wall of sound, you could hear everything individually, and it wasn't quite the right idea.

Hudson: You mentioned words "hard" and "rough-edged" in your article in *Guitar Magazine*. It got me thinking. Once in Midem in Cannes, I said to a fellow from Scotland, "I see a connection among music styles from Scotland, Australia, and Texas." He grinned and said "Well, of course, lassie, we all live on the edge." Your music does have an edge. You don't sand it all off.

Winter: It's true. If you try to make what I do too commercial, then it's going to take all the things that I like out of it. I like the rough edge, I like mistakes.

Texas Twister

Johnny Copeland

My way of life, the way I think, the way I feel and how I feel, that's the major influence on any person who prays to be an individual. I must be an individual. I don't want to be directly like nobody, but like everybody that's done it right.

I first talked with Johnny at St. Mary's Bar and Grill in San Antonio in 1987. He came out in the parking lot before the show. I turned on the recorder, and we talked. We met up at the Navasota River Bottom Blues Festival and concluded our series of talks in the summer of 1996 via telephone. He was awaiting a heart transplant, still touring and playing, and adjusting to a left-ventricular assistance device (LVAD) machine that kept his heart pumping. He was still more than willing to share his story.

His well-deserved title "Texas Twister" explains some of the story; this man loved to perform. He's been on several labels, most recently Verve of Polygram. Rounder, a roots-oriented label in Massachusetts, provided a good home for several of his albums. His fellow Texan compadre, Albert Collins, "The Iceman," ended up on Alligator Records in Chicago, a label known for "Houserockin' Music." Johnny Winter also recorded with Bruce Iglauer at Alligator. These labels have one thing in common—they produce artists with substance who love what they're doing, and they allow the artist to have a say in the final product.

Johnny had a say wherever he was. Dr. Mehmet Oz of Columbia Presbyterian Hospital has long been interested in the relationship between music and healing. Inspired by the dramatic impact Johnny's music has had on the patients and staff, Dr. Oz has expanded his investigation into the role of music in healing. The distinctions between healer and patient became blurred in Johnny's case.

Johnny had early dreams of becoming a boxer. The fighting spirit is personified in Johnny "Clyde" Copeland. Talking to Johnny was being in the presence of love; he loved Texas, he loved playing, he loved the blues, he loved people. And Johnny fought for what he loved right up until the end on July 3, 1997. The following interview is a combination of several conversations over a ten-year period.

Hudson: Give us the whole story. Where did you start, and how did you get to where you are today?

Copeland: I started in Haynesville, Louisiana, on a farm called Prentice Meadows. My daddy was a sharecropper and a blues singer. He would play over the weekends and farm through the week. When I was one year old, my mother left my father, and we moved to Magnolia, Arkansas. That's where I started school. About the time I was eight years old I went back for a while to my father in Louisiana. That's where I fell in love with the guitar. I went on a job with him one night when he played. I was interested but not really too interested in it. Two or three years later he passed away, and his last words were, "Be sure that he gets my guitar." So I got the guitar in Arkansas, and I messed around with it. I hadn't really learned a whole lot on it, but due to the way things were, I was always surrounded by musicians. I had a guitar, so musicians came to see me a lot, and they would play country blues for me.

Hudson: How does Texas fit into the story?

Copeland: When I got to Texas, I was confronted again by my good friend Joe Hughes, who was beginning to play music. We was young kids. I think I was fourteen, and he was almost fourteen. There's about three months difference in our age. Eventually me and Joe put a band together called the Dukes of Rhythm. We worked all around the Houston area. We worked San Antonio, Galveston, Port Arthur, Leesville. We was a traveling act. Then we broke the band up, I think, around '54. I decided to go another way and work with Albert Collins's band. Joe kept the Dukes of Rhythm together. Then we were two out in the world, me and him. We had a good thing going for a long time because we were always competitive with each other. He was my teacher, and you always want to beat the teacher. We went on like that. If he saw me, and I had put a good band together, he would get pissed and go put him one together. Finally he got rid of the Dukes and got him a whole new crew. He didn't want none of them in the band. He's cooking today, that's what I was telling you, he is cooking. So it looks like me and him are back on that same level, fixing to do the same thing again because I've been listening to him, and he sounds so good.

Hudson: Who else did you work with in the beginning?

Copeland: I did a lot of work with Percy Mayfield, T-Bone Walker, Lightnin' Hopkins.

Hudson: What do you consider the major influences on your music?

Copeland: My way of life, the way I think, the way I feel and how I feel, that's the major influence on any person who prays to be an individual. I must be an individual. I don't want to be directly like nobody, but like everybody that's done it right.

Hudson: Did that Louisiana stuff stay with you?

Copeland: I didn't learn a lot about the Louisiana stuff, I tell you, because the only one that I remember my daddy did was "Baby, Please Don't Go." My dad did that, I do that. I do it a little different than my daddy did it because my daddy had it jumping. I do it a little different, but I can still do it like my dad did it, too. Hey, what can I say? I've played Texas blues, I've had a wonderful life, I had a happy childhood, I had a good family life. The only times things got rough was after I got grown.

Hudson: Some people associate the blues with the real down-and-out periods, but I've talked to a lot of performers who express real positive things through the blues.

Copeland: How can music be anything but positive? Anytime you can go in and do something and make everybody happy, if it's not for but five minutes, you've accomplished something. Whatever you're doing, if you can make a mass of people happy that really means something, because five minutes of happiness is sometimes a lifetime.

Hudson: What about your association with Rounder Records?

Copeland: My association with Rounder Records has been great. I think that Rounder Records is one of the greatest things that could happen to our music. If it's traditional music, it's big with Rounder, and I like that. Whatever background you come from, the Rounder company will have some music that will please you, if you want to hear it. And that's good.

Hudson: With all the diverse influences in your background, including your trip to Africa and that sort of production, it all adds up to a performer often described as the premier Texas blues artist, the cornerstone of the Texas blues. Where does Texas fit in?

Copeland: I am a Texan. The whole world knows T-Bone Walker, but he didn't push the fact that he was from here. Neither did Lightnin'. But I got the Texas flag on the top of my guitar, and I got "Texas" all up and down my guitar strap. I learned my music in Texas, and I love some of the guys that I grew up with playing the blues around here. Hey, I think everybody should be aware. You must talk about who came along with you and what you did when you came along. It's quite obvious that I wasn't the best of them. I'd have to be something special to be the best of everybody that come along with me because there's about ten or fifteen guitar players that came along at the same time.

Hudson: You were in a good crowd.

Copeland: I was in a good crowd, but I wasn't the greatest of them. They should all get a shot to go out into the world. How do they get that shot? It's once somebody takes that giant step and calls back and says, "Hey, y'all, come on."

Hudson: Opens some doors for everybody else.

Copeland: Right. When somebody takes that giant step and moves with the understanding that this is what he must do. If you make the giant step and don't have the understanding that that's what you must do, then things stay the same.

Hudson: How'd you get the nickname, the Texas Twister?

Copeland: A kid named Ashley Cohen, disc jockey at Columbia University. I was going to join his show one evening. I was living in Harlem at the time. I was walking through Central Park and there was snow swirling everywhere. I was running a little late, and when I get to Columbia, I open the door and all this snow is blowing and there he is waiting for me out in the hall. He says, "Are you Johnny Copeland? I'm the Cincinnati Kid." So I say, "Well, I'm the Texas Twister." He never let me forget that.

Hudson: You've certainly had a long, varied, and diverse career in music. You haven't stayed in one spot.

Copeland: Because of the guys that went before me, I've had a long, diverse period in my music. They didn't do enough talking about me, you know.

Hudson: You've carved out your own spot successfully.

Copeland: Like I say, I'm happy with myself in a lot of ways. I don't like some of the songs I write, but I'm working on that, too.

Hudson: How long have you been writing songs?

Copeland: A long time. I've been writing now for as long as I've been playing the guitar. Writing is the greatest part of my ambition. I like to write. I like the creation of new ideas.

Hudson: How do you know when it's time to write a song?

Copeland: It's always time to write a song. It has no time.

Hudson: Do you have to get into any special situation to write?

Copeland: I'm writing a song now. I'm always writing a song. Through my conversation with you, you might give me another chorus in it.

Hudson: Do you have any favorites?

Copeland: I did a song called "Catch Up with the Blues" on the last album and another one called "Rainbow." They've never missed with an audience nowhere in the world. They go, "Wow, man, we *all* get way off into it!" I went and sat in the forest and I had a little talk with a tree. Then you could chop it down, cut it up, put it in a fire to burn, but if you didn't dig up the roots, the tree would live on. And then, I had a little talk with the sea, and every grain of sand that's in the ocean gets washed up on the beach to lay in the sunshine sometimes. In the next verse I went to sit on a mountain, and I had a little talk with the sky. It showed me a beautiful rainbow, and said, "Johnny, that represents life. Life got to shine like this rainbow." I also like all of the tunes on *Copeland Special*. I like them all on *Texas Twister*. But I don't really have a special one. These are my creations. These things come out of my head.

Hudson: Have there been any real special moments that have just stood out for you?

Copeland: Well, a lot of them. I've had a lot of special moments. But I guess one of the greatest thrills of my life was to be in the Congo in Africa and watch the multitude of people dancing all on top of the houses and up in the trees. It looked like the world was shaking, getting carried away in the tradition of beats. It took some kind of effect on me. It really did. It had me jumping. I didn't know what was going on, except I had to be just moving. It had a real positive effect on my mind, body, feet. The next thing I knew I was out in the middle of the field dancing, too, saying, "Y'all get over and let me show you how we do it over there." I was dancing. That's the hardest thing to get, that effect on the audience. If I don't get that effect it makes me feel kind of bad. I work hard, but sometimes you can work hard, hard, hard, and you still can't get it.

Hudson: Change directions?

Copeland: It's just that the blues ain't right; the people are in another frame of mind. You got certain nights that you can get them going real good, and certain nights that you can't get them going because they more serious on this night than they were before. You have people going out on Friday night. They are out having a good time. But the next night they are out with their husbands or people they're serious about, and they're a little more laid back. And Sunday night, that's the day everybody worships God, and they are a little more laid back then.

Hudson: How did you end up going to Africa?

Copeland: We went on a State Department tour and the Congo was the first stop we made. All of a sudden I realized, "I'm in Africa, and this is where I'm from. Wow!" Then I found out that 80 percent of all the black people in America came from the area that I went to. Eighty percent of them. Twenty-nine million of them.

Hudson: It must have really created a sense of roots and tradition.

Copeland: Up until that point, my mind could go back to Haynesville and to Prentice Meadows Farm. Some guy might say, "Where are you from?" I would say, "I'm from Prentice Meadows Farm," but I couldn't go past that. Now that blank spot is gone. I'm seeing farther now. I've erased that spot where it stopped, where everything stopped. Though I knew it didn't stop there, I had no knowledge, no way of seeing past it. But playing in Africa showed me how to see past that. It showed me so much about the nature of my people that I love so much. It just showed me everything. Now I do have a broader perspective. It taught me how to deal with other nationalities of people because I can relate to them better. I walk the streets all over the world, and I can relate to the Africans now because if they come from the country that I've been to, I'm glad to talk to them, and they're glad to talk to me. That makes it great.

Hudson: It sounds like your career has been one of excitement and growth and change. Have there been any of those low periods that you've had to struggle through?

Copeland: Well, yeah. I think everything is a struggle. But if you love what you are doing, are you struggling? If you're doing what you love, then you're never struggling. It's all too interesting for me to be struggling. Because I'm interested in everything. So if I'm struggling, it don't matter because I love to struggle, too. You love all of it.

Hudson: It's the challenge; it's all part of it.

Copeland: Well, it's sweeter when it pays off. I remember when we got through with *Copeland Special*, and I had to go to Boston to talk to the Rounder company. We picked up some money. I don't remember how much, but it was more money than I had been used to having. I looked at the money, and I said, "This money comes from my music. When I get to New York the first thing I'm going to do is go buy me a big meal." In the beginning I had really been through some changes to try and get my music to move. Once it did move I said, "Hey!" It's good to say, "Hey!" 'cause everything I'm doing now I'm doing with the money from my music. I finally got past that, but it was a great feeling to move where I didn't have to go look for money from other places or other sources to keep doing what I love to do.

Hudson: What's it like being based in New York? There are so many places you could have chosen, but that's where your career really went into high gear.

Copeland: I think God sent me there. I tell you, if you intend to go nationwide or around the world, you must go to New York. Other than that, you're regional, and you'll never be nothing but happy within yourself like I was here. I was a happy person in this place. There was so much I didn't see and so much I didn't know. What you don't know can't hurt you no way. But there is so much you don't know.

Hudson: Do you enjoy touring in Europe?

Copeland: I've enjoyed great audiences in New York, Philadelphia, and throughout California and Texas. But some of my greatest times have been in Ireland. When I tour Europe, I always have a good time. I focus on Europe first, really, to try to make our music known over there. Europe sends it back here to us threefold. So we pound Europe hard. We all did. Albert Collins, Stevie Ray, myself, the Thunderbirds, we all went. Now a lot of guys who never went anywhere before are beginning to go there because of what we did. That's another good feeling.

Hudson: Opening some doors.

Copeland: Opening doors for people from home. Names you been hearing all your life, and suddenly you look up, and there are those names up on the boards. Texas blues is moving up with Chicago blues. We have given folks another choice. Let's put it this way: I believe everybody should be given at least two choices. When it's just one choice, that ain't right. Texas blues offers the world another choice.

Hudson: What's unique about Texas blues?

Copeland: We have nothing against Chicago blues, but the specialty of Texas blues is flavoring. Let's say the way you would cook a chocolate cake is not the way I would cook a chocolate cake. If I cooked one, I may want more chocolate, and you may not want so much. It would be a little different in taste. In Texas we're pulling from a Kansas City swing in a New Orleans funk. So we got a little different twist going there.

Hudson: What about guitar players?

Copeland: Delta blues players have a tendency to play slide a lot. Though they play a lot of slide, and they play it great, you wouldn't hardly hear a great slide player in Texas. But you can hear some great slide players out of the Delta. I mean *great.*

Hudson: Some folks talk about a special sound and a special kind of energy in Texas guitar players. That run of notes.

Copeland: Special sound, special flavor. They flavor their music with pianos, horns, and things like that where Chicago could be slide guitar, harmonica, all kinds of different things. Because it was more to the roots. When you say Delta blues you are talking about the real roots of our people, people who come out of the hard core of oppression. I'll put it that way. I'm not being radical, but I'm saying the way it was. Our people were outnumbered. The oppressors had to use cruelty to maintain control. Delta music was really hard-core and depressed, which produced a different sound.

Hudson: I just wonder about the atmosphere in Texas—the frontier, the space.

Copeland: Out here in this area we had a lot of that to go on, but in Texas back when I come into the business, we was playing in clubs all around the state. We were integrated. In '53, '54, '55 everybody was coming to one club to hear the music. It wasn't like the whites go here, the blacks go here, the Spanish go here. Everybody was going to the same club, which amazed me when first I came to San Antonio. That was one thing that really tripped me out, to see everybody coming to hear the music. And they were sitting together, and they were drinking together, and they was having a good time. Then I went to Corpus Christi, and I saw the same thing. I went to Kingsville and saw the same thing.

Hudson: What about your guitar style?

Copeland: I've never been what you would call a great guitar player. It got to bugging me once how some guys can go up and just play so much stuff on the guitar. I just play what corresponds to the song. I'm more an all-the-way-round person. I accumulate the writing, the singing, and the guitar playing, and, of course, I love my audience. I love playing the blues festivals. I just played one in Pittsburgh, then Minnesota and Iowa.

Hudson: What about your CD, *The Jungle Swing?*

Copeland: That's an old Willie Dixon song from 1954. We recently did a beautiful tour through Europe called the Spirit of Africa, with a jazz player named Randy Weston and a group from Marrakesh, so I decided I wanted to record another African-descended blues thing.

Hudson: You're recording with Verve now [1996]. What are you working on? What's your most exciting project?

Copeland: I'm trying to find a lady who wants to sing the blues with me. I wish I could find one. I've been wanting to talk to Etta James because she sings so pretty. When she was at the Grammy awards, I could have grabbed her and kissed her. She sounded so good. Or maybe the great Miss Koko Taylor. I'd like to do a record with a lady so we could sit back and talk. So we could talk to each other through the music, you know. That's better than trying to do it with a guy.

Hudson: How many albums do you have out now with Rounder?

Copeland: Eleven. We just brought one back dedicated to the greats that I did when I was younger. They released it in London, and that's on the market now. And I'm glad. I like the record. I told the guy, "Hey, I'm going to push this record 'cause I like it. So I'm going to get behind it." I'm working on a live record right now.

Hudson: Where are you recording?

Copeland: Different places. We've got some cuts from over in Europe and just around everywhere. And we're going to put that on the market.

Hudson: You've won a lot of big-time awards: the W. C. Handy Entertainer of the Year from the American Blues Foundation and the Grand Prix du Disque de Montreux for blues, soul, and gospel. Was there one among the others that stands out?

Copeland: The Grammy is one of the greatest wins you can make. How did that feel? Like I was floating. By the time I got through floating, I done floated all out of the picture! It's always great to win. You can always say, "I did my part," because your time don't belong to you, and your time is limited. You have a certain time to get so much done. And you have to go in and get it done. I'm glad I'm having fun, because it would be hard to do if I wasn't. Everything you win and everything you do is good for you if you know what to do with it after you win it.

Hudson: Describe Texas music.

Copeland: Texas music is a feeling that goes back to the beginning of the blues. Fannin Street in Houston played some of the greatest blues in the '30s that have ever been played, including Leadbelly, Blind Lemon Jefferson, and all of these guys were all right around Texas. We don't have to mention Lightnin'. Lightnin' speaks for hisself. Lightnin' was that star out there by itself. That light that shines. Way over, the Eastern Star, he was way out there. His blues is so humorous you couldn't listen to it without laughing.

Hudson: Did you ever get to spend time with him?

Copeland: Oh, yeah. Let me tell you a story about his last days. I was in New York and he had a gig there at Tramp's. I called him up and said, "I need to get myself together for this trip," so he says, "Come on out to the show," and then he adds, "I've been sick." Now I was flying to Europe the next day, but there was something in his voice, so I say, "I'll be there." I never figured that would end up being his last performance. He was a great brother, real nice.

Fears and Dragons

Ray Wylie Hubbard

"Our fears are like dragons guarding our most precious treasure." . . . A line that touches more than just the physical. I needed to let other people know about it. One way to do that is to put it in a song. I can't just go around knocking on doors saying, "Hey, this is the truth here. This line is really cool." So then I wrote the whole song around that. Once I got that idea, the rest of the song came pretty easy.

Ray Wylie Hubbard has documented the changes in his life through the songs he writes. He knows how to tell a good story. Like many other talented Texas writers, he's often been looking for a label. He's never quit performing. Playing at an inaugural ball at the White House, and at every single one of Willie Nelson's famous Fourth of July picnics, he is known as a consummate showman. He entertains Texas style, and Buffalo (Terry Joe Ware) plays guitar in a way that defines Ray's style. Ray also went on the road for a while with another guitar legend, Bugs Henderson. Often called "renegade" or "underdog," Ray just keeps capturing the attention of music critics even as he always keeps his audience—with or without radio play. One headline read, "Ray Wylie Hubbard: In Search of a Genre." Like many Texas writers, he does not fit into a niche. He constantly redefines himself and creates his own place. He has paid his dues. Two of his albums can be found on Dejadisc in San Marcos. The others are collector's items. Our first conversation was in 1985 at a hotel in Kerrville. I had been listening to him for years in the Fort Worth–Dallas area.

Hudson: Let's talk about your roots.

Hubbard: I went to high school in Dallas at W. H. Adamson High. Michael Murphy and B. W. Stevenson were both there, and Larry Gross, who wrote "Junk Food Junky." We all got involved in a folk music scene and started playing acoustic guitars at assemblies. Through Michael Murphy I discovered a club called the Rubaiyat. I used to go down there and hang out. That's where I ran into Johnny Vandiver and Jerry Jeff Walker. Through those people I got turned on to Woody Guthrie, Cisco Houston, Jimmie Rodgers, and Lefty Frizzell. Johnny Vandiver would do a song. I'd say, "Where you get that song?" He'd say, "Cisco Houston." Then I'd go listen to all the Cisco Houston songs. My first influences were primarily folk and country blues.

Hudson: You've really gone through a lot of changes in your music. How much was conscious effort and how much was natural growth?

Hubbard: It's all a learning process. I've gone through complete changes, playing first with the Cowboy Twinkies then the Gonzos. Now I'm playing with Bugs Henderson and some full-tilt rockers. In each band you change. Bugs will be playing some wild screaming guitar, but then we'll turn around and do a Doc Watson song. Pretty typical in the Texas music scene, actually.

Hudson: What do you find easiest when you write?

Hubbard: None of it's easy for me. Sometimes a song will come in fifteen minutes; sometimes I work for years. I wrote "Redneck Mother" in about fifteen minutes. Last night we did it during the first set. A bunch of folks came in later and asked for it again so we did it Reggae style. Then halfway through we changed to Joan Jett rock 'n' roll. I never write down a set list because I want to keep that freedom. I don't want it to become mechanical.

Hudson: Remember when you visited my English class in Aledo, Texas, at nine in the morning? That principal turned on his speaker system just so he could monitor this unusual guest speaker I brought in.

Hubbard: That was a great discussion. I enjoyed it. And I appreciated the Flannery O'Connor book you gave me. I was an English major in college. Just didn't get the degree because I hadn't finished the Spanish requirements.

Hudson: Do you have some favorites of the songs that you've written?

Hubbard: I really like the song I wrote called "Jazzbo Dancer," but we hardly ever do it.

Hudson: What about the direction of Texas music?

Hubbard: I think there's always going to be a magic about Texas music. I don't think Texas music has ever been headed in one direction. It's so diversified.

Hudson: What is it about writing songs that keeps you going?

Hubbard: Boy, I thought this was going to be easy. It's not. I'll be driving along and get a little melody in my head. All of a sudden I know there's a song to be written. Something that hadn't been said before. Sometimes a phrase will hit me. I was reading *King of the Gypsies*, and I came across the story that a gypsy stole the nail that was for the heart of Jesus. I said, "Man, there's a song in that." And I wrote "Gypsies Have the Right To Steal." The idea comes first for me—sometimes a phrase—and I hear the whole song. It happens at strange times.

Hudson: Who are some significant songwriters in Texas?

Hubbard: The early Willie Nelson songs, man, they kill me. They're incredible. His new songs are good, but some of his older songs will just destroy you. Johnny Vandiver didn't write a lot of songs, but what he did write was really good. I really like Townes. I haven't bought any of his records, but my record player doesn't work. I try not to listen to other people. I'm afraid I'll hear a phrase then I'll unconsciously use it years later. Bugs Henderson has some great songs. My favorite now is "Stabbed in the Back," by Bugs. Guy Clark, Michael Murphy, Gary P. Nunn are great writers. There's just so many. Don't forget Freddie King.

The next conversation took place in my Schreiner College English class in 1994.

Hubbard: I'll start off with a song I've recently written, "The Messenger." I was reading a book by Joseph Campbell, there was a line in there where he quotes Rilke. I thought the line was so good that at first I stole it. Then I felt guilty and gave him credit for saying it in the song. "We all have a message to stand and deliver. The message I bring is from Rainer Maria Rilke. 'Our fears are like dragons guarding our most precious treasures.'"

Hudson: We could dismiss class now, since this song may just answer all our questions.

Hubbard: A line like that touches more than just the physical. I needed to let other people know about it. One way to do that is to put it in a song. I can't just go around knocking on doors saying, "Hey, this is the truth here. This line is really cool." So I wrote the whole song around that. In the last four years I've really gotten into reading a lot about writing and creativity. A lot of times these songs seem to just fall out of the ceiling on to the kitchen table. And you can write them down. If I can just get the ego out of the way, the song will come out a lot easier. Sometimes I'll be writing a song and get a spot where I just can't get the next line, so I just forget about it for a while. Then it comes.

Hudson: Here's another book for you by Rilke. He talks about love, the need for solitude as part of the creative process. Is there anything else about Campbell that interests you?

Hubbard: It's all this stuff I missed when I was in college. I was trying to take over the dean's office, protesting a lot. I was in college from 1966 to 1969 in Denton and Arlington. It was a very exciting time actually. Music was changing then. I was an English major, but that was just something to write down so you didn't end up on a rice paddy in Vietnam. I missed a lot. Now I'm enjoying the learning, absorbing all that.

Hudson: That song wasn't written with hopes of getting it on the radio, was it?

Hubbard: No, I've never really been interested in that. Some people can write songs, get them in front of the right people, get the label and get the money. I've never really concerned myself with that particular focus. I wrote what meant something to me. I got involved in the trapping of it and really got into music. I became a working musician.

Hudson: And a consummate performer. I remember once at Billy Bob's where, even wearing a back brace, you threw yourself on the floor, wildly singing a song. Such a show.

Hubbard: I can't deny that. I had a very high-energy band. The Cowboy Twinkies at the time—cowpunk, a thrash band at the time. What we lacked in talent, we made up for in attitude. We'd go into these serious country bars and play Hendrix. Just to see what kind of reaction we could get. That was part of it. Some Merle Haggard songs with a break full of feedback. We didn't get a lot of airplay. Still don't. I've never been able to be a Nashville briefcase writer. A lot of songs seem to exist to make money for the record label. I don't mean to sound bitter about that—if possible, I might be part of that. But, it doesn't work for me.

Hudson: Other influences on you?

Hubbard: In high school I got into folk music, Bob Dylan, Woody Guthrie, Cisco Houston, Eric Anderson, Joan Baez. In Texas you can't get away from country music, so I heard Bob Wills, Hank Thompson, and that whole cadre. Then there's Freddie King, Mance Lipscomb, and Lightnin' Hopkins. It was an incredible time for music in the '60s. It was all there. When I sit down to write, I just write and see what happens. I don't deliberately choose a type of song. The MTV *Unplugged* has brought back an awareness to what's underneath the slick performance. Now we're getting into more interesting music.

Hudson: Another comment on "Redneck Mother"?

Hubbard: Yeah, Jerry Jeff did that, and I got paid. If you're going to write a song, you'd better be able to play it for twenty-five years.

Hudson: Why have you called that the "albatross" around your neck?

Hubbard: When I wrote it, it was a throw-away song. We never rehearsed it. I wrote it in about twenty-five minutes. I have no knowledge of its "author." Somebody else wrote it, I'm sure. It was the late '60s. The country was divided into camps. If you had long hair, you weren't American. Merle Haggard wrote "Okie from Muskogee." Willie Nelson had not yet performed at the Armadillo World Headquarters to bring the hippies and rednecks together. It was a time when traveling through West Texas with long hair provoked fear. People I knew had been hassled out there. Long hair was an un-American thing to do. It was a weird time, and this was a weird song. It makes no sense to me. [He reluctantly sings the song for my English class.]

I was in Red River, New Mexico, with a bunch of folksingers sitting around trading songs. It was my turn to go get the beer. I went to a place called D-Bar-D Bar, a real redneck bar. It was serious at the time. I expected to get hassled and I did. But it was by a little gray-haired woman and her son. We didn't get down and wrestle in the mud or anything. When I got back it was my turn to sing a song. I sang, "He was born in Oklahoma. . . ." And I wrote the song. We always made up the verses as we went. Bob Livingston, a bass player, left, went to California, and started playing with Michael Murphy. He started playing with Jerry Jeff in Austin after that. One night Jerry Jeff broke a string, and Bob sang a song. That's the one he sang. The next thing I knew people started pouring beer on each other and fighting. Jerry Jeff said, "I'd better learn this song." We only had a first verse and chorus. Bob would spell "mother" and make it up as he went along. When he got ready to cut at Luckenbach, Jerry Jeff called me for a second verse. So I wrote the second verse right then over the phone. I wrote about three verses. They recorded it. Every now and then I'll get a royalty check from Australia for $9.30.

Hudson: It's good to hear all the various stories about how we create.

Hubbard: There's always an opportunity for change. I started playing in high school. I never took a lesson. Then I started writing. All of a sudden, I got a band together and just got out there and did it. Thrown out to the honky-tonks. About six years ago, I changed the way I thought about things. I was on a pretty bad road as far as excess is concerned. Six years ago I quit drinking. I had some help. I got straight. Then about two years ago, I started thinking it's about time to grow up and decide what I'm going to do. I started looking carefully at this idea of being a songwriter. I decided I needed to learn to play the guitar better. So I took my first-ever guitar lesson. It's kind of like that line about our fears being like dragons. The idea of taking a guitar lesson at my age brought up fear. I just went through that fear and found a guy who could teach me. I wanted to learn to finger pick. The other side of that fear was this treasure. The ability to write these other songs.

Hudson: Have you and Buffalo written together? [Terry Joe Ware—his longtime partner.]

Hubbard: Yes. The other thing about Terry as a guitar player is that he has good taste. He plays really tasteful stuff. And he's a producer as well. He has a studio up in Norman, Oklahoma. We've been playing together a long time.

Hudson: I remember Terry taking that long lead on "Desperados Waiting for a Train," at the Rubaiyat on Maple in Dallas.

Hubbard: Yeah, we used to do that song by Guy Clark, but at the end we never knew how it was going to end up. Terry would take the lead on the guitar. I could walk off the stage and go get a salad. These guys would play from five to twenty minutes. Grateful Dead stuff.

Hudson: The chorus of "The Messenger" is a description of an aesthetic life style. Is that part of your experience?

Hubbard: It's one of those times when I realized what's more important to me—when I took a close look at priorities in my life. "I'm not looking for loose diamonds."

Hudson: You once said to me that we're really all messengers.

Hubbard: Sometimes there's better messages than others. At one time I thought you had to self-destruct to be creative. When I was eighteen my heroes had died at twenty-nine in the back seat of a Cadillac with whiskey or pills. Then you try to do it, too. Who's next, Hemingway? Oh yes, I can do that, too. My perspective has changed. You really don't have to self-destruct to create.

Hudson: Is there a moment when things turned around for you? Stevie Ray Vaughan talked to me about that moment—when he fell off a stage.

Hubbard: Pretty much the same deal for me. I used to take it pretty much to the edge. Stevie Ray actually came out and talked to me. He was the first to talk to me from that perspective. About two weeks later, something clicked. It was the second time I ever met him. I saw him a year later, and he asked how I was doing. Sometimes it just takes one person who cares.

Our next conversation took place in Kerrville on October 5, 1995. Ray came to town to play the wedding of Greg McLaughlin and Renee Moore, former students of mine. He also played a small bar in town. He had a small but avid crowd, fans willing to listen to the songs. He joked about being for "hire." We talked briefly at the wedding reception.

Hudson: The first time we talked was ten years ago.

Hubbard: That was back when I knew it all.

Hudson: Let's talk about now.

Hubbard: It's pretty good right now. I feel comfortable with my writing. I'm coming up on my fiftieth birthday and nine years of clean and sober on the same day. It's time to look back. I had my last drink November 12, 1987. November 13 I turned forty-one. I feel like my career is still moving forward. It doesn't feel dead in the water. Especially my writing. Hey, I'm the guy who wrote "Redneck Mother." Hopefully that guy's come a long ways since then. There's been a lot of growth. Some time after I got straight, I developed a conscience. I decided to contribute to life instead of just taking from it. I didn't write all the songs on *Loco Gringo* because I had a record deal or because I thought anyone would hear them. I didn't have a reason other than the writing. I didn't know at that point if I'd ever have a record deal.

Hudson: There are several strong labels in Texas. I was glad to see it on

Dejadisc out of San Marcos. Their press kits are works of art. What does it feel like to just write for the writing?

Hubbard: It's an urge to create. That's a cliche, but there's a lot of truth in cliches. There's a divine creative spark within everybody. Some have to be nurtured. I had to nurture that spark and bring it forth. I did that by doing certain things. Try to get the ego out of the way when I'm writing. Somewhere in there, not to get too deep, somewhere in my writing I stop thinking of God as a noun and think of god as a verb. Let "Be" be. Tap into that source, the divine creative spark. I do certain things to appease the muse.

Hudson: You didn't pick up that approach hanging out in bars.

Hubbard: I read a lot. But I hate to talk about this because, when it's in print, it ends up looking pretentious.

Hudson: Maybe we won't print it.

Hubbard: If I sound smart, go ahead and use it. If I sound pretentious, cut it out [laughter]. Being a writer you understand that. The oral quality of this conversation may not translate into print.

Hudson: Do you see yourself as a storyteller?

Hubbard: It started out just Buffalo and I doing acoustic work. I have this ability between songs to keep it going with some of the goofy stuff I say. I really appreciate storytellers. I enjoyed Mark Twain growing up. A lot of the songs I write do tell stories. When you start writing a song, you don't know how it's going to develop. When I started "Dust of the Chase," it started with one line; "I came down from Oklahoma with a pistol in my boot." The story-song just evolved. One thing about writing: you can do the crime, you don't have to do the time.

Hudson: I heard you at Willie's picnic in 1996. You sang a song with the line "Condemned by the gods to write." I love that song.

Hubbard: I write because I feel I'm condemned to write. I write whether or not I have any success with it. It's not like I'm writing to have hits or writing for a record deal. "There are some who can rise above blind fate. There are others who just can't seem to pray. And there are those condemned by the gods to write. They sparkle and they fade away." That's where I am. You write and flourish whether or not you get famous. Sometimes you just slide away.

Passion on the Road

Johnny Rodriguez

I wrote "Riding My Thumb to Mexico" in about thirty minutes when I was twenty-two. I feel like I'm going somewhere in that song. I get that traveling feeling.

Johnny Rodriguez always commands the stage, whether it's an arena stage or the stage at an open mike in a small Texas town. Known for his voice, his performance, his presence, Johnny is a writer who takes his craft seriously. His heart and soul are part of each performance. Always dressed impeccably in subtle Texas fashion, jeans and a starched shirt, he gives everyone in the audience a way to relate. My last conversation with Johnny took place in 1996 in Austin at Shoal Creek on Lamar. His road to success has been rough and rocky, often leading him away from a stated goal, but he's always stayed on that road. His latest album on Hightone Records has been reviewed as his best.

Johnny's career began when he met Tom T. Hall. His debut album was followed by fifteen number one hits. He has thirteen albums on Polygram, eight on Epic, one on Mercury/Polygram, and one on Capitol. His Hightone record, out in 1996, is the first on an independent label. In addition to the hits came industry accolades, awards, and even television and film roles. Heady stuff for a kid in his early twenties from Sabinal, Texas, a small town ninety miles from the Mexican border. He drifted away from the great music that had been part of his life. The Hightone album project brought him back.

Hudson: You've been involved in the music business a long time for your young age, and you've had a lot of different experiences. Is there any one sort of magical moment that stands out above all the rest?

Rodriguez: Probably playing guitar on the stage with Jerry Lee Lewis.

Hudson: When did that happen?

Rodriguez: About every time I see him. I seldom get to see him, for some reason or another, but we're pretty good friends. He's a funny guy. I get a kick out of knowing him. I don't know why he invites me up. I'm the worst guitar player in the world, but he always says, "Hey, come on and play guitar."

Hudson: Are there any other particular performers that have been a real strong influence on you?

Rodriguez: Roger Miller, Mickey Newberry, Tom T. Hall, and Willie Nelson as far as writing, 'cause I'm always doing them. I'm interested in writing.

Hudson: How do you know when it's time for you to write a song?

Rodriguez: It's hard to say. You either have to be hurting enough or be happy enough. It's an extremity, the feeling I have to have.

Hudson: Do you have some songs you've written that are closer to you than others?

Rodriguez: No. I talked to Dolly Parton about that one time. We used to travel together and visit and talk about songwriting. She said when somebody asks you what your favorite song is, that's the hardest question in the world to answer. She had the best answer I have ever heard. She said, "The songs you write, they're like your children, they're your kids. If you ask someone who is your favorite kid, what do you say?" That's how I feel about my songs. I do enjoy performing "Pass Me By" because it was my first hit.

Hudson: And eleven other hits followed that one. How do you feel about that period in your life?

Rodriguez: I didn't even have time to think about it. Fourteen number one hits in a row. It just happened before I even knew it.

Hudson: How do you account for that success?

Rodriguez: I believe in God for one thing. I think he had a lot to do with it.

Hudson: What do you think people like best about your performances?

Rodriguez: I think when I do my best and people know that I am doing my best. I'm never satisfied with what I do. Every time I make a record or perform, I always manage to find something wrong. I'm always critical of myself.

Hudson: Do you have any particular time of day that you write, any kind of schedule?

Rodriguez: At night or when I am moving, traveling, like riding in a car or in an airplane. Moving, you know. I don't know why.

Hudson: Is there anything other than the extremes of emotion that triggers that impulse to write? Do you hear words, language that catches your imagination?

Rodriguez: Yeah, but I'm not a disciplined writer. Like some people can just hear something and sit down and say, I'm going to write this. I procrastinate. I put things off a lot. I'll just think about this idea. Sometimes I lose ideas like that. But if it sticks in my mind long enough, if it's good enough for me to remember, I figure it's going to make a good song. That's more or less how I do it. When I get time, I sit down and just write it. It don't take long, it don't take over thirty or forty minutes.

Hudson: What are you looking forward to in the future?

Rodriguez: Just what I'm fixing to do right now. I'm working on writing a couple of movie scores. I'm fixing to do a movie with Elliot Gould. I play a friend of a couple of convicts. I'm writing some of the music for that, and I'm doing the music for a movie with Nick Nolte. I spend quite a bit of time with him. That's what I'm trying to zero in on right now. It's challenging.

Hudson: If you had to describe Texas music . . .

Rodriguez: It's down-home, it's earthy.

Hudson: That describes your music too, right?

Rodriguez: I hope so.

Johnny and I talked years later at Shoal Creek in Austin. Then we joined Larry Trader and headed out to Flores Mexican Food. There we heard Johnny Gonzalez sing. I watched Johnny Rodriguez get passionate about the music. He even decided to sing along. Heads popped up in the restaurant as folks tried to decide where that "voice" came from. Johnny kept sharing stories with me. He was passionate about his stories as well. He knows he has a gift, and he knows he needs to give it back.

Hudson: We meet again. Let's talk about your interests now. What's a current passion of yours?

Rodriguez: The movie I'm working on. The main thing is to send a message to young Latino gangs. I was in a gang when I was a kid. So when I see them out here, I think they don't know what they're getting into.

Hudson: So, you know what it feels like to want to be part of a group?

Rodriguez: That's why I'm interested in this project. There was almost no place for me to go as a kid except out in the streets. You've got to belong to something. This movie is called *Down from the Barrio*. It's about four different characters. The one I play is the worst killer—the Boogie Man. Even this kind of guy goes down. That's the main thing the movie is saying.

Hudson: How did you meet the producer?

Rodriguez: I met him at Willie's Fourth of July picnic in Luckenbach. Little Joe plays a priest in this movie. He keeps trying to save my soul, and I keep running him off. I'm in prison, and I finally die by lethal injection. True story.

Hudson: Do you have a sense of your own heritage as distinct?

Rodriguez: I feel a responsibility to aim right at my heritage.

Hudson: Every time we talk I have a sense of a driving force in you.

Rodriguez: Yeah, I know for one thing I haven't come up to my full potential in singing and songwriting. I know I've been screwing around and not taking care of myself.

Hudson: Every time I've seen you, your performance has been wonderful. Ironic for you to feel this way. You've been the superstar; you've had the hits; you've had the crowds. People see you that way. But you know there's more?

Rodriguez: Philosophically speaking, there's so much more I want to learn. Other venues are opening up to me. I'll probably be doing more and more work with films. I want to do some community work that really makes a difference. I know I should be giving something back right now. Sometimes I'm just hanging out.

Hudson: When has it been "perfecto" for you in this business?

Rodriguez: Really, never. I always find something wrong.

Hudson: How do you keep getting in touch with what you have to say?

Rodriguez: That's a good question. Most of the time if I go directly from my heart to writing it down—if I don't go to my head too much—that's how I get to it. Does that make any sense?

Hudson: Perfect sense.

Rodriguez: A magical performance for me was when I played Carnegie Hall and my mother was sitting in the front row.

Hudson: Is there a particular Texas club scene that you like?

Rodriguez: Billy Bob's in Fort Worth. I love staying on the Northside when I play there. You see all those cowboys and all that western stuff. I love it there.

Hudson: Some writers spend time alone when they write. Others like the city. One time you told me you could write on the road. How is it now?

Rodriguez: It doesn't work that way now. Now the best time is with a co-writer. I get motivated that way by other people. I like to do that in the morning, and it doesn't matter where.

Hudson: Do you see yourself as part of the Nashville scene?

Rodriguez: I guess. I've been living there for twenty-four years. I like Nashville. It's changed a lot. For the better, I think. There's more diversity in music, for one thing. Before it was just country music. It's not that way anymore.

Hudson: What's the biggest frustration for you?

Rodriguez: Having to stay in front of the public. If I'm going to be a professional about it. I stayed out of doing interviews for a long time. That's when I got miserable.

Hudson: It's obvious to me that you like relating to people.

Rodriguez: I do.

Hudson: But there's so much possibility for pain in your profession—rejection, misperceptions.

Rodriguez: I know I can't control all that, but if I'm going to do something stupid, it better not be in front of somebody. If things are going to change, it's important to do some footwork.

Hudson: What's the hardest work you've ever done?

Rodriguez: Therapy.

Hudson: Do you have any songs that address that?

Rodriguez: No. Maybe I should write one. I hadn't thought about that. I wrote a song called "These Excuses." That song addresses behavior patterns, for sure.

Hudson: From 1988 [our first conversation] to now [1996], what's the biggest shift that's occurred for you?

Rodriguez: When I went in to do this album I said, "You're forty-four years old now. You need to prove yourself. Prove you can do what you were aiming at." That involves discipline. What really helped out was the fact that the two producers who started with me twenty-five years ago produced this album. They know me better than I do. I didn't write anything on this album for Hightone. I didn't feel confident enough yet. The next time I will. I felt pretty disconnected. All the great opportunities I had in Nashville to write with some great songwriters. What did I do? Nothing. But for some reason, I just got motivated last year.

Hudson: I think there's an important starting place many people miss—to start by being with who you are. Forget all the "shoulds." Really getting with who you are, then working out of that.

Rodriguez: Yeah, and some get in trouble by taking it all too far.

Hudson: You're bound to have been shoved into a few boxes.

Rodriguez: They've tried.

Hudson: Do you like who you are?

Rodriguez: Yeah, but I had to work at it. I can find any excuse in the world to make myself feel guilty. Then I start beating myself up. I used to feel guilty because I made more money than my brothers and sisters, or because I was doing better than some poor guy at the end of the street. Feel guilty instead of saying "Thank you." That's what I needed to do—say "Thank you."

Hudson: You've got struggles and gifts others don't have. What's the biggest misperception about you out there?

Rodriguez: One of the things I had to learn to do was ask for what I need. Otherwise, you don't get it.

Hudson: Here's a standard question: What advice would you give to songwriters and musicians?

Rodriguez: Don't overprice yourself. Let the promoter make money. And write. That separates you from everybody else.

Hudson: Did you write all your number one songs?

Rodriguez: No, I wrote about five—"Riding My Thumb to Mexico," "Dance With Me," "You Always Come Back To Hurting Me," "Down on the Rio Grande," and "Fools for Each Other." That one only went to number seven.

Hudson: Do number one songs mean a lot now?

Rodriguez: I want to enjoy life now. See my family. Many of them will be at John T. Floore's on Saturday night. The president of the record label told me a story that Robert Earl Keen told him that I didn't even know. He said when I played the Astrodome in 1975, Keen was in school. They had a contest in his class to write the best essay about why Rodriguez was the best songwriter in the world. He lost. The winner got a chance to meet me. [A Keen song came up on the jukebox.] Later, I met Keen, and it was at the Astrodome.

Hudson: Let's have a story about one of your songs.

Rodriguez: When I was a kid, I always wanted to travel. I started hitch-hiking when I was thirteen or fourteen. We used to hitch-hike to Mexico because we could go over there and get drunk. You could drink if you could reach the bar. I wrote "Riding My Thumb To Mexico" in about thirty minutes when I was twenty-two. I feel like I'm going somewhere in that song. I get that traveling feeling. I showed it to Tom T. Hall and questioned the title—look how it looks: "Use it," he said. They'll laugh at it.

Hudson: I read Kerouac's *On the Road* one summer at Naropa, a Buddhist school in Boulder, Colorado. I love the road image.

Rodriguez: So do I. There was a couple of times when nobody would pick us up. It was hotter than hell in the summer. We'd just get on the other side of the road and go.

Hudson: What's the story that's going to stay with you for the next twenty years?

Rodriguez: They won't know how I survived that long. I'll be sixty-four.

Hudson: What other activities do you enjoy?

Rodriguez: I like fishing and hunting. I love the outdoors. I love fall.

Hudson: Is there anything you want to talk about that we haven't hit on yet?

Rodriguez: One time this writer, Gail Burkholder, and I were going out to visit someone in Hendersonville. Our car stalled on the side of the road. A car stopped and Hank Cochran got out. I didn't even know it was him. Gail did though, and she told me. Then we go out to Guy and Susanna's and told them the story that Hank gave us a ride. That was the first time I heard "Pancho and Lefty." I was turned off at first to that song because it wasn't right about Pancho Villa. Townes wrote the song, and he says it's not about Pancho Villa.

The Business

Holly Dunn

Communicating with the audience is important. I don't feel like I've done a very good job if I haven't connected with them, if we haven't broken down that barrier between us by the end of the hour. I want to leave them a little warm and fuzzy. I want them to feel good about me. The only way I know how to do that is to get down there amongst them. I don't just run up and down the aisle. I go down for three or four songs.

Holly Dunn sat alone in her booth at the end of the 1987 Nashville Radio Seminar. She smiled warmly at me, and I felt welcome. She willingly shared ideas with me about her projects, her writing, and Texas music. She seemed overjoyed to be in the business.

We talked again at Aqua Fest in Austin, Texas, in 1988—this time after a rousing performance to a packed crowd. No empty rooms for Holly Dunn. Every step in her career seemed carefully orchestrated. An aura of confidence surrounded her as she talked about her latest album and current hit single. I heard Texas in her songs, for good reason. She had written six out of the ten songs on the album. She played them enthusiastically for that Texas crowd.

In 1995 *Life and Love and All the Stages* was released on Polygram and distributed by River North. This album showcases a recharged Holly Dunn. Her story includes a long list of awards: three Grammy nominations, CMA Horizon Award, BMI Songwriter of the Year, ACM top new female vocalist (1986), and star on Hall of Fame Starwalk (1994). She has scored four number one hits and ten Top Ten singles. Although she left the recording studio in 1992, she never stopped touring. She joined River North because longtime fan and label president Joe Thomas asked her to be the flagship artist for the new label. Her first single was "I Am Who I Am," and she means it. Holly says, "There's a large part of me in everything I write—either me or someone that I care about, or something that I've seen up close and personal."

She played the YO Social Club in Mountain Home, Texas. Her warmth was readily apparent when she agreed to photos—one with each of the twenty board members. Many said, "She sings as good as she looks."

I have experienced her complete willingness to keep telling her story. Family, tradition, and strong roots are evident in the life and music of Holly Dunn. She always has time to talk—no canned answers, no superficial chatter. This woman is as real as the streets of San Antone, the winds of Lubbock, the back roads of the Hill Country. First we talked in Nashville.

Hudson: You have a current duet on the charts with Michael Martin Murphy, "A Face In The Crowd." How did that association come about?

Dunn: I met his wife about a year ago, and we hit it off. When Michael was trying to decide on a duet partner this time, she brought up my name. He called me, and that was it.

Hudson: How did it feel when that phone call came?

Dunn: It was great.

Hudson: Let's talk about your other singles.

Dunn: My last single was called "Daddy's Hands," which earned me two Grammy nominations. In fact, we're going to the Grammys in a couple of days. It went to number seven on the country charts. "Daddy's Hands" was my fourth single. It's the one that put me on the map.

Hudson: Let's talk about the influences on your work.

Dunn: A lady I worked with this morning has been a big influence, Miss Emmylou Harris. I brought her in to sing background on one of the cuts on my new album. It was a real thrill to be that close to one of my all-time heroes. There are so many wonderful women in country music—men too.

But being a female, I think the women have influenced me more than anything.

Hudson: What was your background?

Dunn: I didn't play San Antonio at all before I left to go to college. I was only eighteen when I left there. I'm a preacher's kid, so I didn't go out to the clubs much when I was growing up. I'm kind of working in reverse. Now I'm going back home and playing the clubs that I probably would have played when I was growing up.

Hudson: What do you enjoy about a Texas audience?

Dunn: I love Texas, period. The people are open and really warm and wonderful. Being a Texan playing the San Antonio market inspires a great response. I feel a lot of warmth and love coming back to me from the stage.

Hudson: What comes to mind when I say, "Let's describe Texas music"?

Dunn: People like Jerry Jeff Walker, Michael Martin Murphy, Willie, and all the folks you would expect somebody to say. There's so much wonderful music happening in Texas all the time. It's been happening for years and years, starting with Bob Wills.

Hudson: Is there a special characteristic of Texas music?

Dunn: In listening to songs for my new album, I noticed that a lot of really great songs that caught my ear weren't a lot of moon, spoon, June love songs, but were from Texas songwriters. I don't know what it is. It may be something in the water down there. Songwriters like Guy Clark have such a unique way of looking at things.

Hudson: It may be the space.

Dunn: It could be. There's definitely a genre of music that is typically "Texas."

Hudson: Are you doing a lot of writing now?

Dunn: I'm trying. Really, I'm probably writing less right now in this part of my career than I ever did because for the past eight years that's all I did—songwriting. I was a songwriter twenty-four hours a day, seven days a week. Now I'm on the road all the time, and if I'm not on the road, I'm doing interviews. Of course, I love to write. I write when I can, usually on the road these days.

Hudson: What causes you to put everything down and start to write?

Dunn: I get driven to it. I have to do it. Something starts happening in my brain and wants to come out. If I don't sit down and do it right then, I lose it. It just has to be done. A lot of times I find now, when I'm on the road, writing in the van or the bus is the best time for my mind if there's not a lot of other music in the car at the time. My mind is free to wander. You're being visually stimulated. When I'm doing something mindless like riding down the road or getting dressed in the morning, that's when I'm most inspired. My mind is free to drift.

Hudson: Is there a song that is special to you?

Dunn: It would have to be "Daddy's Hands." I wrote it for my dad four years ago as a Father's Day present. I had no expectations that it would have commercial appeal. The Whites recorded it first, then I did. I was a songwriter for CBS and somebody pitched it to Sharon White. She heard it and broke into tears and recorded it immediately.

Hudson: How did you become part of this songwriters' pool?

Dunn: I moved here to Nashville and did all sorts of odd jobs like everybody else for about ten months before I got on with CBS.

Hudson: Ten months isn't a long time.

Dunn: You're right. I've known people who've been here ten years and still don't have a writer's deal. I signed with CBS for four years, then went right to MTM as an artist and songwriter over there. I really have been lucky . . . and blessed. Once I got into the business, I never missed a day being employed doing what I love to do. I can't say I've had to struggle and suffer like some I know.

Hudson: You're on the right track.

Dunn: Right on my track. I know where my train's going [laughter], or I hope I do!

When we talked at Aqua Fest in Austin in 1988, Holly had a new album out on MTM, *Across the Rio Grande*.

Hudson: I loved that ballad you sang tonight, "Across the Rio Grande." Let's talk about that song first.

Dunn: It was written by two really fine writers in Nashville, Chick Raines and Don Cook. It's been recorded before, but I didn't care. I just loved the song when I heard it. It really did take me back home to San Antonio and the Mexican-American friends I had there growing up. It gave me the opportunity to sing in Spanish a little bit—a verse or two.

Hudson: Tell me about the new album.

Dunn: It just came out and I'm real proud of it. This is my first official co-production. I worked on it with brother Chris Waters and Warren Peterson. We're all three dyed-in-the-wool Texans. It's my best work ever. We probably went through fifteen hundred to two thousand songs of mine and Chris's and everybody else in the world that we could think of. I ended up writing six of the ten on the album.

Hudson: What's the relationship between the writing process and the performing?

Dunn: When you work with a song from the first letter all the way through the last letter of it, lyrically, and the first note through the last note, it's a very intimate thing. You get to know every syllable, every phrase, every breath, every "T" and "I." You really get involved with it. It's like your child. If I pick another's song to use, it's got to be one that makes me slap my forehead and go, "Why didn't I think of that?"

Hudson: I see a lot of strength in your life, both in your career and in your performance. How do you account for that?

Dunn: I've thought a lot about it because really I shouldn't be as strong-willed as I am. I'm the baby, the only girl in my family, totally sheltered, a marshmallow. I don't really know where I got the determination. Maybe because I had so much done for me, I was determined to stand on my own two feet at some point and prove that I can do it myself. I like to be in control of my life. I don't have to be an absolute dictator, but I do like to have a certain amount of say in what I do, how I look, where I sing. Nobody really tries to tell me what to do—they "try" [laughs] only once, only once, then they never try again. I've always had a real clear sense of who I am, and who I am musically. People know that and respect it.

Hudson: How are you going to balance the performing and the writing?

Dunn: That really is the key word—*balance*. When you become a recording artist, your life suddenly is totally off balance because you are on the road two hundred plus days a year. Aside from the personal stress it causes you and the homesickness, you have a dual career, of songwriter and singer, and something suffers along the way. Last year my songwriting time just went down the tubes. I had to scramble around in December, January, and February, before we cut the album, and write fast and furiously. That's not the way I like to do it. I like to know I have a stockpile of songs already written to choose from. So this year I've already been writing. We're putting songs aside for the next project. And you're right, balance is the key, and it's tough. You really have to make a time to do what you need to do. Look ahead.

Holly's career went as far as it could in one direction. MTM closed. She signed with Warner Records and put out four albums from 1989 to 1992. Then she took a break. The following conversation took place at a time when she decided to sign with another label, River North Nashville, and get back to work, staying in touch with her own direction, her own sense of purpose. It was August 1996.

Hudson: Great to keep up with you this way. Let's talk about the story you tell of those years between 1988 and 1996.
Dunn: It's been character building.
Hudson: What I know about character building is that it involves coming up against obstacles and being willing to overcome them, no matter what.
Dunn: Exactly.
Hudson: What's it been like? Have you gone down some dead-end roads? Did you have to know when to turn around?
Dunn: It's been an interesting road. I mean, it's been a very rocky and twisting road, and there's been so much happening. My relationship with Warner Bros. was a little strange. There was a lot of struggle creatively to get me to leave my partnership with my brother Chris. We had most of my hits together. Why should I walk away from a fruitful partnership? Just to try something else? I finally tried it, and the resulting album really hit the wall and did nothing. I asked off the label in 1992 and decided to kick back and get my head together. It had been a debilitating relationship for me creatively and emotionally. I was in a real bad place in my psyche to go out and try to start all over again. I talked with my management, saying, "I know it's a gamble, but I want to take twelve months off from the label search and just tour and write songs and center myself a little bit before I launch back in to pursuing a record deal somewhere else." They said fine, and as life does sometimes, it takes longer than we anticipate to get the ball rolling. I was enjoying not having the pressure of a record deal, and I kind of enjoyed it a little bit too much. I toyed with the idea of not recording again. I was just out there on my own. Just being Holly Dunn and doing my music and doing it without anybody expecting anything from me. When River North approached me—after two and a half years out

there—it felt right. They're actually based out of Chicago. They've had a successful run with black gospel music. At one point they had ten out of the top twenty songs on the chart on the black gospel chart. They look at me to be the veteran country artist on the new label started up in Nashville.

Hudson: Did you write all the songs on the album?

Dunn: Yes. I had two years of material backlogged and, as a writer, I think it's some of my finest material. It was a rare time to write without a label breathing down my neck. I was as free as I was in the very beginning. I hadn't been tainted by everybody's expectations. It's a rare individual who could care less what other people think, and I'm not such an animal. I wish I was, but I care too much sometimes about pleasing other people.

Hudson: I want to hear more about balancing the expectation that comes with being a mainstream artist with lots of hits and just being Holly Dunn.

Dunn: It's hard. I look to other people to inspire me. Emmylou Harris, Patti Loveless, and Mary Chapin Carpenter have all maintained their integrity in this business. They somehow managed not to sell their souls to the devil and still have the popular success. It's really tough to do. Patti Loveless is on top of the world, but the business is pretty scary. If you want to play the big league and hit the home run, you really have to be careful as you pick the songs you're going to sing. It's a dicey thing to pick material. You don't want to wince every time you hear your song on the radio, and it's harder now because who knows what the radio will play.

Hudson: I've talked before about the influence of location, family tradition, outlaw tradition, and space. Which of your many influences matter most to you?

Dunn: All those things. Dad was a preacher and I grew up singing. I learned to sing harmony next to my mom in a Church of Christ. We had no choir and no instrumentation in the church. Our singing was a cappella. Music was very strong in my family. Mom's a painter. We were very much into the spoken word, the sung word, and art. I grew up in a rich musical place. Of course, San Antonio has that wonderful mixture of Mexican-American culture that permeates everything just like the Cajun culture permeates Louisiana and New Orleans. I find some of my rhythms have a Spanish flavor.

Hudson: Are you working with your brother again?

Dunn: Yeah, and I'm real excited about it. I'm also working with Don

Cook. We've come full circle because the first album Chris and I did together was called *Across the Rio Grande*, and Don, a Texan, wrote that song. Now he's a big music executive and producer of the universe with Brooks and Dunn and the Mavericks. This is the first album I haven't really co-produced in an official way. I've just kind of let them run with it because I feel like I'm in such good hands. I obviously make suggestions, but I'm not getting official credit. I'm totally fine with that.

Hudson: Let's talk about one of the songs you're working on now.

Dunn: "We've Got the Love" is a song Chris and I wrote. It had a real Tex-Mex sensibility to it. A maverick feel. I just love that song. I've been doing it live for the first few months just to see how people would react to it. It's a real sweet song. I wanted to write a positive song about relationships. It seems like we keep writing about broken hearts and being lonesome. I decided I wanted to write a good positive song. "We've got the love to make it. We've got the love to take it all the way. If we've got us to lean on, we've got enough to keep on, you know, we're here to stay. We've got the love." It's a really simply worded song with a beautiful melody. I started the song with the first verse and melody congealing. Then Chris and I had a writing appointment, and he really brought the song home. It was a real magical moment, musically and lyrically.

Hudson: You mention an "appointment." Is that one way you structure the creative process—to set aside time?

Dunn: I get to write with some of the best writers in Nashville, and often they're booked up for six months in advance.

Hudson: What about your road work? Are you playing festivals, clubs, concerts?

Dunn: All kinds of stuff. It's a real typical country music mixed bag. One night we'll be headlining at a fair with eight or ten thousand people in the stands. The next night we'll be opening for some other major artists in a concert setting. Some nights we'll be in a club.

Hudson: Any preference?

Dunn: I actually like the clubs. They're very intimate, and I really feel the people. My favorite venue is a small theater where they're seated. I enjoy going out into the crowd. I can go up and down the aisles and shake hands and sing to them. Literally sing to them instead of just being this little person up on the stage.

Hudson: Sounds like you're still interested in what you're communicating to people.

Dunn: It is important. I don't feel like I've done a very good job if I haven't connected with them, if we haven't broken down that barrier between us by the end of the hour. I want to leave them a little warm fuzzy. I want them to feel good about me. The only way I know how to do that is to get down there amongst them. I don't just run up and down the aisle. I go down for three or four songs sometimes.

Hudson: Do you see yourself as part of a group of women?

Dunn: A nice thing has happened in my life the last few years. The girls— did I say girls—the women I started out with grew up somewhere along the line. Kathy Mattea, Patti Loveless, and Lori Morgan were all women of my graduating class. When you start out you're very protective of your turf. There's competition going on whether you know it or not. Time mellows us, and it's like a new understanding. Things make more sense now.

Hudson: Do you have some heroes?

Dunn: There's a lot of women I admire. I really admire Mary Chapin Carpenter. I admire her articulateness and the depth of her music. She's been noncompromising. I admire Reba McEntire in the way she's handled her career. She's an incredible businesswoman, and she's incredibly good to her fans. She's so giving to the nth degree. Minnie Pearl was still alive when I was inducted into the Grand Ole Opry. She really blew me away as a person. Through the Opry I've gotten to know all kinds of wonderful people. I do that show about six times a year now.

Hudson: Is there anything in Texas that you miss, living in Nashville?

Dunn: Everything. My momma and daddy and everything else.

Hudson: Do you visit often?

Dunn: I have lately. Dad's been very ill.

Hudson: What's your source of strength?

Dunn: I'm stronger than I was. After you get hurt enough times, you either get numb or you start accepting things the way they are. If I were the only artist out there right now struggling to get on the radio, I could take it personally. When I started making records in '86, there were about forty people with recording deals. Six labels, I think, and about forty artists. Now there's about twenty labels and three hundred and sixty artists that have deals right now. It's a physical problem. We can blast and bash radio all the time. They can only play so many artists. But the labels aren't helping any by signing everybody and their dog without spending the time and effort to develop the ones they have. It's just disposable now. I just heard of a group of great artists who got dropped from the label. I feel grateful to have a label that's young and hungry and can't afford for me to fail. I'm ten years into this business, and I've still got a deal, and new things in the pipeline.

Hudson: David Halley, a songwriter from Lubbock, said in one of his songs, "The rain doesn't fall for the flowers when it falls. Rain just falls." I like to think of that when I observe all that happens in our lives.

Dunn: It just falls and gets everybody wet, and that's just it. There's just a lot of factors that are involved in whether a song is going to make it or not. Sometimes it's not fair. That's just life. As long as you know you're doing the best you can, what else can you do? There's a certain lack of control you have in this end of the business, and you just have to pass that football off to somebody else at some point.

Hudson: You're so easy to talk to, we could write a whole book on you. Thanks for all the many visits we've had.

Dunn: When I don't have to worry about working in this business anymore, I will tell the whole story. Because it's a whole other story, let me tell you.

That'll Be the Day

Sonny Curtis

I have to say a big part of it is liking it. You've got to like it to do it. I like to get my guitar. In the winter time I sit downstairs in front of my fireplace with a roaring fire, and it's snowing outside, and boy I can just get inside myself. I could just sit for hours and think, and I love to do that. And when I get it written, I like to rewrite it and just get it right, man. And it takes a long time, but I have the patience for it. I love to think real long thoughts.

Sonny Curtis came to Kerrville to play the annual folk festival. He willingly gave me hours of his time to tell his story, eyes shining as he recounted story after story. After a long journey through all aspects of the music business, he shared his positive outlook on life. We met up several years later at Midem in Cannes, France. We had dinner with Guy Clark, and I heard even more stories.

He continues to play with the Crickets, and he appeared in and wrote the theme song for "The Real Buddy Holly Story," a documentary about the singer's life, produced by Paul McCartney and the British Broadcasting Company.

Sonny is a significant part of the history of Texas music, and he is still a viable force in country music.

Hudson: You have been associated with some very important traditions in Texas music. You've not only been associated with them, I mean you probably are one of the important traditions in Texas music, so I'd like to hear you describe your part in the development of one aspect of Texas music.

Curtis: Well, I don't know if I played that big of a role in the development of music in Texas. I come from West Texas, I say West Texas, up in the Panhandle near Lubbock, I come from a real small town called Meadow, Texas, about thirty miles southwest of Lubbock, and I started out very early playing. My uncle Ed Mayfield was a guitar player who played with Bill Monroe and the Blue Grass Boys. He had a tremendous influence on me. Then I guess when I was about a freshman in high school, I became aware of Chet Atkins, who was a real influence on me. Once I learned that Chet Atkins lick that was all I did all day long, every day, was to play like Chet Atkins. I didn't study or anything like that at school. I didn't feel that was necessary. A friend of mine moved from Meadow up to Lubbock, and he became acquainted with Buddy Holly. He went to the same school Buddy did and Bob Montgomery, who was a friend of Buddy's, and through him I met Buddy and Bob. I joined their band. I played fiddle and guitar, and we had a country band, and while we were still in high school, Elvis Presley came through Lubbock, and this was when he first started out. As a matter of fact, I have heard that Elvis made seventy-five dollars for that show that night in Lubbock; that's how early it was in his career. He made twenty-five for himself and twenty-five apiece for Scotty and Bill. He didn't have the drummer D. J. Fontana at that time. Bill Black just played a percussive kind of bass called the slap bass. We had a guy in our band, Don Guess, who played that kind of bass real well. And of course we fell in love with Elvis Presley at that time, mainly because he had girls all over him, and we saw a bit of value in that [laughter]. We could see that happening to us. Of course it didn't happen to us quite on the grand scale that [laughter] we imagined. But I played of course the Chet Atkins thing I was telling you about. Scotty Moore's style was really Chet Atkins's style. And so I could play those licks the next day after Scotty left town—I could play all that stuff. I could just listen to it on the record, and I had it down because I was used to taking stuff off of Chet Atkins's records and his style was much more difficult. Buddy sang and learned all those songs, and he played my Martin guitar, and I played his Fender guitar, and the next day Elvis left town. We started booking out and playing all of Elvis's music. All of us were still in high school. So we did that for a long time, and we graduated pretty soon after that. Buddy landed the deal with Decca Records in Nashville. We were kind of a rock and roll group, and everybody in those days was trying to capitalize on that rock and roll stuff. So that's what they wanted from Buddy. So Buddy and Don Guess and myself went to Nashville and recorded these records, early records on Decca.

Hudson: Did you record any of your own songs then?

Curtis: One of my songs was "Rock Around with Ollie Vee." We were really kind of Elvis clones, if that's a good word for it. And we weren't satisfied with those records even though listening to them these days, they feel great. Because we all felt good about our music, but we didn't like those records. Buddy, in particular, didn't like them. We, of course, thought we would be instant stars. That's how ignorant and naive we were about the music business in those days, but we came back around Lubbock, Texas, from that trip and you know they played our records around Lubbock on the radio, and that was about it. So we were in about the same boat we were in before we went.

Hudson: Where did you play in Lubbock?

Curtis: I played the Cotton Club with Tommy Hancock. I was in two or three different bands. You know Charlene Hancock and Connie and Tracy. What a wonderful family! I was in Tommy's band, Roadside Playboys, and I played out there with him in the Cotton Club a lot. But I played with Buddy around car-lot openings and grocery-store parking lots.

Hudson: Advertising campaigns and so forth?

Curtis: Yeah, really they'd do remotes from the radio stations. KDAV and KLLL, and they'd have us come out, and we'd set up on the back end of a trailer, and we would play. We did a lot of that. We did fair booster trips. We would get on a tour and go all over the South Plains. We would get off and do fifteen minutes in a town, and they would advertise the fair, and we would go to the next town. We would go to Colorado City, Post, Snyder, Brownfield, and all those towns advertising the fair. We did that sort of thing, and we played roller rinks. Bamboo Club was one of the names of the joints. I left Buddy because Slim Whitman came through town looking for a guitar player, and he paid real money, and for a change I was going to make some money. I remember my salary was a hundred dollars a week. Whew! Wow, that was heavy duty. I was only with Slim about fifteen minutes, but I left Buddy and the guys, and it was probably the best thing that ever happened to Buddy because it threw him out of the Elvis kind of sound and put him into playing his own lead, and he developed that wonderful style which was so great. The chord lead kind of deal. The reason he did that was because he didn't have anyone else to help him, and he and Jerry Allison, the drummer, they played roller rinks around there, like teen hops or whatever you want to call them. Just the two of them, and man, they got so tight playing drums, just drums and guitar.

Hudson: That's an interesting combination.

Curtis: Necessity is the mother of invention. But they got so good, and they could just feel what the next one was going to do. And that's where that great chord lead kind of stuff like "Peggy Sue" and all that stuff came from. He just had to fill it out. And those things really felt good. So they went on and made it real big. I floated off to Nashville, and I lived down there.

Hudson: You floated off to go ahead and write some of the most well known songs in the business.

Curtis: [laughter] Well, I didn't do that right away.

Hudson: Were you aware something significant was happening in Buddy's group?

Curtis: That's sort of a hard question, but I don't think so. Man, at that age we didn't even plan ahead far enough to know about lunch. All we wanted to do was see our name on a record. We loved to play, I will say that. And we loved music. We ate, slept, and breathed music, just lived it all day long and did an awful lot of hanging out, and once in a while we'd get a gig and make a little money. I remember Buddy's brother. He was a contractor; he got us all gigs from time to time. I was a bricklayer's helper once and just about worked my socks off, man I worked about three days and made about twenty-five bucks, and that weekend I went with Buddy to the Clover Club in Amarillo, which was owned by Bob Wills at the time, and we made twenty-five dollars apiece. Went up there and played Saturday night. Well it didn't take me long, you know I may be dumb, but I'm not that dumb, to figure out twenty-five dollars for Saturday night picking at the Clover Club is a lot more fun than working three days to get it as a bricklayer's helper. So I really started concentrating on music. But I don't think we were aware that we were doing anything special. We were just wanting to play and sing and record and try to make a little money.

Hudson: I'd like you to speculate on what is the most significant contribution Buddy Holly has made in music.

Curtis: I don't know if I can or not. I do feel like he had a real influence on early rock and roll music, and he was an influence on the Beatles and that English movement. The Beatles recorded "That'll Be The Day." I believe that was their very first record. Not for sale, but it was a demo. But Buddy was certainly a real influence on the Beatles, and they have even said so. You know Paul McCartney is to this day a real Buddy Holly fan. He has the thing in England he does every September called Holly Days. I have been three times. When I was with the Crickets we went over in 1977 and did a show. And we went back in '79 and did another one with Wings, Paul's group, and some English rock and rollers. Don Everly went with us and Albert Lee and Bob Montgomery. We were all part of one big show. Paul has made a documentary with the BBC about Buddy's life and career, and I, of course, was a big part of that. They sent a crew over from England to Nashville and came out to my house and went over to Jerry Allison's and Joe B. Maudlin's house, and we talked about when we first went to Nashville and that sort of thing.

Hudson: Reminisce a little bit. You drifted off from the group, played with Slim Whitman, made a little bit of hard cash, right? That was a little bit of the motive.

Curtis: [laughter].

Hudson: And then you came back to play with the Crickets after that fateful day?

Curtis: Actually, let me see: I moved to Nashville, and I was with the Philip Morris Country Music Show with Carl Smith, Red Sovine, and Goldie Hill, and then I went to Los Angeles for a while, and I played up in Colorado Springs in a nightclub up there for a while. Then I went to New York and stayed up there for a while.

Hudson: Was your career just always moving and growing?

Curtis: No, it was standing absolutely still.

Hudson: Did you feel like you were treading water?

Curtis: It was standing still.

Hudson: Did you play with Waylon during that time?

Curtis: Waylon and I were good friends back in Texas, and his career was about like mine, but at least he had a job. He was a disc jockey. And that was a talent that I couldn't quite get together.

Hudson: Were you writing during that time?

Curtis: Yeah, I was writing. As a matter of fact I had a minor hit with Webb Pierce which was my very first record. I had written some songs, but a song called "Someday" was recorded by Webb Pierce, and that was kind of a minor country hit. It got in the Top Ten, I think. It was the backside of a honky-tonk song which was a Mel Tillis record. But I met up with the Crickets when they came back from England in 1957, I believe it was, and I was up there recording. I had gotten a recording deal, but it didn't work. They put me with a New York band. Everyone showed up and read the music and smoked, and I didn't feel anything. It wasn't me at all. And I'll never forget going into my first big recording session in New York. Man, I put my suit and tie on like I was going to church, you know? [laughter] But anyway, I was really green. I shouldn't have been up there. It was really dangerous. I was nineteen at the time. It is too dangerous for a guy like me to be lost in New York City. But Buddy and the Crickets really made it pretty big, and we got together and started hanging out. And Buddy and the Crickets split in the summer of '58 because Buddy wanted to live in New York, and he was older than the other guys. He was a little older than all of us, and he had a bit of a sense of direction which the other guys didn't have at the time. The rest of the group wanted to stay in Lubbock and ride motorcycles.

Hudson: They didn't have any space in New York, that's one thing they had in Lubbock.

Curtis: They had small hills in Lubbock to ride your motorcycles. Jerry Allison called me, and I was just totally out of something to do. I was just odd-jobbing-it here and there and making a little money picking here and throwing back cotton and, if you can believe this; I was a salesman at one time. I went around selling advertisements in a brochure for a little fair that they were doing, went around to cotton gins selling these things, and oh, what an awful gig! [laughter] But when you have to make some money, you have to make some money. But Jerry Allison called me and said how about joining back up with the Crickets, and of course I jumped on that right away.

Hudson: Was this with Buddy Holly?

Curtis: No, Buddy had left. He'd moved to New York. He got married, and Jerry got married, and I think a lot of times when people get married, it sort of changes their attitude. It's broken up a lot of groups, and I'm not suggesting that's what broke up their group, and I think for the most part it was a real friendly split. Because they even maintained contact with Buddy. But we played a little bit here and there but mostly hung out and rode motorcycles. But after Buddy died on February 3, 1959, we didn't have very much happening at all and didn't know quite what to do. You know it was a real shock to all of us because Buddy was a real good friend. So the Everly Brothers called us and wanted to know if we would go on the road as their backup band. Everly Brothers had a habit of picking up a band wherever they were. But one night in Florida a couple of years earlier when Buddy was still alive, they didn't have a band, and the Crickets said, "Shoot! We'll be your band tonight," and after they did their show, they went on and backed the Everlys, and the Everlys just loved it. And evidently it went down great, and so they called and wanted us to be the backup band. I did that gig until I got drafted, and that was about a year, and we went to England and Australia, and I was having a good ol' time. The word got out that the Crickets were backing them, especially in England. That's when I realized how important the Crickets were in England, because when we were over there playing the tour with the Everly Brothers, all of a sudden in the *New Music Express*, one of the big major magazines in England, our picture was in there. There I was.

Hudson: Is there any sort of clear way to summarize the history of the Crickets?

Curtis: I guess the best way I can explain it to you is if we had a show and had all the Crickets, everyone who has been a Cricket, we would outnumber the audience more than likely [laughter]. Because there have been a lot of Crickets. Jerry Nayler was a singer for the Crickets for a brief period there around '62. And Earl Sinks, who goes by the name of Earl Richards now, he was a singer when I joined backup for the group.

Hudson: How long did you stay with them?

Curtis: About twenty-five years [laughter].

Hudson: So you were the mainstay part of the group.

Curtis: Well, I joined the group to play guitar, but I was a little too country to sing, so I've always been a little too country for rock and a little too rock for country. I was somewhere in the middle there.

Hudson: Sounds like a good description of Texas music to me.

Curtis: [laughter] But I joined to play guitar, and I sang harmonies and that sort of thing. Earl Sinks was a terrific singer. He had a good feel and had a sound similar to Buddy's, and he left the group, and Trini Lopez was in the group for about fifteen minutes, and he came out to Los Angeles and we played a few gigs with him. Tommy Allsup, he was in the group. Buz Cason was a singer with the group, and after we went through all these singers, it sort of boiled down that we had gigs to pick and somebody had to sing this stuff, and I was sort of elected. It was at one time Glen D. Hardin, Jerry Allison, and me. And Glen D. played piano with his right hand and a new piano bass invented by Fender Rhodes with his left. He played that keyboard bass, and we went on the road like that for a while. We retired three or four times, but there is always something to get us to come back together. And when we moved to Nashville, we weren't playing that Cricket game at all, and Waylon called and said "Hey, let's go on the road this weekend and do some shows out in Arizona just for the fun of it." So we said okay. We went out to Phoenix, Flagstaff, and Tucson for the weekend, and it went so well that we stayed five years. This was in '79. It was right after we had moved to Nashville from L.A. We kind of made a major thrust back in '72. We had what I think was the best rock and roll band the Crickets ever had, except when Buddy was in it. We had Albert Lee playing guitar and singing harmonies, and we had Glen D. Hardin playing piano for us. We had to kind of book our gigs around Elvis's schedule so we'd get Glen D. to go with us, and sometime they conflicted, but Albert filled in pretty well when Glen D. couldn't make it, and Jerry played drums, and I played guitar and fronted the band and sang our songs, and we had a great band. I mean it just cooked. But the sad part is that everywhere we played, people said, "Hey man, play 'That'll Be The Day.' You guys don't sound like the Crickets. What's the deal?" And so, maybe we should have changed our name.

Hudson: People have a habit of wanting to hear what's familiar, and I think when you are going with a real known name or reputation, it's probably harder to get something new across to them.

Curtis: You're exactly right. That was the whole deal. It was a hard lesson for us to learn, and we kind of hung it up from that, and then we all sort of moved to Nashville. But I was writing all this time and studying music.

Hudson: Were you having hit songs along the way?

Curtis: *The Mary Tyler Moore Show* theme just kind of fell in my lap, and that was a good deal for me. It was a real prestigious lick, and it opened up a few doors for me. And I had done some session guitar work in L.A., but

I never did quite get into that too heavy duty, because I'm not that great a reader. I'm still not a great sight reader, and in L.A., you pretty well have to be. It was a good experience, but I started from the *Mary Tyler Moore* theme: it was a springboard into jingles, and I did jingles for about four years before I moved to Nashville, that's all I did. I really would have loved to come back to Texas, and at some point I dream about coming back to Texas. 'Cause I'm a Texan and probably, if I come back to Texas, it will be in the southern part, because Lubbock is a little bit too cold and windy and all that. I hate winters, and I love it in Austin and San Antonio because your winters are only about fifteen minutes long. But Nashville, I get depressed around the middle of February. I just want to slash my wrists because the winters are so long, and the trees are dead and the shadows are long.

Hudson: Are you pursuing anything specific in Nashville?

Curtis: Oh yes, I'm pursuing a career like a songwriting career, a music career, an artist career, you know.

Hudson: But to most folks, you have one.

Curtis: Well, I do. I do, but I'm still pursuing.

Hudson: What are you pursuing? More of the same?

Curtis: [laughter] More of the same. Well you know, life is an ongoing thing; it's something you have to plan daily. You have to say, where am I going to get the money to buy this loaf of bread? Well, I'd better write a song. But it's an ongoing thing. I have a little writer's room down on music row, and I live about an hour out of town. I have a fairly happy existence. I have a farm, and I've always dreamed of that.

Hudson: Do you have a record label right now?

Curtis: I do in England. Record deals are kinda hard to come by over here. But that's all right. My songs get cut. I could go on all day about the music business. The real central music business to me is boriiiiing. Mainstream radio is boring. DJs don't have any regional personality. The DJ in Wichita Falls sounds like the one in Toledo with their radio voices and on and on. Where's Wolfman Jack when we need him? It's like a factory in ways. It's so sterile, I can't believe it. I started my own label just as a tool mainly to perpetuate myself into a record deal. It's called Rabbit Ranch Records.

Hudson: Sounds like you're on the track that's going to make a difference.

Curtis: I tell you what. It doesn't matter if it makes a difference or not, because I am making it. And I mean I'm a music biz guy, and I go out and do my thing. Either they can accept it or not.

Hudson: There is a real appreciation of the songwriter now. Do you feel that in Nashville?

Curtis: Yeah, Nashville is full of great songwriters; the competition is pretty fierce.

Hudson: What do you notice about Texas songwriters?

Curtis: They're not in the mainstream. They're not afraid to put out a record with a "p" pop on it. They're not afraid of a little noise. They're not afraid to use a fiddle on a classical piece.

Hudson: Exactly, all the edges haven't been polished off.

Curtis: That's right man. For myself, I pick good music, and I put my heart into it. I've been doing it forever, and I know what it's about. Don't sign me if you're not going to do something for me. I don't want it, I don't need it.

Hudson: You're getting ready to go judge twenty new songwriters at Rod Kennedy's Folk Festival. Describe your own writing process.

Curtis: Well, I used to write songs on the bus when I was on the road with the Everly Brothers. But it is awfully hard to do that. It's really hard to write on the road. I just create a writing phase now. I block out this time. I get up in the morning, and I go to work and take my cup of coffee downstairs and look at that blank page and go for it.

Hudson: Where does it come from?

Curtis: I don't know. I guess my process is similar to others. I get inspired by good music that I hear. I like classical music, Chopin and Mozart. I'm always on the lookout for hook phrases.

Hudson: So, language triggers your imagination?

Curtis: Yeah, it just comes out of the air. I keep a pad around all the time, even when I'm watching late-night TV. I'm always looking for ideas. I have to say a big part of it is liking it. You've got to like it to do it. I like to get my guitar. In the winter time I sit downstairs in front of my fireplace with a roaring fire, and it's snowing outside, and boy I can just get inside myself, and just, you know, I could just sit for hours and think, and I love to do that. And when I get it written, I like to rewrite it and just get it right, man. And it takes a long time, but I have the patience for it. I love to think real long thoughts.

Sonny and I met up again in 1996 in Cannes, France, at Midem. He was still happy with his life, exuberant about his writing, excited about his career. This life has sustained him.

My Way

Lyle Lovett

The most important part about trying to write anything is having a decent idea to write about. But it also becomes a matter of editing. I find I have a lot to choose from when I have a really good idea. But if I've got a bad idea, I can't think of the next line to save my life.

I first heard Lyle sing around a campfire at the Kerrville Folk Festival. The following interview is a compilation of several conversations we've had over the years. He may be, to borrow a line from one of his signature songs, the ultimate "walking contradiction," and he represents that aspect of Texas music that is eclectic, quirky, and eccentric. Roxy Gordon, publisher of *Picking Up the Tempo*, says, "He's pop country—always has been."

My first conversation with Lyle was at Riverfest in San Antonio in 1986. He was gracious and warm as we talked backstage. He told stories of college life at Texas A&M (he has a background in English and journalism, which he shares with fellow songwriter Robert Earl Keen).

Seeing Lyle return to the folk festival in Kerrville for a knockout performance, then watching him command the entire Majestic Theatre in San Antonio in 1995, serves to remind me that Lyle delivers magic on any stage, opening his arms wide enough to embrace the varied elements of Texas music—with his large band, with his cello player, with his own guitar.

Lyle is part of that literary tradition in the Texas music scene. He has many stories to tell, and the stories on his album *I Love Everybody* include topics like penguins, fat babies, "creeps like me," and skinny legs. His unique sound is ever changing, combining gospel, rhythm and blues, Texas swing, and country and western influences. His self-deprecating style and keen sense of humor are ever present in all of his songs. Now add surrealistic and quirky.

The one constant with Lyle is a wry sense of humor. His story about Texas music adds a dimension; he enlarges the playing field. Lyle has found the audience he has created.

Hudson: How did it all get started for you?

Lovett: I started by playing other people's songs, Texas songwriter songs. My first single was called "Farther Down the Line" and Jerry King—I'll tell you, you need someone like that when you're just getting started—added it to the list of songs playing on the radio that first week it came out. That was a big help, and because he was playing it, some other stations started playing it. That's what it takes, a lot of help from a lot of people.

I've been very lucky, too. With the early record albums I was somewhat conscious of trying to have something to get on the radio. My first two records were played mostly on country and western stations, and so I have always tried to have two or three songs that could work in a country format. With the third album I didn't have much luck at it, but thankfully the songs have gotten played on other kinds of radio. Each new album has really been a combination of old songs and new ones. With the third one I finally got to record some of the blues songs that I've wanted to do for some time. The large band thing was something I've really been wanting to do since I made my first record, which came out in 1986. There's a song on that first one called "The Wedding Song," which had the kind of arrangement that I always wanted to return to.

Hudson: Is that your favorite on the album?

Lovett: Actually, the very first tune. It's a Clifford Brown song called "The Blues Walk." The band played it, and I had absolutely nothing to do with it other than listen to them do it.

Hudson: Unlike a great many songwriters, you seem to have a remarkable degree of freedom in the studio.

Lovett: The record company has been really good to me. They've given me a free hand and enough rope to hang myself. Actually, it's the most wonderful feeling in the world to be able to have a record out on a label like MCA and to be able to have written all the songs. That's all you could ask for if you are a songwriter, getting to sing your own songs on a record. That's everything, everything. It's shooting for the moon.

Hudson: What are your roots in Texas music?

Lovett: I'd grown up in Texas and have been here all my life. My family has been in Texas since the 1840s—on the same piece of ground even. I got really interested in learning how to play guitar by listening to some of the great Texas songwriters—Guy Clark, Townes Van Zandt, B. W. Stevenson, Steven Fromholz, and, of course, Willie Nelson and Jerry Jeff Walker. All those guys were playing around Austin in the '70s. I started out playing their songs. I also play Willis Alan Ramsey and Uncle Walt's Band songs. Then I started making up songs myself. I've always tried to play places where I could play my own songs. Getting in the Kerrville Folk Festival was one of the first big breaks for me. I used to wander from campfire to campfire just playing and learning. Years later I had the chance to play the main stage. Throughout the state there have been great opportunities to play in places like the Waterloo Icehouse and the Cactus Cafe in Austin and Anderson Fair in Houston and the smaller songwriter clubs.

Hudson: Do you have any favorites among the legendary Texas honkytonks?

Lovett: I never really played the honky-tonks. I got to play a few dances but didn't hardly do it that way. I always enjoyed getting to play at Gruene Hall. I got to play on Sunday afternoons, the songwriter shows. But getting in a day early to go hear Clay Baker play on Saturday nights is always great. Getting to actually dance, too. That's one of my favorite spots. There's a place at home in Cypress, Texas, that I used to go to all the time—my mom even used to go there. Everybody calls it the Tin Hall. They had the dance there every Saturday night, so those are the legendary spots around Texas for me. They're a lot of fun to go to.

Hudson: How do you know when you are ready to write a song?

Lovett: I wish I knew. I wish I could make myself ready. Writing songs is really the hardest thing for one to do. It has to be just so, particularly for me, since I really write from personal experience. It helps to be off by myself, and it really helps if I have time just to be able to think about what I want to write. As for what comes first, the words or the music, it all just comes together for me at the same time. I wish I could figure it out better. Maybe I'd write more songs.

Hudson: Do you have anything you rely on like facing a blank wall or hiding out in Colorado?

Lovett: No. I'd like to try that though. I write songs when I spend a lot of time on the road driving, getting to think about things. I get a lot of things started while I'm driving my truck.

Hudson: Let's talk about your songs.

Lovett: I couldn't really say which song has been the most difficult to write, but some songs will be finished in ten minutes and others I work on for several months. Sometimes I get started with an idea and don't finish with it until months later. I work best if I can take time off. But dropping out and taking time off gets kind of scary, too—that puts a lot of pressure on me. I have to organize my everyday life to allow me to always be working on trying to write. If I just try to block time off and do it, it doesn't always work. But if I can organize every day in a way that allows me to think about wanting to write something, it seems to help.

Hudson: How do you find a topic?

Lovett: The most important part about trying to write anything is having a decent idea to write about. But it also becomes a matter of editing. I find I have a lot to choose from when I have a really good idea. But if I've got a bad idea, I can't think of the next line to save my life.

Hudson: What about critics?

Lovett: They have a right to their own opinion, but I'll tell you a funny story. I did an interview with a guy in England who asked me about recording "Which Way Does That Old Pony Ride." He decided I was trying to say something about sexual preference, which I thought was really funny because the song is definitely not about a bent cowboy. Actually I was helping an old girlfriend of mine move, which was a pretty tough deal—not from the emotional standpoint but just the work. Helping somebody move is really hard, and I was thinking of trying to escape, looking for something that would take me in the right direction away from the work. That's all it was, really.

Hudson: Your music often exceeds expectations. Among other surprises, there's a lot of jazz sound, and I've seen you play on more than one occasion with conga drums.

Lovett: Playing in songwriter clubs early on, I couldn't afford to have a band with me. James Gilmer, who lived in Houston, started sitting in with me, and I enjoyed having a beat going on along with my playing. John Hagan would play with me when I was in Austin. So we started putting it all together, the three of us, and I've really enjoyed playing as a trio. Hutch Hutchinson, who has played bass for me, has also been great. He's from the Bonnie Raitt band and played for years with the Neville Brothers and just seems like he's been around the world. They've helped me a lot with my sound.

Hudson: It's still Texas music.

Lovett: You bet. Texas music is from the heart, and it's music about people. It's not necessarily music to be on the radio or music to sell records—it's music about real feelings. That's what I try to do when I write a song.

The Road Goes On . . .

Robert Earl Keen

Laughingly, I might say because I'm inept at everything else. Truest reason is there's nothing I love more than being involved with music. And being involved in the entertainment business. If I'm not entertaining others, I can entertain myself by writing a song. I derive enjoyment and satisfaction from that.

When I met Robert at the Bluebird Cafe in Nashville, he had one self-produced album. Six albums later, and many great concerts behind him, he signed with Arista Austin and began the major label experience. His attitude and his experience parallels that of many Texas songwriters. His independence and his willingness to follow his heart are shared with many other writers. He watched fellow writers Steve Earle, Nanci Griffith, and James McMurtry go on to other levels, and he kept creating his career amidst the struggle. He did the stint in Nashville and returned to Texas. Known for his humor, he now has a following for his serious writing as well. One night at the Scott Theatre in Fort Worth, at a gem of a concert produced by Dan Chandler, I watched two young men, self-proclaimed "Keenoids," get up and act out a choreographed routine as Keen sang. At Luckenbach I watched busloads of students from A&M, his alma mater, push up to the stage and sing loudly along with each song. He's played the Majestic Theatre in San Antonio, John T. Floore Country Store, Willie Nelson's Fourth of July Picnic at Luckenbach, and Leon Springs Cafe. He's played everywhere he wanted, and he's toured Europe. Still accessible to crowds, still willing to interact with fans, Keen is still on the rise. And his writing just keeps getting stronger.

Hudson: I first met you at the Bluebird in Nashville in 1987. Let's do a 1996 update.

Keen: I'm in Athens, Georgia, now working on my first album for Arista Austin. After six on independent labels, this is a different experience for sure. Arista came to Austin and produced Latin records, but they always said they would go to the English-speaking world sooner or later. I always kept in touch and sent them material. I'd give them calls and invite them to shows over and over and over. They decided to sign me. Our office manages me and another guy, Jimmy Perkins. Jimmy Perkins facilitated this deal with Arista Austin. Jimmy and Cameron Randle (Arista Austin) and my wife and I sat down and settled this.

Hudson: I think it's a great match. You have really created a business around your own career, managing yourself and promoting yourself. Now you sell your own work, send out newsletters, and truly have an active fan club. It seems possible to become part of the family. How did that evolve?

Keen: I started sending out simple little cards letting people know where I was playing: "I'm playing at the Acapulco Mexican restaurant." Every "single" act does that. It just started building. I always tried to keep a handle on it, knowing that over the years, fans come and go, but there's a core base that just continues to grow. Being in touch with the fans and being accessible is the key to my success.

Hudson: That's a strong stand to make, rather than Robert Earl Keen waiting around until someone tells him he's good.

Keen: If I had ever done that, I'd be doing something else. I've always believed in myself, and I've been the only one at certain times. That has served me well.

Hudson: You stayed with that. What has given you the strength to do that?

Keen: Laughingly, I might say because I'm pretty inept at everything else. Truest reason is there's nothing I've loved more than being involved with music and being involved in the entertainment business. If I'm not entertaining others, I can entertain myself by writing a song. I derive enjoyment and satisfaction from that.

Hudson: Sounds like a "follow your bliss" statement. What has given you the inner resources to do that?

Keen: I would say my mother never pushed me to do anything but what I wanted to do. She never put a huge price on having to make money. She has a high respect for education and reading and always hinted at that. She had a lot to do with my ability or willingness to say, "This can happen. This can work." You know how parents are. They can say one word and crush you. She never did that. And I'll always be grateful.

Hudson: Everyone talks about your storytelling ability and your photographic representation of a scene. Would you briefly tell the story of your own life as if you were standing outside it?

Keen: In a Shel Silverstein sort of way, there was this kid who heard there was a rainbow on the other side of the mountain. He kept walking and walking, and he stopped by the pond, and there was the turtle and the frog. They said, "We've heard about it, too. But we don't know anybody who's been there." You keep on walking; you walk through deserts and forests and start climbing up this mountain. You start to see a glow along the way which makes you believe there's a possibility of getting there. All along, there's obstacles. The creeks, ravines, lions and tigers and bears. The hardest things to narrate are a person's own self-doubts. We only seem to read about those in an autobiography after the person is dead. All along, the internal battle never seems to stop, along with the external battles. Like people not believing in you. People who say you ought to go back to Texas and get a real job. In some ways in the last three or four years, I've realized all the goals I've had. Willie Nelson recorded my song, along with the Highwaymen. I got four birds with one stone. I've played on huge stages with lots of acts. Done a lot of stuff. Signed with a major label, which I always thought was a big deal. Now I have people congratulating me all the time. Other people think it's a big deal as well. It's almost a harder struggle having racked up six albums on independent labels and then coming to a major label.

Hudson: There's bound to be some new challenges.

Keen: The new challenges for me are with myself and with writing. Where am I going? What am I doing? Now that I have some recognition, I want to sit down and write a piece of music or a song that's really astounding. I can't just repeat what I've done.

Hudson: Standing on the top of success creates many expectations. How do you keep moving?

Keen: I could spend 365 days a year at home. In the past there were so many things I wanted to see and do, so many people I wanted to play with. My goals now are to become a better writer. I've proven to myself that I do have this talent. A lot of times, it was just me in a fantasy land saying, "Yeah, I can do it." Not really knowing. You have to spend time by yourself collecting those thoughts and making them work.

Hudson: Do you have more say about your time now?

Keen: No, my time is completely eaten up. I'm really going through a lot of frustration. I've been here for six weeks, and I can't stand it. The result is going to be wonderful. The producer, John Kean, is a really meticulous and gentle sort of man. He really works and works with the stuff. He's gotten some things out of me and the other musicians. He's presented a challenge which really makes it work.

Hudson: Is your longtime pal Brian Duckworth with you on the project? He really fiddles away at the live performances.

Keen: He's at home. We went through this early on. I've used the other members of the band, but sometimes I have problems with him on recording projects. We don't see eye to eye. It's not a democratic band. I've brought him to a lot of other recording projects, and it doesn't work. He's pretty unhappy about it. I hope he gets over it. I've really gone with what I feel like are the best decisions. I went out on a limb by using my whole band. The record label didn't want me to do that. It's turned out great. I've been vindicated.

Hudson: Did you write some songs for the album?

Keen: Yeah.

Hudson: Guy Clark told me he waits until he has ten good songs and then does an album. James McMurtry said he had to write songs in the studio for the album.

Keen: I'm somewhere in the middle of that. I split the difference. I go in with most of the songs. I went in with eight of the ten songs. I wrote four and dumped two. I'm doing one of James's songs, "Levelland." I wrote seven of the ten songs on the record.

Hudson: That adds texture.

Keen: I did a Dave Allen song called "Fourth of July," and a song by someone no one knows, but I've done it a long time.

Hudson: There seems to be a literary bent in this Texas songwriting. In an old interview with you, you had just bought three Cormac McCarthy books for Christmas presents. I know you have an English degree.

Keen: Cormac is so powerful. He's a real writer in the '90s. Writing sort of shut down with the death of Steinbeck and Hemingway. I got hooked on that whole Cormac thing because he was writing about something I was familiar with, Menard County.

Hudson: Who are you reading now?

Keen: Actually I'm reading Steinbeck again. *Cannery Row*. I go back to that when I can't find anything else.

Hudson: I'd love for you to come be on our speakers series in the Honors Department at Schreiner. It would be a chance for you to share yourself in a little different context.

Keen: Sounds like fun. So far this whole album process is a completely different experience for me, so I can't say what's going to happen with my time. I'm not in control at all. Before, I would call the record label, get some money, and do an album. This deal is different. I had a good thing going before, you know. I'm not doing this because something was wrong before. The main thing a major label offers is a publicity machine which I could never duplicate, never hook into. Love or money won't buy that machinery. That's what record labels provide.

Hudson: It takes a certain amount of bravery to take that next step.

Keen: I'm definitely ambitious.

Hudson: What's something you've imagined that you haven't done? Are you going to write a novel?

Keen: [after hesitating] Yeah, I haven't done that. I used to write it off that my prose was lousy, but I've become a better editor over the years. And I'm a lot more interested in that these day. I think if I got started, I could roll on and make it happen. Other than that, I would like to raise some cows.

Coda

As I bring this collection of stories to an end, I want to repeat that the collection is not definitive, nor does it claim to be inclusive. What we have here is a group of varied and distinct voices, sometimes saying the same thing, sometimes not. These voices address some similar issues even as each speaks alone. My ambition was to talk to songwriters who are passionate about what they do, who would do what they do no matter what. I found that group in Texas. I wanted to give each a chance to talk about significant moments, and I didn't want to guide the conversation in a particular direction. As you can read, many of these conversations seem to overlap and many seem to repeat. That's the nature of the beast. Often the project threatened to overflow all banks. I kept having to make decisions—what to keep, what to cut away. I was encouraged by stories of Michelangelo's work habits: chisel away the excess marble until the shape emerges. I had that opportunity with this material; there was plenty of excess. I cut out many of my own contributions to the dialogue, since at times I traded my share of stories and theories. Many heard the same stories from me.

Shaping the dialogue from oral to written form was a challenge. We do not write as we speak, and I wanted to be sure the distinct quality of each interviewee was preserved in the writing.

Each interview stands alone in its contribution to the collection, but after reading the entire collection one can see many patterns emerge. Some shared notions include that of following your heart, being true to yourself, standing where others fear to stand, taking risks, and walking on the edge. Every artist in this book is following a dream—no accidents here. Most are in touch with their own vision and are willing to keep expressing it in story and song.

We talked about how writers work, how theme gets expressed, how location influences writing, how the business occurs for each, how family and church are part of a Southern heritage, how the Texas mystique shows up, how writing becomes a chance to say "what is," and how passion can keep us alive. It can also kill us. Since the manuscript came into being, Stevie Ray Vaughan, Townes Van Zandt, Blaze Foley, Jimmie Dale Court, Jubal Clark, Johnny Copeland have all died early deaths. Each of these men gave their all to their choice to perform. The life on the road killed Townes, while an accident on the road killed Stevie Ray. Blaze was in the wrong place at the wrong time. Johnny Copeland's heart gave out; Jubal fought cancer to the end. Jimmie Dale had a heart attack at age forty-five.

This collection gives a perspective, often from the edge, of lives willing to take risks. The courage to take risks is an integral part of the creative process, of "telling stories, writing songs."

Biographies and Selected Discographies

Ball, Marcia. Born March 20, 1949, in Orange, Texas, Marcia calls Austin home now. She is a blend of East Texas blues and southwest Louisiana swamp rock, having grown up in a place that produced such blues greats as Janis Joplin, Johnny and Edgar Winter, Clifton Chenier, and Kenny Neal, to name a few. Professor Longhair is a major influence. She began playing piano at the age of five, played in a psychedelic band, Gum, during college, and played a part in the cosmic cowboy revolution with Freda and the Firedogs. She also hails Patsy Montana as an influence. Marcia did a series of albums for Rounder and a collaboration with Lou Ann Barton and Angela Strehli for Antone's label. She is an educated businesswoman as well as a songwriter and performer. Marcia has established herself as an important player in the blues scenes in both New Orleans and Austin and continues to work at festivals throughout the United States, Canada, and Europe.

Selected Discography:

1980 *Freda and the Firedogs Live* (Big Wheel)
1983 *Soulful Dress* (Rounder)
1985 *Hot Tamale Baby* (Rounder)
1989 *Gatorhythms* (Rounder)
1990 *Dreams Come True* (Antone's)
1997 *Let Me Play with Your Poodle* (Rounder)
1998 *Sing It!* (Rounder)

Clark, Guy. Born November 6, 1941, in Monahans, Texas, Guy now lives in Nashville and writes songs. He spent time in Houston, met Townes

Van Zandt and Lightnin' Hopkins, and generated a distinct voice as both songwriter and performer. His first recording contract was with RCA in 1975, and the album was *Old # 1*. By the mid-1980s his songs had been made into hits by country stars such as Johnny Cash, Ricky Skaggs, George Strait, Vince Gill, The Highwaymen, and David Allan Coe. He tours regularly and has a following in Europe.

Selected Discography:

> 1975 *Old #1* (Sugar Hill)
> 1976 *Texas Cookin'* (Sugar Hill)
> 1978 *Guy Clark* (Warner Bros.)
> 1981 *South Coast of Texas* (Warner Bros.)
> 1983 *Better Days* (Warner Bros.)
> 1989 *Old Friends* (Sugar Hill)
> 1992 *Boats To Build* (Elektra/Nonesuch)
> 1995 *Dublin Blues* (Elektra)
> 1997 *Keepers* (Sugar Hill)

Clark, Jubal. Born March 17, 1929, in Bailey County in the Texas Panhandle, Jubal moved to Austin in the early 1950s after a stint in the navy. He quickly became part of the "Outlaw" country music scene. His friendship with Willie Nelson resulted in numerous appearances at Willie's picnics and Farm Aid Benefits, as well as roles in several of Willie's movies. Blaze Foley also became a friend and sometime housemate. There were several flirtations with commercial success, but signed deals never materialized. A six-song cassette, *Gypsy Cowboy,* was released on Outhouse Records in 1990. Two weeks before his death on May 16, 1997, Jubal gave final approval for a digital remix of *Gypsy Cowboy* that also includes three live cuts recorded at the Austin Outhouse in 1993. The legacy of Jubal Clark includes hundreds of original songs, his beloved fifteen acres in the Hill Country, and the many friends and fans of the man and his music. His life and songs are mirrors of each other.

Selected Discography:

> 1990 *Gypsy Cowboy* (cassette/Outhouse Records)
> 1997 *Gypsy Cowboy* (CD/remix)

Copeland, Johnny. Born March 27, 1937, in Homer, Louisiana, he died July 3, 1997. He was the son of sharecroppers, and his father died when Johnny was very young. His first gig was with friend Joe "Guitar" Hughes. Soon after Hughes became ill, the young Copeland discovered he could be a front man and deliver vocals as well as anyone around Houston at that time. He also took up boxing when his family moved to Houston. He relocated to New York in 1974 and found receptive audiences. He recorded seven albums for Rounder Records, beginning in 1971. He discovered a congenital heart defect during a hectic tour in 1994. Even after being put on a waiting list for a heart transplant and being dependent on an LVAD (a recent innovation for patients suffering from heart defects), he continued to tour. As he struggled with his heart problems, Johnny Copeland became a living symbol of the perseverance and determination that are the basis of so many great blues lyrics.

Selected Discography:

1977 *Copeland Special* (Rounder)
1983 *Texas Twister* (Rounder)
1986 *Bringin' It All Back Home* (Rounder)
1992 *Flyin' High* (Verve)
1993 *Further Up the Road* (AIM)
1996 *Jungle Swing* (Verve)
1996 *Live in Australia 1990* (Black Top)

Court, Jimmie Dale. Born July 22, 1951, in San Antonio, Texas, Jimmie Dale died October 9, 1996, just a few short weeks after the Kerrville tribute to his grandfather, Jimmie Rodgers. A drummer and songwriter, Jimmie Dale performed a mixture of his grandfather's tunes, originals, and blues-country-rock standards around Texas. Based in Austin most of his life, Jimmie Dale traveled to Meridian each year for the annual tribute to Jimmie Rodgers and was the focus of the tribute each September in Kerrville. He is survived by two sons, Austin and Cody, living in San Antonio.

Selected Discography:

1996 *Jimmie's Texas Blues* (Inherited Productions, Austin)

Curtis, Sonny. Born May 9, 1937, in Meadow, Texas, Sonny began performing as a teen on local radio in Lubbock, playing fiddle on the popular *Buddy and Bob* show, which featured a young Buddy Holly. Waylon Jennings was a DJ at the station. Sonny joined Holly's band, the Three Tunes, in 1956, as a fiddler, guitar player, and backup singer. In 1959, after Holly's tragic death, his band, the Crickets, asked Sonny to become their lead guitarist and singer. He was drafted in 1960 and was stationed in Fort Ord, where he wrote the song "Walk Right Back." He had his biggest success as a songwriter, his repertoire including "I Fought the Law"; the theme song for the *Mary Tyler Moore Show,* "Love Is All Around"; the theme song for "Evening Shade," and many more. In the early 1980s, he and two former Crickets, Joe B. Maudlin and Jerry Allison, reunited and performed with Waylon Jennings' show. In 1991 he was inducted into the Songwriters Hall of Fame.

Selected Discography:

> 1968 *1st of Sonny* (Viva)
> 1969 *Sonny Curtis Style* (Elektra)
> 1980 *Love Is All Around* (Elektra)
> 1987 *Spectrum* (Nightlite)

Dobson, Richard. Born March 19, 1942, in Tyler, Texas, Richard has a college degree in Spanish and served a stint in the Peace Corps—and many stints in Nashville. He tours Europe regularly with albums on Brambus Records in Switzerland. His songs have been recorded by David Allan Coe, Guy Clark, Lacy J. Dalton, Nanci Griffith, Kelly Willis, Rick Densmore, and Pinto Bennett. He spends his time "on the road," and when he lands, he writes. *Don Ricardo's Life and Times* is his newsletter, and he's just finished a book project about his life on the road with many other Texas songwriters.

Selected Discography:

> 1986 *True West* (RJD Records, Nashville)
> 1990 *Richard Dobson and the State of the Heart* (Brambus Records, Switzerland)
> 1993 *Blue Collar Blues* (Brambus Records, Switzerland)
> 1994 *Amigos: Richard Dobson Sings Townes Van Zandt* (Brambus Records, Switzerland)

1996 *Love Only Love* (Brambus Records, Switzerland)
1998 *Salty Songs* (Brambus Records, Switzerland)

Dunn, Holly. Born August 22, 1957, in San Antonio, Texas, Holly had barely graduated from college when she found herself soaring to success with her first group, Freedom Folk. She moved to Nashville in 1978 and, after working odd jobs and singing demos, signed with CBS. In 1984 she was hired as a songwriter for MTM, and several top female singers recorded her songs. Her debut album appeared in 1986, around the same time "Daddy's Hands," her breakthrough hit, was released. During the 1990s her popularity declined, resulting in Dunn's departure from Warner in 1993. In 1995 she released *Life and Love and All the Stages* followed by *Leave One Bridge Standing* in 1997. She began working with her brother, Chris Waters, and ended up working with him again after leaving Warner Bros. She made her debut as a producer in 1988 with *Across the Rio Grande*.

Selected Discography:

1986 *Holly Dunn* (MTM)
1988 *Across the Rio Grande* (MTM)
1989 *Blue Rose of Texas* (Warner Bros.)
1992 *Getting It Dunn* (Warner Bros.)
1995 *Life and Love and All the Stages* (River North Nation)
1997 *Leave One Bridge Standing* (A&M)

Earle, Steve. Born in Virginia, Steve was living in San Antonio, Texas, by the time he was two. He started playing guitar at thirteen and was touring the state playing by the time he was sixteen. He spent time in Houston, where he met Guy Clark and Townes Van Zandt. In 1974 Steve moved to Nashville. After several years there he moved back to Texas and continued south to San Miguel de Allende in Mexico and kept writing songs. In 1979 he moved back to Nashville and, with producer Tony Brown's help, came to MCA. With long hair, beard, and shades, Steve kept pushing the limits of country music with 1988's rock-influenced *Copperhead Road*. And he began making headlines for more than his music. In 1994, after his release from prison on heroin charges, Steve released three albums in three years. He and longtime friend Jack Emerson started a label, E-

Squared, which was picked up for distribution by Warner Bros. His final album in that trilogy, *El Corazon*, is a statement from his heart and more evidence that he is back to stay and with a vengeance. He is working on a book of short stories.

Selected Discography:

1986 *Guitar Town* (MCA)
1987 *Early Tracks* (Epic)
1988 *Copperhead Road* (MCA)
1990 *Hard Way* (MCA)
1995 *Train a Comin'* (Winter Harvest)
1996 *I Feel Alright* (Warner Bros.)
1997 *El Corazon* (Warner Bros.)

Ely, Joe. Born February 9, 1947, in Amarillo, Texas, Joe grew up in Lubbock. He got his start in the early 1970s, working with Butch Hancock and Jimmie Dale Gilmore in a group called the Flatlanders. He later formed his own eclectic group and signed with MCA in 1977. *Honky Tonk Masquerade,* the album that followed, was considered one of modern country's most ambitious. He has received attention from rock fans and garnered ecstatic reviews in country and pop magazines. After being dropped by MCA in 1983, he lay low, touring and writing, until 1987 when he signed with Hightone and released *Lord of the Highway*. He later re-signed with MCA, releasing *Love and Danger* and *Letter from Laredo*. In February of 1998 he played to a packed house at Gruene Hall. Teye, a Flamenco guitar player, added just the distinct sound to garner Ely even more attention. He calls Austin home now.

Selected Discography:

1977 *Joe Ely* (MCA)
1978 *Honky Tonk Masquerade* (MCA)
1979 *Down on the Drag* (MCA)
1980 *Live Shots* (MCA)
1981 *Musta Notta Gotta Lotta* (MCA)
1984 *Hi-Res* (MCA)
1987 *Lord of the Highway* (Hightone)
1992 *Love and Danger* (MCA)

1995 *Letter to Laredo* (MCA)

Foley, Blaze. Born December 18, 1949, Blaze lived an unconventional life, followed his dreams, and died February 1, 1989, in what was called "an unfortunate homicide." Lucinda Williams said, "Blaze Foley was a genius and a beautiful loser." His death came during the rebirth of his career. He had recorded *Live at the Austin Outhouse* cassette and was nearly finished with the overdubs at Bee Creek studio for a new album on Heartland Records. He was often heard to say, "I only write songs because I feel them."

Friedman, Kinky. Born in Palestine, Texas, on October 31, 1944, he attended the University of Texas, served three years in the Peace Corps stationed in Borneo, and by 1971 had founded his band, Kinky Friedman and His Texas Jewboys. A wild and colorful group, known for songs like "They Ain't Making Jews Like Jesus Anymore," they toured with Bob Dylan's Rolling Thunder Revue. After the band disbanded in the late 1970s, Friedman moved to New York and played the Lone Star Cafe. He turned toward writing and not only wrote for *Rolling Stone* magazine, but also became a mystery writer of tales such as *Greenwich Killing Time, A Case of Lone Star, Elvis, Jesus & Coca Cola, God Bless John Wayne* and *Roadkill*, a mystery generated around Willie Nelson and family on the road. Kinky traveled with them during his research.

Selected Discography:

1973 *Sold American* (Vanguard)
1974 *Kinky Friedman* (Varese Saraban)
1976 *Lasso from El Paso* (Epic)
1983 *Under the Double Ego* (Sunrise)
1992 *Old Testaments & New Revelations* (Fruit of the Toon)
1995 *From One Good American to Another* (Fruit of the Toon)

Hester, Carolyn. Born in 1937 in Waco, Texas, Carolyn was an important figure of the early 1960s folk revival. Her albums were produced by Norman Petty (Buddy Holly's producer), Tom Clancy, and John Hammond. Her first Columbia album is notable for one of the first appearances of Bob Dylan on record (playing harmonica). In the 1980s Carolyn became a mentor for budding talent Nanci Griffith, whom she met at the Kerrville Folk Festival. Based in California, Carolyn serves on the board for the Kerrville Folk Festival and travels to Texas several times a year.

Selected Discography:

1962 *Carolyn Hester* (Columbia)
1963 *This Is My Living* (Columbia)
1964 *That's My Song* (Dot)
1965 *At Town Hall* (Dot)
1990 *At Town Hall* (Bear Family)
1996 *Texas Songbird* (Road Goes On Forever)

Hinojosa, Tish. Born December 6, 1955, in San Antonio, into a large family, Tish went to parochial school, listened to the songs of her parents as well as the Beatles and Woodstock, and left Texas for Taos, where she further honed her songwriting. Next stop was Nashville. She found that incorporating her ethnic heritage into her music was a problem at that time (early 1980s), and she returned to New Mexico in 1985, where she recorded *Taos to Tennessee*. She moved to Austin in 1988 and continued expressing her social concerns. "Something in the Rain" is a song about the danger of picking pesticide-laced crops, told through the eyes of a small boy. Tish also has a loyal following overseas.

Selected Discography:

1985 *Taos to Tennessee* (Independent)
1989 *Homeland* (A&M)
1990 *Culture Swing* (Rounder)
1992 *Taos to Tennessee* (Watermelon)
1994 *Destiny's Gate* (Warner Bros.)
1995 *Frontejas* (Rounder)
1996 *Dreaming from the Labyrinth* (Warner Bros.)
1997 *Soñar del Laberinto* (Warner Bros.)

Hubbard, Ray Wylie. Born November 13, 1946, in Soper, Oklahoma, Ray was a leading figure of the progressive country movement of the 1970s. He and his family moved to Dallas during the mid 1950s. He formed a trio called Three Faces West which played regularly in Red River, New Mexico, a musical hotbed for artists like Steve Fromholz and Bill and Bonnie Hearne. The success of Jerry Jeff Walker's rendition of Hubbard's song "Up against the Wall Redneck Mother" guaranteed him instant cult status at the same time he formed a group called the Cowboy Twinkies, which included Clovis Roblain and Terry Joe "Buffalo" Ware. They were a "cowpunk" group, playing Merle Haggard and Led Zeppelin. He cut a live album with the Bugs Henderson Trio. He continued to tour constantly for about eight years, then in 1992 issued *Lost Train of Thought* on his own label, followed in 1995 by a Dejadisc release of *Loco Gringo's Lament*. Ironically, he then found a label for his album *Dangerous Spirits* in Europe, and Rounder picked it up here for distribution. The fate of a songwriter walking on the edge—always looking for a home. He has also been a guest at Schreiner College, sharing his insights on songwriting and life with English classes.

Selected Discography:

1978 *Off the Wall* (Lone Star)
1994 *Loco Gringo's Lament* (Dejadisc)
1995 *Lost Train of Thought* (Dejadisc)
1997 *Dangerous Spirits* (Philo/Rounder)
      Ray Wylie Hubbard and the Cowboy Twinkies (Warner Bros.)
      Caught in the Act (Waterloo)
      Something about the Night (Renegade)

Keen, Robert Earl. Born in Houston in 1956, Keen now lives in Bandera, Texas. He graduated in 1980 from Texas A&M, where he developed a friendship with Lyle Lovett. An interest in bluegrass led to an interest in songwriting, and he co-wrote "This Old Porch" with Lyle. Robert had a short stint in Nashville, but decided Texas was a better base. He has developed a loyal following of fans, many from his alma mater, Texas A&M. Lyle Lovett, Nanci Griffith, Joe Ely, Kelly Willis, and the Highwaymen are some of the acts who have recorded his songs. Known for his ability to tell a story and to entertain a crowd, Robert is a songwriter on the move. Guy Clark, Jerry Jeff Walker, and Townes Van Zandt were also influences on his writing.

Selected Discography:

1984 *No Kinda Dancer* (Philos)
1988 *Live Album* (Sugar Hill)
1989 *West Texas Textures* (Sugar Hill)
1993 *Bigger Piece of Sky* (Sugar Hill)
1994 *Gringo Honeymoon* (Sugar Hill)
1995 *Merry Christmas from the Family* (Sugar Hill)
1996 *Number 2 Live Dinner* (Sugar Hill)
1997 *Picnic* (Arista)

Lovett, Lyle. Born November 1, 1957, in Klein, Texas, near Houston, Lyle was raised on a family horse ranch in a town named after his great-grand-father, a Bavarian weaver. He began writing songs in the late 1970s while attending Texas A&M, where he studied journalism and German. He didn't pursue a musical career in earnest until he returned from touring Europe (while studying in Germany) in the early 1980s. He then showed up at the Kerrville Folk Festival as a regular around the campfires. Guy Clark heard a demo tape of Lyle's songs in 1984 and directed it to Tony Brown (a producer who has worked with many Texas artists) at MCA Records. Lyle signed with MCA/Curb in 1986, releasing his first album, *Lyle Lovett*, which received excellent reviews; five of the songs reached country Top Forty. His second album, *Pontiac*, revealed how eclectic and literate Lyle was and expanded his audience in the pop and rock markets. His country audience started shrinking. He assembled a large band and recorded his third album. He settled in California and pursued a variety of projects: producing Walter Hyatt's *King Tears* album, an acting debut in *The Player* by Robert Altman, singing on an album with Leo Kottke, and donating a cover of "Friend of the Devil" to the Grateful Dead tribute album. His fourth album, *Joshua Judges Ruth*, is his most successful album to date, peaking at number fifty-seven and going gold. In 1996 he released *Road to Ensenada*, an album that performed strongly on country charts, entering at number four.

Selected Discography:

1986 *Lyle Lovett* (Curb)
1987 *Pontiac* (Curb)
1989 *Lyle Lovett and His Large Band* (Curb)

1992 *Joshua Judges Ruth* (Curb)
1994 *I Love Everybody* (Curb)
1996 *Road to Ensenada* (Curb)
You Can't Resist It (MCA)

McClinton, Delbert. Born November 4, 1940, in Lubbock, Delbert was to achieve his first success in music through his harmonica. His harmonica work on Bruce Channel's hit, "Hey Baby," got him on the big-time circuit. He eventually toured England and gave harmonica lessons to a young John Lennon. He fronted the Rondells in the 1960s and charted in the 1970s with Glen Clark as Delbert and Glen. With roots in Fort Worth, he is also part of North Texas musical history. He has released many albums on various labels and guested on albums with everyone from Roy Buchanan to Bonnie Raitt. His album on Rising Tide Label, along with the video that aired on Country Music Television, created a stir. Gary Nicholson, another songwriter with roots in Fort Worth, wrote or co-wrote all but one song on this album.

Selected Discography:

1975 *Victim of Life's Circumstances* (ABC)
1978 *Very Early Delbert McClinton* (Lecam)
1980 *Jealous Kind* (Capitol)
1989 *Honky Tonkin'* (Alligator)
1989 *Live from Austin* (Alligator)
1992 *Never Been Rocked Enough* (Curb)
1993 *Delbert McClinton* (Curb)
1997 *One of the Fortunate Few* (Rising Tide)
Honky Tonk'n Blues (MCA)

McMurtry, James. Born March 18, 1962, in Fort Worth, James comes from a literary background. His father, Larry, gave him his first guitar at seven, and his mother, an English professor, taught him how to play it. He spent time in a boarding school in the East and began performing his own songs while a student at the University of Arizona. He moved to San Antonio and played the small-club circuit and entered the New Folk Contest at the Kerrville Folk Festival, where he was chosen as one of the six winners. John Mellencamp received a demo tape and, duly impressed, served as co-producer on McMurtry's debut album, *Too Long in the Wasteland*. Now based in Austin with his wife, Elena, and son, Curtis, James has completed a three-album contract with Columbia and is on Sugar Hill, a label which also lists Guy Clark and Townes Van Zandt.

Selected Discography:

1989 *Too Long in the Wasteland* (Columbia)
1992 *Candyland* (Columbia)
1995 *Where'd You Hide the Body* (Columbia)
1997 *It Had To Happen* (Sugar Hill)

Moffatt, Katy. Born November 19, 1950, in Fort Worth, Katy started out singing Leonard Cohen's "Dress Rehearsal Rag" in a local coffeehouse. She has worked in radio, on films, and with several record labels in both country and rock fields. Her pop album, *Kissin' in the California Sun* (1977) came out while she was opening for Charlie Daniels, Warren Zevon, Muddy Waters, and Steve Martin. She also worked with Willie Nelson, John Prine, Jerry Jeff Walker, and the Allman Brothers. During the early 1980s, she sang with Tanya Tucker, Lynn Anderson, and Hoyt Axton until she gained a contract with Permian Records in 1983. Her partnership with producer Jerry Crutchfield spawned three impressive singles. In the mid-1980s, when Permian folded, she moved to Rounder, where she recorded a duet with her brother, an excellent songwriter, Hugh Moffatt. She has a loyal following in Europe and debuted at the Wembly Festival in England in 1990. She lives in California and continues to write and perform.

Selected Discography:

1976 *Katy Moffatt* (Columbia)
1976 *Walkin' on the Moon* (Philo)
1978 *Kissin' in the California Sun* (Columbia)
1992 *Indoor Fireworks* (Red Moon)
1993 *Greatest Show on Earth* (Philo)
1994 *Hearts Gone Wild* (Watermelon)
1996 *Midnight Radio* (Watermelon)

Nelson, Willie. Born in Fort Worth on April 30, 1933, raised in Abbott, Willie spent the 1960s writing songs for stars like Ray Price ("Night

Life"), Patsy Cline ("Crazy"), Faron Young ("Hello Walls"), and Billy Walker ("Funny How Time Slips Away"). During the early 1970s he became part of the burgeoning "Outlaw" country movement. A genuine star, recognizable in both pop and country circles, he has never played it "safe" musically. Always ready to take a risk, he borrowed from a wide variety of styles and created a distinctive sound. No one sounds like Willie Nelson, and he is easily recognizable. He continues to be a prolific writer and performer, entertaining huge crowds each year at his annual Fourth of July Picnic, now held in Luckenbach, Texas. In 1993 he was inducted into the Country Music Hall of Fame. He also has movie credits. After receiving a bill for $16.7 million in back taxes, he lost most of his assets and released a double album, *Who'll Buy My Memories? The IRS Tapes*. By 1993, his debts paid off, Willie had launched another phase of his recording career with *Across the Borderline*, a project with Don Was featuring cameos by Bob Dylan, Bonnie Raitt, Paul Simon, Sinead O'Connor, David Crosby, and Kris Kristofferson. One of Willie's many commitments in life is to help out with the plight of the American farmer. In 1985 he founded Farm Aid, and he continues to do charity work.

Selected Discography:

1962 *And Then I Wrote* (Liberty)
1971 *Willie Nelson and Family* (RCA)
1974 *Phases and Stages* (Atlantic)
1978 *Stardust* (Columbia)
1980 *Honeysuckle Rose* (Columbia)
1982 *Pancho & Lefty* (Columbia)
1993 *Across the Borderline* (Columbia)
1996 *How Great Thou Art* (Fine Arts)
1997 *Willie* (RCA)
1997 *Songs from the Songwriter* (CBS)

Nunn, Gary P. Born December 4, 1945, designated as "Official Ambassador to the World" by Texas governor Mark White in 1985, Gary P. Nunn began his musical career as a seventh grader in a garage band in Brownfield, Texas. He attended Texas Tech University and South Plains College while pursuing music on the weekends. In 1968 he transferred to the University of Texas at Austin and immersed himself in the local music scene. He joined the "Outlaw" music scene in 1972 when Michael Martin

Murphey, Jerry Jeff Walker, and Willie Nelson all moved to Austin. At one time he was playing bass for all three. He led the Lost Gonzo Band, honed his songwriting skills, and became an integral part of Texas music history. Gary moved out on his own in 1980, assuming responsibility for his own career without the aid of an agent or manager. Now he performs forty-eight weekends out of the year with his band, the Sons of the Bunkhouse, maintains the A-O Ranch, an eight-hundred-acre cattle ranch in eastern Oklahoma and site of the Terlingua North Summer Social Maverick Chili Cookoff and Music Festival, and enjoys a near folk hero status in Texas. Known for his accessibility, his songs, his association with the state of Texas, his warm smile, and his lively and danceable performances, Gary P. Nunn has never met a stranger.

Selected Discography:

1980 *Nobody But Me* (Turnrow Records)
1984 *Home with the Armadillo* (Guacamole Records)
1989 *For Old Times Sake* (A-O Records)
1991 *Rendezvous* (Gonzo Records)
1993 *Totally Guacamole* (Campfire Records)
1994 *Roadtrip* (Campfire Records)
1996 *Lost Gonzo Band—Dead Armadillos* (Demon Records, UK)
1997 *Best of Gary P. Nunn* (Campfire Records)

Powers, Freddy. Born October 13, 1931, in Duncan, Oklahoma, and raised in Seminole, Texas, Freddy got his musical training in West Texas honkytonks. His career covers a wide range of styles—comedy, Dixieland, country, and country-jazz. His favorite stomping grounds are the Nevada lounges, but he's played many Nevada main showrooms. In the 1980s, he co-wrote songs with Merle Haggard. During this association, Freddy received five BMI Awards for number one songs; CMA's prestigious Triple Play Award for writing three number one songs in a twelve-month period; and Nashville Songwriters Assoc. Award. He's also written for Ray Charles, George Jones, Janie Frickie, and Willie Nelson. In the 1980s, Freddy sang, played guitar on, and co-produced Willie Nelson's *Somewhere Over the Rainbow* million-seller album. Well-respected in the business as one of the best rhythm guitar players around, Freddy says one of his favorite accomplishments is his *Country Jazz Singer* album. Freddy has appeared on many national TV programs, including *Austin City Limits*. He and his band have toured and opened the show for Merle Haggard.

Selected Discography:

1995 *The Country Jazz Singer* (In Orbit Records)
1997 *The Hottest Thing in Town* (Powerhouse Music)

Rhodes, Kimmie. Born March 6, 1954, in Lubbock, Kimmie says her daddy gave her dimes to sing gospel songs for his buddies when she was six years old, and she hasn't stopped singing since. She moved to Austin in 1979, where she met producer and husband, Joe Gracey. In 1981 she recorded her first album, *Kimmie Rhodes and the Jackalope Brothers*, when Willie Nelson invited her to use his studio on the Pedernales River. In 1985 she recorded her second album, *Man in the Moon*. Her third album, *Angels Get the Blues*, recorded in the original Sun Studio in Memphis, was released in 1989. These records, released on an English label, led to a series of British and European tours that received rave reviews. She has been a regular at the Willie Nelson picnics and recorded two of her originals for his album *Just One Love* on Justice Records. Kimmie's CD *West Texas Heaven* features twelve of her original songs and includes duets with Waylon Jennings, Townes Van Zandt, and Willie Nelson. Kimmie now lives in Austin and performs with the acoustic band that she has assembled to promote the new record, which features Joe Gracey on bass, Gabe Rhodes on guitar, and Kimmie on rhythm guitar and vocals. Yes, a family affair.

Selected Discography:

1985 *Kimmie Rhodes and the Jackalope Brothers* (Jackalope Records)
1988 *Man in the Moon* (Heartland Records)
1993 *A Lot Like Texas* (Red Moon Records, Switzerland)
1996 *West Texas Heaven* (Justice Records)
1997 *Jackalopes, Moons & Angels* (Jackalope Records)

Rodriguez, Johnny. Born December 12, 1952, in Sabinal, Texas, Johnny got his first guitar when he was seven as a gift from his brother. By the time Johnny was eighteen, he had been in jail four times. Happy Shahan, a promoter at Alamo Village, heard of him through a Texas Ranger named Joaquin Jackson and hired him for his shows at the village. Johnny was nineteen. Tom T. Hall and Bobby Bare heard him and took him to Nashville. His first single, "Pass Me By," reached the Top Ten in 1973, beginning a string of fifteen consecutive Top Ten hits that ran through 1977. When he signed with Epic in 1979, his career was entering a period of decline, but he continued to have Top Forty hits into the mid-1980s. His Hightone album in 1996, *You Can Say That Again*, marked a return in his career. He also began working on a movie with Little Joe Hernandez, performed at fundraisers, and continued to battle with some of his own personal demons.

Selected Discography:

    1973 *Introducing* (Mercury)
    1973 *All I Ever Meant To Do Was Sing* (Mercury)
    1979 *Rodriguez* (Epic)
    1986 *Full Circle* (Epic)
    1988 *Gracias* (Capitol)
    1993 *Run for the Border* (Intersound)
    1993 *Tienen Sabor* (Combo)
    1996 *You Can Say That Again* (Hightone)
          Ridin' My Thumb to Mexico (Polygram)
          Desperado (Mercury)
          Coming Home (EMI Latin)

Royal, Darrell. Thirty-two years old when he took the head coaching job at the University of Texas in December of 1956, he came to the Austin campus with a folksy sense of humor that produced a phenomenon called "Royalisms" and an innovative style of football that produced almost instant success. In 1962 he assumed the dual role of athletics director and head football coach, and when he resigned from the football job following the 1976 season, he remained as director of athletics for three years. In January 1980 he left the Athletics Department and became a special assistant to the university's president, Peter Flawn. Royal is a music lover and hosts songwriters circles at his house, insisting that everyone listen and everyone share a song. His friendship with Willie Nelson is legendary in the lore of Texas. Lyndon Johnson once wrote, "I'm not a football fan, but

I am a fan of people, and I am a Darrell Royal fan because he is the rarest of human beings."

Shaver, Billy Joe. Born September 15, 1941, in Corsicana, Texas, Billy Joe has the upbringing he wrote out in the song "I Been to Georgia on a Fast Train." He lived on his grandma's old-age pension, worked on his uncles' farms, lost part of his fingers during a job at a sawmill, and got his country learning "picking cotton, raising hell, and bailing hay." He tried his luck in Nashville and had songs recorded by Kris Kristofferson, Tom T. Hall, Bobbie Bare, and, later, the Allman Brothers and Elvis Presley ("You Asked Me To"). His real breakthrough came in 1973 when Waylon Jennings recorded *Honky Tonk Heroes*—considered the first "Outlaw" album. Shaver had an abrupt change of lifestyle, a religious experience, and wrote "I'm Just an Old Lump of Coal." John Anderson took it to number one on the charts. Shaver moved through several labels and began working regularly with his son, Eddy, who also toured with Dwight Yoakum. *Tramp on Your Street*, released on Zoo/Praxis, featuring Eddy on lead guitar, was quickly recognized as one of the strongest and hardest country records to hit the shelves. He tours regularly, is currently signed to Justice Records in Houston, works with his son Eddy, and appears in a movie with Robert Duvall, *The Apostle.*

Selected Discography:

1973 *Old Five and Dimers Like Me* (Monument)
1977 *Gypsy Boy* (Capricorn)
1981 *I'm Just an Old Chunk of Coal* (Columbia)
1982 *Billy Joe Shaver* (Columbia)
1987 *Salt of the Earth* (CBS)
1993 *Tramp on Your Street* (Zoo)
1996 *Highway of Life* (Justice)

Throckmorton, Sonny. Born in New Mexico in 1941, son of a Pentecostal minister, Sonny played guitar and sang in church from an early age. He graduated from high school in Wichita Falls, Texas, and later dropped out of college after an English professor told him writing would never be his profession. He knew differently. After a stint in Los Angeles, Sonny moved to Nashville and began working with several publishing companies. He later moved to Texas, success being so elusive in Nashville, and obtained a greater awareness of his own direction. He signed a deal with Tree International Publishing and began gaining the recognition he so richly deserved. In 1978 and 1979 he was voted Songwriters of the Year by the Nashville Songwriters Association International. He was also voted 1977 Cashbox Songwriter of the Year and 1980 DJ's Songwriter of the Year. Sonny was inducted into the Nashville Songwriters Association International's Hall of Fame in 1987 and into the Texas CMA Hall of Fame in 1999. Two major motion pictures have been based on his hit songs, "Middle Aged Crazy," and "Eighteen Again." He has obtained fifteen number one country hits and recorded for Capitol, Mercury, Warner Bros., MCA, Starcrest, and Country Garden labels. His list of hits includes: "Friday Night Blues," "I Feel Like Loving You Again," "I Had a Lovely Time," "I Wish I Was Eighteen Again," I Wish You Could Have Turned My Head," "I'm Knee Deep In Loving You," "If We're Not Back In Love By Monday," "It's A Cheatin' Situation," "Last Cheater's Waltz," "Middle Aged Crazy," "She Can't Say That Anymore," "Smooth Sailing," "Thinking of a Rendezvous," "Trying To Love Two Women," "The Way I Am," "Why Not Me," "Stand Up," and "Where The Cowboy Rides Away."

Selected Discography:

> 1978 *The Last Cheater's Waltz* (Mercury)
> 1985 *Southern Train* (Warner Bros.)
> 1985 *Sonny Throckmorton* (Country Garden)

Tillman, Floyd. Born in Ryan, Oklahoma, on December 8, 1914, Floyd was raised in Post, Texas. Best known for writing "It Makes No Difference Now," which sold to Jimmie Davis for three hundred dollars in 1938 and became a hit for Davis, Bob Wills, Bing Crosby, and Gene Autry, Floyd is a true crossover artist. He began his solo career in the late 1930s and had his first number one hit in 1944 with "They Took the Stars Out of Heaven." Other hits appeared in the 1940s—"Slippin' Around" (the first cheating song on the radio) and "I Love You So Much It Hurts." His last solo success came in 1960 with "It Just Tears Me Up."

Selected Discography:

> 1962 *Let's Make Memories* (Cimarron)

1969 *I'll Still Be Lovin' You* (Harmony)
1975 *Golden Hits of Floyd Tillman* (Crazy Cajun)
1991 *Country Music Hall of Fame Series* (MCA)

Tucker, Tanya. Born October 10, 1958, in Seminole, Texas, she had her first hit in 1972 when she was just thirteen years old. After moving around Texas, her family moved to Las Vegas, where she regularly performed. Eventually her demo tape was sent to Billy Sherrill, who was head of A&R at CBS Records. He signed her; the first song released was "Delta Dawn" (by Alex Harvey), and the song became an instant hit. She moved to MCA in 1975. In 1978 she decided to radically change her image and cross over to rock with her *T.N.T.* album, which went gold the following year. She switched to Arista Records in 1982, moved to Capitol Records, and returned with a hit in 1986. She continued to score a constant stream of Top Ten singles, including four number one hits. And her success continues into the 1990s.

Selected Discography:

1972 *Delta Dawn* (Columbia)
1974 *Would You Lay with Me* (CBS)
1978 *T.N.T.* (MCA)
1983 *Changes* (Arista)
1987 *Love Me Like You Used To* (Liberty)
1988 *Strong Enough To Bend* (Liberty)
1990 *Tennessee Woman* (Liberty)
1996 *Love Songs* (Capitol)
1997 *Complicated* (Capitol)

Van Zandt, Townes. Born March 7, 1944, in Fort Worth, Townes is widely respected and admired as a great songwriter. He died January 1, 1997, after hip surgery. The time between being born and dying was, for Townes, a treacherous road. He often told of the voices he heard in his head. He saw writing as a way of silencing the voices. He spent time in and out of rehabilitation centers and hospitals. A traveler by nature, he spent several years in a military academy and several more in college before becoming a folksinger. He moved to Houston in the mid-1960s and played clubs like Sand Mountain and the Old Quarter (where he recorded one of his finest albums in 1973). He moved to Nashville in 1976 at the urging of his manager, John Lomax (also Steve Earle's manager for a time). He released *Flyin' Shoes* in 1978, then toured for the next ten years. "If I Needed You" and "Pancho and Lefty" became country radio hits. In 1987, Townes was back in business with his eighth studio album, *At My Window*, which came out on his new label, Sugar Hill. His last album was *Road Songs*, on which he covered songs by Lightnin' Hopkins, Bruce Springsteen, and the Rolling Stones. Sugar Hill also released *No Deeper Blue*, his first studio album since 1987. He recorded it in Ireland with a group of Irish musicians. When Bob Dylan played Austin one year, he announced, "I'm going to play a song by one of your great songwriters," and launched into "Pancho and Lefty." No greater tribute.

Selected Discography:

> 1968 *For the Sake of the Song: First Album* (Rhino)
> 1969 *Our Mother the Mountain* (Tomato)
> 1972 *Late Great Townes Van Zandt* (Tomato)
> 1977 *Live at the Old Quarter* (Tomato)
> 1989 *Live and Obscure* (Sugar Hill)
> 1993 *Rear View Mirror* (Sundown)
> 1994 *Roadsongs* (Sugar Hill)
> 1997 *Highway Kind* (Sugar Hill)

Vaughan, Stevie Ray. Born October 3, 1954, in Dallas, he died in a helicopter accident on August 27, 1990, in East Troy, Wisconsin. Raised in Dallas, he began playing guitar as a child, inspired by older brother Jimmie. Vaughan's first real band, after playing in a number of garage bands, was the Cobras. He formed Triple Threat in 1975 and continued as Double Trouble after 1978. They played the Austin area and quickly became one of the most popular bands in Texas. In 1982 they played the Montreux Jazz Festival and caught the attention of David Bowie and Jackson Browne. After laying down the lead guitar tracks for what became Bowie's *Let's Dance* album, Stevie Ray landed a record contract with Epic and began working with John Hammond, Sr. He released three albums and toured with Double Trouble. Alcohol and drugs took their toll, and he checked into a rehabilitation clinic in 1987. His fourth album, *In Step*, released in 1989, became his most successful album, peaking at number thirty-three on the charts, earning a Grammy, and going gold just over six months after its release. In 1990 he recorded an album with his brother Jimmie. It was released posthumously and entered the charts at number seven. This album, *Family Style*, began a series of posthumous releases that were as popular as the albums he released during his lifetime.

Selected Discography:

1983   *Texas Flood* (Epic)
1984   *Couldn't Stand the Weather* (Epic)
1985   *Soul to Soul* (Epic)
1986   *Live Alive* (Epic)
1989   *In Step* (Epic)
1991   *Sky Is Crying* (Epic)
1992   *In the Beginning* (Epic)
1995   *House Is Rocking* (Epic)
1997   *Live at Carnegie Hall* (Sony)

Winter, Johnny. Born February 23, 1944, in Leland, Mississippi, Johnny formed his first band at fourteen with his brother Edgar in Beaumont, Texas, and spent his youth in recording studios cutting regional singles and in bars playing the blues. His discovery came in 1968 with an article in *Rolling Stone*. His debut album reached the charts in 1969. He achieved a sales peak in 1971 with the gold-selling *Johnny Winter and . . . Live*. His albums became more overtly blues-oriented in the late 1970s, and he also produced several albums for Muddy Waters. In the 1980s he switched to the blues label Alligator for three albums and has since recorded for MCA and Pointblank/Virgin. He began a tour in 1998 and played a showcase at South by Southwest Music Conference in Austin on March 21. His complete discography is a long one.

Selected Discography:

1969   *Johnny Winter Story* (Blue Sky)
1969   *Second Winter* (Columbia)
1970   *Johnny Winter and . . .* (Columbia)
1972   *Austin, Texas* (United Artists)
1973   *Still Alive and Well* (Columbia)

1977 *Nothin' but the Blues* (Blue Sky)
1984 *Guitar Slinger* (Alligator)
1985 *Serious Business* (Alligator)
1986 *Third Degree* (Alligator)
1991 *Let Me In* (Point Blank)
1994 *Live in Houston, Busted in Austin* (Magnum)
1996 *Ease My Pain* (Sundazed)
1997 *White Hot Blues* (Sony)
1998 *Live in NYC '97* (Virgin)
1998 *Texas Tornado* (Charly)
1998 *Together Live* (Blue Sky)